The Thin Yellow Line
by William Moore

Fifty-five years have elapsed since the end of the First World War. Yet forty-five more must pass before the official records of the Courts-Martial of those tried for cowardice are open to public scrutiny. Clearly in this case security comes a poor second to embarassment. As long as any relatives of the men who were shot remain alive the authorities presumably feel that it is better to keep the truth hidden away.

William Moore, a journalist of many years experience, does not agree. Cowardice is an emotion which all of us must cope with as best we may and when it determines if a man is to live or die, it merits the closest possible examination. Nevertheless it remains such a delicate subject that even the news that Mr. Moore was writing this book provoked a flurry of controversy in the newspapers.

Mr. Moore persisted and the result is a disturbing and highly readable book in which he examines the attitude to cowardice in battle throughout the ages. It is not an edifying story but it is, as Sir Winston Churchill said of another book on the same subject, "a soldier's tale cut in stone to melt all hearts."

The Thin Yellow Line

The Thin Yellow Line

by

<u>*William Moore*</u>

ST. MARTIN'S PRESS · NEW YORK

CONTENTS

ACKNOWLEDGEMENTS

I would like to put on record my gratitude to those people who played a large part in helping me to sustain the drive required while writing this book. Messrs. Rigby and Suddaby of the Imperial War Museum I came to regard as formidable allies when research difficulties arose. While Martin Mahoney, a colourful enthusiast who co-operated with my friend Martin Middlebrook during the writing of his classic work on the Somme, was tireless in his persistence at the Public Records Office. No-one could have shown me greater kindness and courtesy than the Earl of Harrowby, who took part in the Parliamentary struggle over the Army Act in the Twenties, and Major-General Sir Edward Spears, whose knowledge of the French Mutiny in 1917 is probably unparalleled. The Historical Services Division of the United States Army responded with impressive efficiency via Colonel Georgia Hill, and my good friend Major-General Hubert Essame once again provided many sources of reference. Fleet Street colleagues Michael Christiansen and Ron Ricketts of the *Daily Mirror* and Peter Hopkirk of *The Times* were also most helpful as was John McCallum, now lecturing in Canada. Many old soldiers entered into correspondence among whom were Messrs. 'Paddy' Kennedy (Manchester Regt.); Harold Mason (Royal Naval Air Service); Martin Power (Manchester and East Lancashire Regiments); Fred Bestwick (D.L.I.); Percy Smith (Queen's); Joe Bolge (D.C.L.I.); Jim Peacock (D.L.I.); Reginald Jennings (34th Division); George Banks (Royal Naval Division); W. Oram (Guards); C. R. Milligan (London and Norfolk Regiments); and S. Horsfall (London Regiment). Last but not least I would like to express my appreciation of the facilities afforded me by Bromley Public Library where the staff still found time to provide a corner for me despite the cramped and difficult conditions they were experiencing in temporary accommodation.

INTRODUCTION

This book is not a defence of the men who were executed for cowardice and desertion in the First World War. It is more than fifty years too late for that. Nor is it a denunciation out of hand of the generals who ordered the sentences to be carried out—many of them sincerely believed in the need for the ultimate penalty. As for the troops who fired the volleys; they were as helpless as their victims. It is only the politicians for whom it is difficult to find an excuse.

For years after the Armistice successive governments of all colours smothered the details of a national scandal. With a few notable exceptions, the attempts of the House of Commons to extract the truth about wartime courts martial was feeble in the extreme; just as it was at the time. This investigation is aimed at repairing some gaps in our recent history which certain authorities would prefer to remain unfilled for another thirty years.

In order to understand more fully the background to the military law which applied in 1914, it is necessary to look at its origins. Many regulations can be traced to the time of the Duke of Cumberland and were designed to keep dull-witted, drink-sodden illiterates standing in line shoulder-to-shoulder to kill or be killed. After the Peninsular War, when British troops periodically indulged in orgies of looting, rape and arson, the Duke of Wellington felt obliged to maintain an iron grip.

Thanks to a unique regimental system, the Victorian army flourished despite the restraints placed upon it. Looked on as an extravagance by politicians and despised by the public generally, the soldiers developed their own code of honour. As a consequence, courts martial were rarely called on to deal with questions of courage, although no-one was in any doubt as to what was required of them. When an officer was tried for leaving a small detachment of men and riding to fetch help during the Zulu War in 1879, Sir Garnet Wolseley was so shocked by the acquittal that he issued a special order pointing out that 'the more helpless position in which an officer finds his men, the more it is his bounden duty to stay and share their fortune, whether for good or ill'.

The war of 1914 ushered in horrors and a degree of strain for which there was no precedent. Nervous systems reacted in ways with which the rule book had not been designed to cope. Unfortunately it was the only book available. The line—symbolized by trenches in place of the red-coated ranks of Cumberland's day—had to be held at all costs. So the shootings began. A system of trials had to be improvised.

It was evident long before the Armistice that serious malpractices were common at courts martial in France. But the politicians were in a dilemma. Before conscription was introduced, the news that executions were being carried out at a rate of more than one a week was unlikely to stimulate recruiting. Later, when teenagers were called up, the opposition of their parents, especially those who might be aware of the legal anomalies of courts martial proceedings, had to be considered. A dual attitude was taken by both the Asquith and Lloyd-George régimes. Executions were publicised in France to deter the troops from failing in their duty but concealed at home for the reasons mentioned. It took M.P.s more than three years to obtain confirmation that condemned men were not told of their sentence at the court martial but were informed they were to be shot only a few hours before the execution took place. Consciences may have been salved a little by the setting up of an inquiry in 1919, but the report of the committee, although it criticised some practices, did not name any transgressors.

The details of the trials of the 346 men who were shot at dawn have never been revealed. Today the files are in the custody of the Ministry of Defence who say they cannot be released for 100 years. Having delved into the matter, I can understand the Ministry's reluctance to open the cupboard where they keep their bullet-chipped skeletons. The reticence of Parliament is more reprehensible. Can it be that they are wary of admitting that their predecessors were bamboozled by a military hierarchy? Or do they believe that all unsavoury subjects reflecting on the House should be suppressed until they are merely of academic interest?

PROLOGUE: THE REALITY

For a terror-stricken boy in khaki the end was a kitchen chair hidden in a French quarry.

The men of the 18th Manchesters were glad to be leaving the crashing, flaring chalk uplands of the Somme. They had seen enough of them in the summer of 1916. As the cattle trucks rumbled through the night away from the pulverised villages and splintered woods most of them slept. Some sat and stared, with feverish eyes while a few talked of what they had been through. In one wagon, guards shared their food with a comrade who had been court martialled a short time previously. There was a good deal of chaff and banter. The prisoner had been remanded to await sentence and his captors reckoned that he would be kept on cookhouse fatigue or made sanitary man for 'the duration'. It was the sort of scene one might expect in a Pals battalion.

There was something special about these formations made up of the volunteers who responded to Kitchener's call in 1914. They were so much more than a processed wodge of patriotic ardour. They were real 'pals'—in the 18th (3rd Manchester Pals) all clerks and warehousemen. They had something to be proud of too. On 1 July, when so many other units had lost nearly all their men with little to show for it, the 30th Division, to which the Manchesters belonged, had notched up one of the rare successes of the day.

General Headquarters, which had expressed some doubts about the division before the battle, was delighted. Further deeds of valour were required of the three brigades, one Regular, one of Liverpool Pals battalions and the other of Manchesters. During the remainder of July they struggled to wrench the shattered copses of Trones Wood and the tumbled ruins of Guillemont village from the Germans. It was in one of these gruelling actions that the prisoner disappeared from his platoon. When he reported after the attack he explained that he had become separated from his section during the confusion but had attached himself to a group of men from the 11th South Lancashire Regiment, the divisional pioneers. He had not thought it necessary to get a note from the officer. And he was not sure exactly where he had been. After all he had been lost! When inquiries failed to trace anyone who could corroborate his story—hardly surprising under the circumstances—the soldier's position came under more serious scrutiny. He was 'put back' for court martial and duly tried for desertion in the face of the enemy. The prisoner told his story over and over again on the way from the front to the battalion's rest area. He was not a well-educated man, just an ordinary working lad who had been sent out with the first draft of reinforcements to join the battalion after it arrived in France in 1915. The general consensus opinion was that he would 'click' for the dirty jobs in the next few months.

The men who guarded the prisoner on the train were taken off escort duty at the end of the journey. When next they saw him they were standing with the rest of the battalion formed in a hollow square. They had been expecting to hear some new order or even an exhortation from the General read out. Instead a horse-drawn ambulance had driven up to a table in the centre of the square. The prisoner had been marched to a prominent position near the table where the officers were gathered, his hat had been removed brusquely by the Regimental Sergeant Major, and the adjutant had read out his sentence. His punishment, awarded by field general court martial and confirmed by the Commander-in-Chief, Sir Douglas Haig, was to be shot. The execution would take place the following morning at dawn. At the bark of the R.S.M. the prisoner wheeled about and vanished into the ambulance which rattled out of sight. The 18th Manchesters stood stunned. Faces remained blank but the eyes betrayed a hurt, questioning look. Under steel helmets brains were racing. They'd all heard announcements of the sort before but no-one had really believed them. After all, they were volunteers. They didn't have to be there. Even as they marched away there were plenty of men in the shabby khaki ranks who muttered about appeals and 'They're only doing it to frighten us'. But they were not in the little group which had been assembled immediately after the parade at which the sentence had been promulgated. This unhappy squad had known the serious nature of their errand the moment the captain told them in strangled tones, 'I only hope to God you shoot straight.'

There were, in addition to the officer, a sergeant and ten soldiers. Six of the men were to form the firing squad. The remaining four were to act as stretcher bearers and remove the corpse. The bearers collected a limber and twenty-four hours' rations for the party and drove to a small farm some distance away.

The prisoner was housed in a hut with a Military Policeman present at all times. Not far away the execution squad brewed tea in an old barn. They didn't have much appetite. It had been impossible to conceal their intentions from the farmer's family and from time to time the soldiers bumped into weeping daughters of the household. Not being able to explain to the women that they were only doing their duty and that to disobey orders would imperil their own lives made the situation even more harrowing. Someone asked a military policeman what 'he' was doing. 'Writing letters' was the reply.

At some point the padre arrived to see the prisoner and the firing squad were ordered out and marched to a quarry on the outskirts of the farm. A staff officer was waiting, the red band on his hat providing the only colour in an otherwise unutterably drab scene. The squad filed down steps cut into the side of the quarry and lined up with a lot of nervous shuffling, riflemen in front, the stretcher party immediately to their rear. As the staff officer engaged the captain in earnest conversation all eyes focused on a single object. Some eight or nine paces from the firing squad stood a heavy kitchen chair.

'The prisoner will be placed in that chair in the morning,' the staff officer announced when the squad had been called to attention. 'After you have been brought to the "present" I will give the signal by dropping my handkerchief and you will fire at the mark. Is that clear?'

After a moment's pause a worried looking soldier coughed, swallowed and asked, 'Sir . . .'

'Yes, what is it?'

'Aa doon't think Aa should be on this duty. Aa know the prisoner well. We coom from the same town. And we're in t'same coompany.'

The staff officer and the captain exchanged glances. Then the Red Band made up his mind.

'I can understand your feelings,' he said. 'I am aware this is an unpleasant duty for all of you. It isn't pleasant for me either. But the responsibility is not yours. It lies elsewhere and you've got to obey orders. We all have. So I can make no exceptions. I'm afraid you will have to go through with it.'

The squad stood silent. The Manchester officer bit his lip. 'Right. Shall we try it now?'

The captain barked out the orders, six pairs of unwilling eyes stared down the barrels of six unloaded rifles aimed at an empty chair and an unharmonious clicking announced that six triggers had been squeezed in response to the dropped handkerchief.

After the staff officer had explained that six rifles would be issued the next morning, one of which would contain a blank round, the squad filed up the steps and back to the farm. In the deserted quarry dusk closed over the empty kitchen chair.

In the barn the night dragged interminably. A bottle of whisky had been sent to the condemned man but the guard reported that he had refused to touch it. He was continuing to write his letters. Even at this late hour he did not seem to comprehend his peril. Just before dawn the sergeant shook the dozing soldiers. Stiff and silent they made their way to the quarry filling their lungs with the damp air. A muffled rumble in the distance told them that the war was still going on where the sky was growing paler in the east. The hateful chair stood where they had left it, dark and ominous and damp with dew.

Many men are reported to have faced a firing squad bravely. This man, who had gone 'over the top' on 1 July and endured the terrors of Trônes Wood, was not one of them. The waiting Manchesters saw the shirt-sleeved figure sway at the top of the quarry steps and watched the escort almost carry him down. His body seemed to be rigid as he was dragged to the waiting chair and the Military Police had difficulty as they tied his limbs to the wooden legs and arms. Someone pinned a piece of white cloth over the man's chest and stepped back. In the anxiety to get the business over with the man had still not been blindfolded when the volley crashed out, its noise magnified by the quarry walls.

'Oh, my God!'

The victim's head had fallen to one side but it was obvious that he was still alive. Without bothering to consult the medical officer who had been present throughout the affair, the Manchester captain strode forward muttering between clenched

4

teeth: 'I shall have to finish him off.' With an obvious effort of self-control he put his pistol to the dying man's ear and pulled the trigger.

As the white-faced bearers moved forward one of the Military Police muttered accusingly out of the side of his mouth: 'Your men's rifles were shaking.' But the little party could not take their eyes off the dead man. When they cut the limp arms free and pulled him from the chair one of them noticed that the dead man's hair was 'standing up stiff and straight from sheer terror'. After the firing squad and the officers had left, the heavy stretcher was manhandled up the quarry steps and placed in the waiting limber. At the cemetery near Bailleulment, where they had been instructed to bury the man, the bearer party discovered that nothing had been prepared. So they borrowed the tools and dug the grave themselves, wrapping the body in a waterproof cape. Some months later a visitor to the cemetery reported that the grave bore a cross but instead of the words 'Killed in action', as on similar crosses, it merely said 'Killed' along with the date of the execution. Nothing else.

On the afternoon of the execution the burial detail returned to their billets and, under the gaze of their comrades, swilled the blood off the stretcher. Some of the watchers looked puzzled and resentful. Only 18 months earlier, Sir Douglas Haig had listed the 18th Manchesters in his despatches as among units which had been 'specially brought to my notice for good work in carrying out or repelling local attacks and raids'. Now the battalion would be associated with the execution when it was announced on parades or published in Orders. Both the praise in the despatch and the rebuke implied in the report of the death sentence were essential, it seemed, for the maintenance of good order and discipline ... but no-one could quite see why.[1]

[1] Compiled from an eye-witness account given by P. J. Kennedy, a former private in the 18th Manchester Regiment and Military Medal holder.

PART I

1632-1914

'The Naturall Courage of English Men'
                                        JAMES II

1

After Cromwell—the Mutiny Act

Making examples of unruly, insubordinate or unwilling soldiers is an old-established custom. In England, until the middle of the Seventeenth Century, there were no military regulations in this respect in times of peace. Under a law first enacted by Henry VI in 1439 and subsequently re-enacted by Henry VII and Henry VIII, deserters were handed over to the civil authorities to be tried. So were soldiers who sold equipment that had been provided by their commanders.

During this period there was no standing army, apart from small garrisons and personal retainers of the monarch. The nearest equivalent of regular soldiers were paid mercenaries under captains who had gained their experience in foreign wars. On the outbreak of hostilities, therefore, the raising of ill-disciplined feudal levies, or the impressment of reluctant civilians, made the enactment of special measures essential for the maintenance of law and order. As early as 1385 a complete code was laid down for the army of Richard II. Henry V adopted similar laws during his campaign in France. Under these Articles of War an archer who helped himself to an altar cross before the battle of Agincourt was promptly hanged. Men could see that when the king forbade looting in the country he claimed as his inheritance, he meant it. Death and mutilation were prominent among the punishments laid down by these so called 'Articles and Ordinances of War'.[1] As late as 1639 a persistent blasphemer might have a red hot poker thrust through his tongue. Rape, arson, and 'muttering against' commanders were included among the offences which could incur capital punishment. Although there is little indication that these laws were implemented with any vigour at the time, the advent of the Civil War and the passage of large

[1] Clode, *The Military Forces of the Crown*, Vol. 2, p. 430.

bands of amateur soldiers through the countryside, necessitated firmer application.

At first leaders on both sides confined themselves to reading aloud the dire threats contained in the Articles of War which they had proclaimed.[2] They were greeted with scant respect. At the back of the minds of both Royalist and Parliamentary leaders must have been the thought that harsh treatment could drive potential recruits into the opposite camp. Once it became obvious that lawlessness by the soldiery was alienating the populace, sterner measures were taken. The Royalists hanged two of their soldiers in Birmingham for looting. Parliamentary officers took a strong line with troops who sacked the homes of 'papists', although they still proceeded with a degree of caution in view of their uncertain legal status. Disciplinary officers were appointed and dire penalties were threatened for desertion. They had achieved little when the armies met in the first major battle of the war at Edgehill on 23 October, 1642. Whole regiments broke and fled on both sides. The record for abandoning their cause seems to have been set up by four Parliamentary junior officers who did not draw rein until they reached London where they assured wide-eyed listeners in a tavern that all was lost and claimed they were among the few survivors to escape[3] from the stricken field. Had they stayed they might have been in a position to report more truthfully that the battle was a hard-fought draw in which fortunes varied. As six Roundhead commanders said in an honest letter after the battle (for which they stayed):

'Some of both sides did extreamly well, and others did as ill, and deserve to be hanged, for deserting and betraying, as much as lay in them, their Party.'[4]

After Edgehill, Parliamentary soldiers were reminded of the passage in the Articles of War published by the Earl of Essex which stated:

'A Regiment or Company of Horse or Foot, that Chargeth the enemy and retreats before they come to handy strokes, shall answer it before a Council of War; and if the fault be found in the Officers they shall be banished from the camp; if in the Soldiers, then every tenth man shall be punished at discretion,

---

[2] *The History of the Rebellion and Civil War in England.*
[3] Young, *Edgehill 1642.*
[4] Rushworth, *Historical Collections.*

and the rest serve for pioners and scavengers till a worthy exploit take off that Blot.'[5]

To be fair, the majority of soldiers at Edgehill stayed and engaged in a grim struggle, the infantry in particular distinguishing themselves. King James II who was present, although only a child, later wrote an account of the battle in which he stated:

'The foot being thus ingaged in such warm and close service, it were reasonable to imagine that one side should run and be disorder'd; but it happen'd otherwise, for each as if by mutuall consent retired some few paces, and they stuck down their coulours, continuing to fire at one another even till night . . . nor can any other reason be given for it, but the naturall courage of English men, which prompted them to maintain their ground, tho the rawnes and experience of both partys had not furnished them with skill to make the best use of their advantages.'[6]

The account included the comment that English troops could be relied upon not to run as long as their officers did not set them a bad example.

The experience of Edgehill convinced both sides of the need to take a new line. At the beginning of October, Parliament declared that 'The Laws and Ordinances of War for the better conduct of the Army' would be applied severely and stated that the Lord General would punish offenders 'by death or otherwise, according to their demerits.'[7]

Among those who took part in the battle of Edgehill was Oliver Cromwell, then captain of a troop of horse. Unerringly his eye lit on the weakness of the Parliamentary cavalry who had suffered severely at the hands of the dashing Prince Rupert. The Prince's men, declared Cromwell, were 'gentlemen's sons and persons' of quality' while the Parliament's troopers were mainly 'old, decaying serving men and tapsters'.[8]

'Do you think,' he told John Hampden, 'the spirits of such base and mean fellows will ever be able to encounter gentlemen who have courage, honour and resolution in them? You must get men of a spirit that is likely to go as far as gentlemen will go, or you will be beaten still.'

[5] *Lawes and Ordinances of Warre, Established for the better Conduct of the Army by His Excellency The Earl of Essex.*
[6] Clarke, *The Life of James II.*
[7] Firth and Rait, *Acts and Ordinances of the Interregnum.*
[8] Fortescue, *History of the British Army*, Vol. 1, Book 2.

Although Parliament's leaders did not follow his example, Cromwell proceeded to recruit men of proven good character for his own regiment, mainly farmers, artisans and yeomen. As the value of these high-calibre troops over the local levies became more and more apparent, and as plundering, desertion and indiscipline remained unchecked, to the detriment of the Parliamentary cause, a major decision was taken. On 15 February, 1645, an Ordinance was issued bringing into being the New Model Army, headed by Sir Thomas Fairfax, with Major-General Phillip Skippon as his chief of staff. Cromwell was made Lieutenant-General of Horse.[9] A shortage of volunteers 'likely to go as far as gentlemen will go' led to 8,000 men being conscripted by press gangs to make up the required number of 22,000 soldiers.[10] Any mutinous inclinations were suppressed by two summary executions. Further hangings reduced the pressed men into obedience as the army set out on its first campaign and victory at Naseby. The standards of Cromwell, who as early as 1643 ordered two troopers to be flogged in Huntingdon market for merely attempting to desert, now applied generally in Britain's first standing army. Antisocial behaviour became a military offence. Drunks were made to endure a painful hour on the wooden horse, a triangular baulk of wood with four legs and a crudely shaped horse's head. Weights attached to the ankles, sometimes in the form of muskets, added to the misery. Fines for swearing and flogging for fornication were also instituted, and a portion of a soldier's pay was held back against the possibility of desertion. Harsh though these measures may seem, they had no detectable adverse affect upon the soldiers who were well treated as long as they behaved themselves and who became imbued with a formidable esprit de corps. Perhaps the most impressive reform was the abolition of the practice of buying and selling commissions and the substitution of a merit system. Many on Cromwell's own side disapproved of this egalitarian attitude but, as he pointed out, there was nothing to prevent a man of 'honour and birth' applying for command of a troop of horse. In the absence of sufficient numbers of such candidates, however, the job still had to be done, Cromwell declared, and it was better to have 'plain men' than none. He summed up his view in a famous phrase: 'I had rather have a plain russet-

[9] See Fortescue, Vol. 1, p. 222 for establishment and organization.
[10] Fortescue, Vol. 1, p. 212.

coated captain that knows what he fights for, and loves what he knows, than that which you call a gentleman and nothing else.'[11]

This lack of distinction in social rank resulted in representatives of old aristocratic families such as Fairfax and Montague serving alongside Henson, the cobbler, and Pride, the drayman.[12]

In the King's army the old systems remained. Commissions were still open to purchase. A gallows set up at the Royalist headquarters at Oxford was used in a haphazard way to cow the soldiery. In an uncharacteristic fit of anger the King ordered the execution in May, 1645, of a senior officer, Colonel Windebanke, for surrendering Bletchingdon House. It was a hard fate for a man who had served at Edgehill and Cheriton and later this was acknowledged by Charles I who paid Windebanke's widow a pension.[13] Such random acts were no substitute for the grass-roots policy of Cromwell and the lack of discipline among the Royalists contributed considerably to their defeat.

Where any signs of insubordination appeared among Parliament's troops, retribution was certain to be swift. In 1649 there was a mutiny in London among men with grievances over pay and projected service in Ireland. Fairfax and Cromwell, knowing they could rely upon their own regiments, immediately seized and court martialled fifteen ring-leaders. Five were found guilty and sentenced to death. In four cases the sentence was commuted but the fifth man, Trooper Lockyer, was shot in public outside St Paul's Cathedral. Another outbreak at Salisbury, where the troops for the Irish expedition were assembling, was dealt with just as promptly. After a gruelling cross-country ride, Fairfax and Cromwell surprised the mutineers at Burford, convened a court martial and ordered Cornet Thompson and two corporals to be shot against the wall of Burford Church while their comrades looked on. In Ireland Cromwell saw to it that his instructions against looting and destruction of civilian property were obeyed. Three English soldiers were shot for theft the week before the start of the siege of Drogheda and two more who robbed Irish homes were hanged the following day.[14]

[11] Gardiner, *Oliver Cromwell*.
[12] ibid.
[13] Young, *Edgehill 1642*.
[14] See Fortescue, Vol. 1 and Esson, *The Curse of Cromwell*.

13

Fair as well as strict, the discipline of the Ironsides was aimed at making men instead of breaking them. For their day they were unique. When they arrived in the Low Countries to fight (and defeat) a force which contained Spaniards, Walloons and English Royalists, the inhabitants fled, expecting to be terrorized. They returned to their homes amazed to discover that this strange English army paid for what it required and, unlike other soldiers, did not plunder their homes, rape their daughters or despoil their farms.[15] Equally remarkable was the respect in which ordinary soldiers were held in their own country. Paid adequately, and comparatively regularly, and led by experienced officers not seeking to exploit their positions for commercial ends, the New Model Army secured an honourable place in the community for its 'other ranks'. With the return of the monarchy this enviable position disappeared and has only recently been restored.

Developments after the Civil War did nothing to allay Parliament's suspicion of Kings and at the same time increased the awareness of English sovereigns of their vulnerability. The reaction of William III was understandable, therefore, when the 1st Foot (Royal Scots) mutinied at Ipswich in 1689, declaring for James II and marching from the town with four cannon.[16] Prompted by a former officer of Cromwell's, the king sent a strong force which surrounded the rebels at Sleaford, seized the ringleaders, and despatched the regiment to its destination in Holland where hundreds of soldiers took the opportunity to depart for good. The result of the precipitate action of the premier regiment of foot was the passing of a law which was to affect British soldiers for generations and is still embodied in legislation today.

Three weeks after the Ipswich insurrection, Parliament passed the Mutiny Act, the sting of which lay in the declaration that 'Soldiers who shall Mutiny or Stirr up Sedition, or shall desert Their Majestyes service (will) be brought to a more exemplary and speedy Punishment than the usuall Forms of Law will allow.'[17] Cautiously Parliament put a time limit on the Act but, apart from brief lapses, it was passed annually under various names until brought up to date in 1955 when the procedure for reviving it was also changed.

[15] Fortescue, Vol. 1.
[16] See Fortescue and Clode, Vol. 1.
[17] See *House of Commons Journal* and *Cobbett's Parliamentary History of England.*

William III, the sponsor of the Mutiny Act, was an experienced if unsuccessful commander. (The Battle of the Boyne was his only outright victory.) Few people knew better than he the need for an officer to see that an order once given was carried out immediately. In his view this principle was vital to military law. The maximum 'exemplary and speedy' punishment for deserters and mutinous and seditious officers and soldiers, or men who fostered these offences, was death. Thirteen officers of the rank of captain and above were to constitute a court martial. Nine of them had to concur before sentence of death could be passed. Courts were not to sit and soldiers were not to be executed between the hours of 8 am and 1 pm.[18]

Such fears as Dutch William may have entertained as to the loyalty of his British troops were dispelled by their stout performances at Steenkirk, Landen and Namur, many of the best of them falling in battle. In the Wars of the Spanish Succession that followed, Marlborough had to be content with troops who included criminals pardoned on condition that they enlisted and the impressment of 'persons having no settled mode of living'.

Debtors and other offenders were given their freedom from gaol on condition that either they enlisted or found substitutes.[19] As casualties mounted boys and old men were impressed by unscrupulous officers.

Sweepings of the country's gaols a large section of the army may have been but it is as well to bear in mind that in those days a man might have been imprisoned for trivial offences which would incur a qualified discharge today. Many good men of spirit and not just criminals were therefore forced willynilly to don uniform. In some ways their very boldness in what then passed for crime made them good regimental material just as the deportation of convicts introduced a rich element into the Australian national character. But to keep such a motley throng in some semblance of order was no easy matter. The provisions of the Mutiny Act were implemented fully and the cat o' nine tails was applied liberally—sentences up to 1,500 lashes were given by instalment.

The execution of persistent deserters was a regular occurrence

18 Clode, Vol. 1, p. 142.
19 See Parliamentary Statutes Queen Anne 1702–11; George II, 1744–5, 1756–7; George III, 1778–9.

and processions of red-coats marching with solemn music to Hyde Park were a frequent spectacle. Having shot the unfortunate victim the band struck up a merry tune and the unit marched cheerfully away leaving the tumbril and corpse to follow.[20]

Despite all these afflictions the British soldiers endured and, under the care of Marlborough, who saw to it that they had adequate provisions and regular pay as well as famous victories, earned a formidable reputation. Strong seeds of regimental tradition and pride took root at this time. A genuine affection for their brilliant commander led them to give him the nickname 'Corporal John', a title which might be contrasted with the appellation 'Iron Duke' conferred upon the implacable Wellington. It did not escape the notice of the troops that, although they were expected to fight costly pitched battles, Marlborough achieved many bloodless successes by manoeuvre, demonstration and hard-marching. When he fell from grace and was replaced by an indifferent general in 1712 his veterans showed their discontent openly. After peace was announced three thousand British troops mutinied while marching through Europe on their way home. Forced to surrender by overwhelming force, ten ring-leaders were court martialled and put to death on the spot.[21]

With the peace of 1712, the Mutiny Act was replaced with a less severe code which forbade the death penalty for desertion, mutiny and other serious offences. Courts martial were restricted to sentences which did not 'extend to life and limb'. This made the survival of a soldier marginally safer but, with or without capital punishment, the power of the military authorities was still forbidding: in fourteen years beginning in 1713 a drummer is on record as having received 25,000 lashes, an experience which contemporaries claimed left him 'hearty and well'.[22] After the Highland Rising of 1715, Parliament, mindful of the Jacobite-led Ipswich mutiny twenty-six years earlier, hastily reintroduced the death penalty for the enforcement of military discipline. In the succeeding years the lot of the 'other ranks' deteriorated. Badly housed in taverns and makeshift quarters, despised by the populace at large, and exploited by unscrupulous officers and N.C.O.s, the wonder is

[20] Fortescue, Vol. 2, p. 33.
[21] Fortescue, Vol. 1, p. 551.
[22] Barnes, *A History of the Regiments and Uniforms of the British Army*.

16

that Britain maintained an army at all. Some deserters were spared from the death penalty on condition that they formed firing squads for other runaways.[23]

A particularly cruel punishment known as picketing was introduced in the cavalry in which an offender was suspended from a tree or gallows by one wrist with only a sharpened wooden stake for his feet to rest on. When the first sentence was carried out a number of sightseers were injured in the rush to watch the spectacle.[24]

The battlefield risks inherent in the outbreak of war with Spain in 1739, followed a few months later by a major European conflict, brought a welcome diversion to an army where the addiction of certain colonels to flogging earned regiments nicknames like 'The Steelback'[5] and 'The Bendovers'.[26] But the return of the British Army to the Low Countries in 1742 was hardly auspicious. The dithering of sundry allies left the troops in enforced idleness around Bruges and Ghent and Field-Marshal Lord Stair, an elderly but astute veteran of Marlborough's wars, applied the Articles of War ruthlessly to the rank and file, while scores of officers who obtained leave during the bitter winter months escaped with nothing more chastening than Stair's undisguised contempt. To make matters more difficult for Stair, the volatile and unpredictable King George II joined the disaffected army. With this added burden, and still short of officers, Stair moved via Hanover against the French. Near Dettingen on the Main, a tributary of the Rhine, his bullied and abused red-coat regiments plodded obediently through knee-deep mud to attack their enemy under Marshal Noailles. Raked by a flanking fire and bemused by the antics of their German monarch, who appeared from time to time to shout at them in broken English, the lines of infantry appeared to waver. Twice they were halted 'and dressed' under fire—while their king disappeared temporarily from the scene roundly cursing his horse in his mother tongue as the refractory beast bolted to the rear. Then, with the perspiring George once more present, they relieved their pent-up emotions by giving the French an object lesson in volley firing by platoons. A storm of musket balls crushed some of France's most famous regiments of horse and foot.

[23] Fortescue, Vol. 2.
[24] *Daily Post*, 9 July, 1739.
[25] Northamptonshire Regiment.
[26] Manchester Regiment.

Almost two years later the Duke of Cumberland almost repeated the success of Dettingen at Fontenoy, when two solid ranks of British infantry braved a withering enfilade fire to pierce the dense French columns of Marshal Saxe. Only the failure of flank support robbed them of victory. One consequence of the battle was the court martial on charges of cowardice of Brigadier Ingoldsby who had been ordered to lead four battalions and three guns against a redoubt on Cumberland's flank. Instead, due to a misunderstanding, Ingoldsby joined in the main attack. Severely wounded, he was cleared of the cowardice charge and found guilty only of an error of judgment.

Taken as a whole, therefore, despite the reverse of Fontenoy, the conduct of the troops engaged at Dettingen and Fontenoy, could be regarded as courageous and admirable. It was with dismay that observers saw this prestige and high reputation vanish before 1745 had drawn to a close. The words cowardice and incompetence became common currency when applied to the army during the second Jacobite Rebellion.

2

When the Red-coats ran

Experienced officers serving the Young Pretender found it hard to believe their eyes. In the fitful light of a September dawn they stared across the dank fields outside the village of Prestonpans as the renowned red-coats formed an apparently unbreakable line and dragoons took their traditional station on each wing. It was a grey moment when doubts thrived and many must have reflected that they were facing an army commanded by a veteran of Dettingen—red-coats whose musketry had wrecked the flower of the regiments of France. Then the highlanders charged the dragoons, slashing at the faces of the horses with their broadswords. A group of clansmen with scythe blades lashed to poles cut the legs of animals from under them and mutilated their riders. The handful of British gunners having fled, the dragoons made a token resistance then took to their heels. For a few minutes, while old General Cope bravely rode among them shouting encouragement, the infantry fired ragged volleys. Then they too broke. Cope and other officers, pistols in hand, rallied about five hundred of the runaway cavalry but could not persuade them to attack the smallest body of enemy. In disgust, when all attempts to stem the rout had failed, Cope led these shaken warriors from the field, being of the opinion that there was no other way to keep them together.

'The panic-terror of the English surpassed all imagination,' wrote a Jacobite officer, Chevalier Johnstone, who was present. 'They threw down their arms that they might run with more speed, thus depriving themselves by their fears of the only means of arresting the vengeance of the highlanders . . .'[1]

'Terror,' he added, 'had taken entire possession of their minds.'

[1] Johnstone, *A Memoir of the Forty-Five.*

The rage of ten red-coats, who were tricked into surrender by a single highlander with a pistol in one hand and a sword in the other, could easily be imagined.

'These were the same English soldiers who had distinguished themselves at Dettingen and Fontenoy, and who might justly be ranked amongst the bravest troops in Europe,' wrote Johnstone.

'However, when we come to consider the matter attentively, we can hardly be astonished that Highlanders who take arms voluntarily from attachment to their legitimate Prince and their chiefs, should defeat thrice their number of regular troops who enlist from seduction or a love of idleness or dissipation.'

He concluded that, 'The soldier who betakes himself to a disorderly flight does not do so with the idea of losing his life, but with the hope of preserving it and of being sooner out of danger. But he deceives himself and rushes on death instead of avoiding it. Soldiers are mere machines and we must direct and guide them to prevent them from being tyrannized over by their imagination. In an attack I have seen the same men advance like lions, who, when repulsed, became in an instant as cowardly and timorous as hares.'

In the moment of victory, viewing a field strewn with more than five hundred English dead, it was only natural that the Jacobite officers should revel in their undeniable achievements. General Cope was mocked in a song: *'Hey, Johnny Cope, are ye wauken' yet'*, which is familiar to this day. The red-coats were belittled.

Called before a Board of General Officers to give his opinion as to the cause of the 'shameful and scandalous Behaviour of the Soldiers', Cope replied candidly that they were gripped by 'a sudden Pannick'. The old man was found to have done his duty throughout the whole affair and the Board pronounced his personal behaviour as beyond reproach.[2] It would have been most unjust for them to have come to any other decision, as the Board was fully aware that the 13th and 14th Dragoons who fled were raw recruits mounted on gun-shy horses. As for the infantry, they were untried regiments far removed from the continental veterans and probably outnumbered.

Cope, having been beaten by Bonnie Prince Charlie and exonerated by his fellow generals, retired gracefully to watch the next act of the play. It was not a pretty one. General

[2] *Report of the Proceedings of the Board*, published 1749.

Hawley, appointed Commander-in-Chief in Scotland in succession to the elderly General Wade, was a foul-mouthed brute of a man for whom the more vicious clauses of the Mutiny Act seem to have been specially created.[3] He could joke coarsely as a deserter was hanged within view of his headquarters and his first act on reaching Edinburgh was to order the erection of four pairs of gallows. On paper his four regiments of dragoons and twelve battalions of infantry looked powerful. Of the Foot, nine units had come from Flanders with high reputations. Closer examination, however, filled Hawley with foreboding. He found the ranks contained many half-trained recruits most of whom were in an exhausted state having been involved in long marches and counter-marches under Wade.

'. . . it is not the names of the twelve battalions that will do the business,' he wrote to the Duke of Cumberland.

General Hawley was right. Although with commendable energy he set his army in motion for the relief of Stirling, then besieged, he was forced to give battle on 17 January, 1746, in a howling gale on a desolate heath known as Falkirk Muir. The alarm caught him unawares while he was enjoying a meal some distance from his troops, and Hawley rejoined them so hastily that he did not even stop to pick up his hat which blew away in the storm. Quickly forming his infantry into two lines of battle, Hawley sent his dragoons to attack the highlanders whom he believed were vulnerable to cavalry. But the clansmen waited until the horsemen were at close range before firing a volley and uttering a tremendous cheer. Without waiting for further manifestations of their enemy's intent, the 13th and 14th Dragoons turned tail and fled. The 9th Dragoons, who had not been involved in the Prestonpans disaster, showed more fight and came forward 'at a hard trot'. Many of the highlanders were knocked down but their resistance 'was so incredibly obstinate that the English, having been for some time engaged pell-mell with them in their ranks, were at length repulsed and forced to retire.'[4] Fleet-footed Scots raced among the retreating dragoons with slashing blades. Hawley's infantry, peering into the teeth of the gale which whirled the smoke of the highland musketry into their faces, saw the cavalry emerge from the fog of battle in disorder and lost their nerve. A

---

[3] See Fortescue, Vol. 2; Mahon, *The Forty-five;* Tomasson and Buist, *Battles of the '45.*

[4] Johnstone, op. cit.

scattered volley was fired by men who had been experienced enough to keep their powder dry—then all but two of the line battalions departed. Only the 4th (King's Own) and the 48th Foot (Northamptonshire) stood their ground, one rank kneeling to provide a hedge of bayonets while two standing ranks fired volleys by turn. The 14th Foot (West Yorkshire) quickly recovered and joined these stalwarts.

As the Clan Cameron on the Jacobite left rushed downhill the combined fire of the unbroken regiments threw them into wild confusion and the Scots halted, fearing a trap.[5]

In the breathing space gained, the English, covered by the unbroken regiments which had now been joined by the rallied 2nd Battalion of the 1st Foot (Royal Scots), the 3rd Foot (Buffs) and the 9th Dragoons, retired into Falkirk. It was not until the next day that the Scots were sure they had gained the field, but General Hawley had no such doubts. Writing to the Duke of Cumberland he confessed, 'My heart is broke'. Although he would not concede total defeat—for 'our left is beat and their left is beat'—Hawley considered himself cheated of victory which superior numbers (actually the armies appear to have been fairly evenly matched) should have gained him. But it was the flight of the line regiments which really hurt. 'Such scandalous Cowardice I never saw before. The whole second line of foot ran away without firing a Shot. Three squadrons did well; the others as usual . . .'[6]

Hawley then reverted to type. Five officers were arrested to face court martial, including the unfortunate artillery commander, one Captain Cunningham, whose inexperienced men, mostly civilians, had bolted the moment a shot was fired. After a vain suicide attempt this officer was tried and cashiered. At a ceremony watched by a veteran brigade, sentence was read out, his sword was smashed over his head, sash ripped to pieces and hurled in his face and the final indignity administered by an ordinary soldier. Seventeen years' service were terminated with a hearty kick on the backside.[7] Humiliating though his treatment was, the gunner officer was better off than thirty-two men of the runaway Foot regiments who were sentenced to be shot for cowardice. Thirty-one dragoons were condemned to the scaffold for going over to the enemy and the fate of fourteen

[5] Johnstone, op. cit.
[6] Fortescue, Vol. 2, p. 140-141.
[7] Tomasson and Buist, op. cit.

more deserters was left to the dubious mercy of the Duke of Cumberland.

If Hawley is to be believed, the troops themselves were ashamed of their conduct and had said in some cases that they deserved to be hanged. Many, he declared, had shaken hands and vowed that rather than flee they would all 'dye nexte time'.[8] Cumberland, then a confident young man of twenty-five in whom the troops had complete faith, weighed up the situation quickly when he arrived to take over supreme command. Lack of discipline was the major cause of the defeats, he concluded, with want of training a close second. He took immediate steps to remedy these failings, carefully drilling his infantrymen in the tactics adopted by the 4th and 48th Foot at Falkirk. Experience had shown that it was more sensible for a bayonet man to thrust at the highlander on his right flank rather than to concentrate on an opponent attacking frontally. The arrival of two veteran Flanders regiments, the 21st (Royal Scots Fusiliers) and the 25th (King's Own Scottish Borderers), plus a properly manned detachment of artillery further raised the spirits of the force. But, allowing for the effect of the reinforcements, the greatest contribution to revived morale and discipline was made by Cumberland himself, a remarkable personal achievement which has been obscured by the notoriety of his other acts during the campaign. He gave a final spur to the pride of the red-coats shortly before the conclusive engagement began on 16 April. Spelling out the reason for the war—among other things, he said, in defence of the soldiers' property!—he assured them of victory, 'through the justice of the cause'. But he added, 'If there be any among you who, through timidity, are diffident of their courage or behaviour, which I have not the least reason to suspect, or any others who, through conscience or inclination cannot be zealous or alert in performing their duty, it is my desire that all such should immediately retire.'[9]

Anyone taking advantage of the offer, which one must assume officers passed on to troops out of earshot, would have a free pardon. Cumberland declared he would rather be at the head of one thousand brave and resolute men than ten thousand 'amongst whom there are some who by cowardice or

---

[8] Hawley in correspondence with the Duke of Newcastle.
[9] Tomasson and Buist; see also Fortescue, Vol. 2, p. 145.

misbehaviour may dispirit or disorder the troops, and so bring dishonour and disgrace on any army under my command.'

On a fresh spring day on Culloden Moor, the outnumbered Jacobite army repeated the shock tactics which had proved so successful at Prestonpans and Falkirk. But the regiments who had bolted previously stood their ground. And even when the slashing, hacking highlanders cut their way into the 4th (King's Own) and 27th (Royal Inniskilling Fusiliers) Regiments, the red-coats gave as good as they got. The surprise occasioned by the resolute stance of the English, whom the highlanders had expected to flee, was as demoralizing as the grape-shot and withering musketry.

Chevalier Johnstone recorded that the left wing of the Prince's army was within twenty paces of Cumberland's line when the red-coats opened fire (having protected their musket locks from early morning showers with their coat tails). Wavering then became general flight 'which spread from the right to the left of our army with the rapidity of lightning. What a spectacle of horror! The same Highlanders who had advanced to the charge like lions, with bold determined countenances, were in an instant seen flying like trembling cowards in the greatest disorder.'[10]

Relentlessly harried into their native hills, the highlanders were subdued and the Jacobite rebellion was crushed.

Within a year some of the veteran battalions of Culloden were in action under the Duke of Cumberland at Lauffeld in the Low Countries, where their discipline won the admiration of the French, who gained an inconclusive victory at considerable cost. For many years the influence of Cumberland was to play a large part in the thinking of British officers. His addiction to iron discipline was reinforced by a toughening up of the Mutiny Act. The bare-back procession to the halberds continued—three of the pole-axes then carried by sergeants formed a triangle, propped up by a fourth, to which a man was tied for flogging. Prussian drill became à la mode, influenced by the successes of Frederick the Great, and undue attention was devoted to the appearance of uniforms rather than their utility. Men were left in no doubt as to their fate if they disobeyed orders. Wolfe, hailed as a progressive soldier, had no hesitation in publishing a warning to the 20th Foot (Lancashire Fusiliers) which he commanded at Canterbury in the winter of 1755

[10] Johnstone, op. cit.

when a French invasion was feared:

'A soldier who quits his rank, or offers to flag, is to be instantly put to death by the officer who commands that platoon, or by the sergeant or officer in rere of that platoon; a soldier does not deserve to live who won't fight for his king and country.'[11]

Having spent a great deal of time and energy on restoring the quality of his regiment, which had fallen on hard times with elderly officers, consumptive soldiers and an unusually high number of cases of venereal disease, Wolfe was unfortunate in not seeing the effect of his training in action. For in 1759 the 20th Foot took part in the unique action of Minden where, with five other regiments, they marched irresistibly through a storm of fire and swept away seventy-five squadrons of cavalry and a host of infantry.[12]

In the light of events, the behaviour of the Allied cavalry commander was incomprehensible. Lord George Sackville had ignored repeated orders to charge the enemy with twenty-four squadrons. He was brought before a court martial where, according to Fortescue, 'the evidence produced . . . shows too plainly that on the day of Minden Sackville's courage failed him'. It was not easy to call Sackville a coward, as he had been wounded at Fontenoy (and he had fought several duels) but, said Fortescue, 'The courage of some men is not the same on every day'. Sackville, who had been Wolfe's predecessor in command of the 20th Foot, was dismissed from the army in a special order which stated 'that Lord George is, and he is hereby adjudged, unfit to serve his Majesty in any military capacity whatsoever'. This disgrace did not disqualify him, however, from becoming Minister of War some years later.

General James Abercromby was fortunate not to have been dealt with even more harshly for his conduct the previous year when he sat safely in his headquarters two miles from where his troops were charging the make-shift but formidable defences of Fort Ticonderoga on Lake Champlain.[13] Two thousand of them fell trying to storm a nine-foot high palisade protected by felled trees. Then the troops broke in wild disorder. Abercromby was quietly recalled. His treatment may well have been due to the scandal over the treatment of Admiral Byng a short time previously.

11 Barnes, *A History of the Regiments and Uniforms of the British Army*, p. 56.
12 The other Minden regiments were the 12th (Suffolk), 23rd, 25th, 37th (Hampshire) and 51st (K.O.Y.L.I.).
13 Fortescue, Vol. 2, p. 328.

3

Byng — The Political Sacrifice

The Hon. John Byng was an experienced officer at the time that the wretched, runaway dragoons were being hanged by Hawley. The lumbering multi-gunned men o' war of Vice-Admiral Byng kept the East Coast for King George. During a gale-lashed winter they did the job well and when the rebellion was over Byng was called to other duty. He sat as a member of the court martial which inquired into the conduct of a number of naval officers at the battle of Toulon. The cause of the inquiry was simple. The French fleet had left Toulon and been met by the waiting British. But in the engagement that followed, Admiral Mathews, Commander-in-Chief Mediterranean, did not follow the 'Permanent Fighting Instructions' laid down by the Admiralty as a consequence of Admiral Rooke's successful action off Malaga in 1704. The nub of these was the obligation of a commander to maintain an unbroken line of battle when confronting the enemy. British admirals were expected to attack down wind with their vanguard engaging the enemy's van, their centre the enemy centre and their rear his rear. Only if the enemy showed signs of fleeing could the Line be broken and the signal 'General Chase' be given to enable freedom of action. The effectiveness of the rigid line tactics can be gauged from the fact that out of fifteen consecutive engagements fought in the late seventeenth and the eighteenth century all were draws. Admiral Mathews, then sixty-eight years old, tried to end this impasse by boldly bearing down to attack the enemy centre before the line was formed. His bewildered captains reacted in various ways, some attempting to copy his move and one squadron merely forming the end of what would have been the line opposite a sea empty of French ships. In the farce that followed the faster French ships sailed off unharmed.

Thirteen courts martial were the sequel to the fiasco. One captain was dismissed for not closing with the enemy, his excuse being that his powder bags were not ready for the guns; one who pleaded weak eye-sight was put on half-pay and five were dismissed but later reinstated. A pessimistic captain took refuge abroad and another died naturally before coming to trial. Two were acquitted.

Byng sat on the two remaining courts martial. The second-in-command at Toulon, Vice-Admiral Richard Lestock, was tried first. This officer, because he had stuck to the regulations regarding the line, even though his ships formed up opposite a clear sea, was acquitted. Then, throughout the summer, aboard the man o' war *Prince of Orange* moored at Deptford, the court heard the case against Mathews and unanimously found him guilty of 'divers breaches of duty' which were the 'principal cause of the miscarriage of His Majesty's Fleet'. He was sentenced to be cashiered and barred from taking 'further employ in His Majesty's Service'. The line had been pronounced sacrosanct. To break it meant disgrace.

Eleven years later, in December 1756, Byng found himself on trial in the cabin of the 90-gun man o' war *St George* at Portsmouth. Sent with undermanned, ill-equipped ships to relieve besieged Minorca, he encountered a French fleet off the island. The engagement was a mismanaged affair in which, through trying to have the best of both worlds, the sacred line was broken. Byng's leading ships were pounded and left unsupported by the other ships, including Byng's flagship. Byng actually declined a suggestion which would have brought him more quickly into action by referring to the previous court martial. He did not wish to incur 'Mr Mathews's misfortune', he said—i.e. be accused of deliberately breaking the line. This hesitant approach enabled the clean-hulled French vessels to sail smartly away from his foul-bottomed ships. The following day Byng held a council of war which voted unanimously to return to Gibraltar as it was agreed there was no possibility of relieving Minorca. A much more stout-hearted attitude was adopted by the British garrison of the island whose vigorous defence of St. Philip's Castle at Mahon cost the French 2,000 casualties before the British surrendered with full honours of war.[1] The capitulation and the apparent abandoning of the island to its fate was received in England, however, with an

[1] Fortescue, Vol. 2, p. 294-5.

outburst of anger when the news arrived in July.

Byng was brought to trial on 28 December. The charge stated that he 'did withdraw, or keep back, and did not do his utmost to take, seize and destroy the ships of the French King which it was his duty to have engaged, and to have assisted such of His Majesty's ships as were engaged in the fight with the French ships, which it was his duty to have assisted; and for he, the said John Byng, did not do his utmost to relieve St Philip's Castle.' Finally he was accused of failing to carry out his instructions.[2]

Four admirals and nine captains tried the case which lasted throughout January. The evidence was conflicting and of a partisan nature, but nothing could obscure the fact that, whatever might be said, Byng had failed in his primary mission. As military and naval ventures sometimes, of their very nature, terminate unsuccessfully he did not anticipate any punishment to be excessive. At the worst he might have expected to have been treated like Mathews and dismissed the service. It was with disbelief that he heard that he had been sentenced to death. Having been told the verdict privately he was formally called before the court to hear the Judge-Advocate read the details of the findings. They disclosed that the court found the case against him proved under the 12th Article of War. This laid down that 'Every person of the Fleet who, through cowardice, negligence or disaffection, shall in time of action withdraw or keep back, or not come into the fight or engagement; or shall not do his utmost to take or destroy every ship which it shall be his duty to engage, and to assist and relieve all and every one of His Majesty's ships, or those of his allies, which it shall be his duty to assist and relieve too shall suffer death.'

But there was more to it. The Article in question prescribed death as the only sentence 'without any alternative left to the discretion of the court, under any variation of circumstance'.

By a unanimous decision, therefore, the court had no alternative but to sentence Byng 'to be shot to death, at such time and aboard such ship, as the Lords Commissioners of Admiralty shall direct'.

They 'most earnestly' recommended him to mercy and a petition asking for clemency was sent off to the Admiralty that day asking the Board to recommend to the King to commute the sentence.

[2] Admiralty Court Martial Records.

Many well-founded arguments have been put forward to show that the findings of the court which cleared Byng of cowardice and disaffection, were contradictory and amounted to an acquittal. Yet, whatever basis there may be for believing that Byng was made the scapegoat for the authorities' own neglect, it is difficult to deny that on the broadly-based charge of not doing his utmost, he was palpably guilty. Had the penalty for this been dismissal, the subsequent defending arguments might have been less vehement. But there could be no other penalty. Until 1749 it had been possible for courts finding a person guilty under the relevant Article to pronounce death or 'such other punishment as the nature and degree of the offence shall be found to deserve'. This qualification had been dropped, however, following the Baker Phillips case.[3] A young lieutenant of that name had taken command of his ship when the captain was killed in action and struck her colours when she was no longer able to fight. There was little doubt that negligence on behalf of the dead captain was responsible for the destruction of the ship but Baker Phillips was found guilty under Article 12 and sentenced to be shot. An outcry followed the execution, critics pointing out that senior officers guilty of much greater offences were invariably treated leniently by their service colleagues. The amendment in the law that followed was intended as a concession to the principle of fair play.

Under the circumstances, a reprieve for Byng was hardly acceptable to the Admiralty or to the politicians. Twelve judges, at the request of the King, considered a plea for a ruling on whether or not the sentence was legal, and upheld it. Other attempts to persuade George II to reprieve Byng were rebuffed, the King pointing out that he had received petitions from civil authorities throughout the country asking him to punish those responsible for the fall of Minorca and for the weak state of Britain's defences. On the advice of his ministers he had publicly promised to do so.

The Admiral was shot on the quarter deck of the *Monarch*, a captured French 74, on 14 March. He entertained visitors the night before, rose early, breakfasted well and, dressed in a light grey coat with a white waistcoat, walked calmly to the appointed place at noon. Sailors packed the yards of surrounding ships to watch. Kneeling on a cushion set on a deck spread with sawdust he tied a blindfold over his eyes and gave the

[3] See Admiralty Court Martial Records and *Encyclopaedia Britannica*, 1911 Edition.

signal to fire by dropping a white handkerchief. Six marines shot him at a range of two yards. Three more, who stood behind the firing squad in case they had to give Byng the *coup de grâce*, were not required. The entry in the log of the *Monarch* for that day disclosed that 'Mr Byng's coffin was brought aboard at 9 . . . Ye boats mand and armd came along side to attend the Execution of Mr Byng: Ye Marines were all under arms at 11 . . . and at 12 Mr Byng was shot dead by 6 Marines and put into his coffin.'

There seems little doubt that Byng died not 'to encourage the others' as Voltaire put it, but because political reasons made it inconvenient to spare him. He might have revealed the sorry state of the ships and crews he had been given. Nevertheless, although the execution was not exemplary by intent, it had a striking effect. In the years immediately following Byng's death British Admirals showed unparalleled zeal establishing 1759 in the history books as 'The Year of Victories' and 'The Wonderful Year'. The clause which permitted courts martial to order 'such other punishment as the nature and degree of the offence shall be found to deserve' was not restored to Article 12 until 1779.

4

The Hand of Iron

The condition of the British army reached a state of un-surpassed wretchedness towards the end of the eighteenth century. Its reputation was lost with the American colonies. The contempt of their countrymen added a sour spice to the short, miserable life red-coats could expect. Enlisted for life, with a private's pay fixed at 8d a day (reduced by various deductions to around 3d) they could look forward to a licence to beg if they were lucky enough to live to be discharged. And this abject condition was perpetrated upon a soldier while the country thrived, canals and steam engines developing the commerce of the growing empire.

Although conditions for some of the labouring classes, in the south in particular, were poor, few were reduced to even con-sidering a soldier's life. Thousands of patriotic spirits who had been tempted to take a calculated risk and enlist under Special Recruiting Acts in 1778 and 1779 were offered their discharge (whether or not they had completed their term) at the end of the American hostilities. Almost without exception they quit. Out of 700 men serving in the Royal Scots, 500 departed with alacrity. A bounty of a guinea and a half for any man who re-enlisted proved a ludicrous inducement. Nothing could compensate a man for service on fever-ridden West Indian islands where regiments were sent in the sure knowledge that they would be 'broken' by disease within two or three years. A bounty of three guineas offered to recruits in 1787, with another two guineas per man for recruiting officers, had no effect on enlistments but greatly increased the numbers of officers seeking them.

At home, the appalling condition of billets in the absence of adequate barracks and the persistent exploitation of men by officers who bought commissions for speculative reasons, did

31

nothing to encourage service in the ranks. Until 1783 a colonel authorized to raise recruits received the money for their pay and uniforms in a lump sum. The opportunities for abuse were obvious. Scandals abounded. Resentment was widespread. Attempts to make up the required numbers by recruiting Irishmen proved futile. There were so many desertions that special depots were set up at Cork and Dublin to deal with them. Most of them were sentenced to perpetual service abroad which was tantamount to being condemned to a slow death. Over everything, as far as the ordinary soldiers were concerned, lay the menacing shadow of the Mutiny Act, with similar Articles of War holding the Royal Navy in thrall. An increase in the number of Marines at this time was a sure indication of the unreliable temper of the crews of His Britannic Majesty's men o' war. Indeed it was a mutiny by the despairing seamen that finally induced the Government to raise the pay of the army in 1797, more as a preventive measure than anything else. Privates in line regiments drew a new rate of a shilling a day, less stoppages.

But the rot went deep. In 1798, when facing a French invasion force in Ireland, the 6th Dragoon Guards fled. Then the distinguished 5th Dragoon Guards were found to be full of disaffected troopers who favoured the Irish cause. Mainly as an example to the officers of other regiments, the 5th were disbanded. Although they could boast honours won at Blenheim, Ramillies and Fontenoy, their place was left vacant in the Army List as a reminder to others that disgrace could be their lot. When they reappeared it was as the 5th (Royal Irish) Lancers.

It was fortunate for the army at the turn of the century that Frederick Augustus, Duke of York, used his position and influence as Commander-in-Chief to secure reforms, such as the pay rise already referred to, the appointment of a proper barracks administrator, improvements in hospital conditions, alterations in the clothing regulations and a number of purely military innovations. With a flash of Cromwellian perspicacity he discerned the imperative need for highly trained and responsible officers who would care for their men. During his tenure of command, therefore, not only was the Royal Military College established but progressive officers of the calibre of Sir Ralph Abercromby (who gave orders as he was dying that the very blanket on which he lay should be returned to the private soldier who owned it), Sir John Moore and Wellington came into prominence. It is incongruous that the Duke of York should have been obliged to resign for a period because his mistress[1] was using her privileged position to run a thriving traffic in cut-price commissions.

The Duke's reforms, which included the development of light infantry and rifle units, produced a better spirit than the army had known for years. The ordinary soldier, the man who carried the musket and wielded the bayonet, at last began to register as something more than a mere cypher. Colonels who reported casualties in figures only received a sharp message from the Horse Guards, in Whitehall, where the Duke had his headquarters, requiring them to name the dead and wounded on active service so that inquiries from next-of-kin could be answered.

Despite all the unpleasant aspects of soldiering, the other ranks had never been entirely bereft of some consideration for their rights. A private of the Middlesex Militia, for example, obtained £600 damages from his colonel on the ground that he had been wrongly flogged.[2]

In the Devon Militia a soldier who won an appeal against his officers in 1797, after he had been found guilty by a court martial of mutiny and given 1,000 lashes, was awarded £500.

An even more remarkable case is recorded in respect of the Royal Navy in 1743. A lieutenant, who had been given a sentence of fifteen years' gaol and dismissed, managed to get his case placed before the Privy Council and the punishment was remitted by the King. Having successfully sued Sir Chaloner Ogle, the president of the court martial, for damages (he received £1,000), he was told by Chief Justice Willes that he could sue any other members of the court. In a bid to do so, he served writs on two of them as they left the trial of Admiral Lestock, referred to earlier. In high indignation, the entire court wrote to the Lords of Admiralty demanding satisfaction for the insult from whoever had advised this course of action. The Chief Justice himself was the subject of some of their derogatory comments which received the veiled approval of the King when he received the complaint via the Admiralty. Within a short time of being informed of this censure, the Chief Justice enforced the arrest of all members of the court and they were obliged to make the most abject apology to him.

---

1 Mary Anne Clarke—subject of a Parliamentary inquiry in 1809.
2 Cited in *Taunton's Reports* 1807–19.

It was read out publicly at the Chief Justice's instruction 'as a memorial to the present and future ages, that whosoever set themselves up in opposition to the law or think themselves above the law, will in the end find themselves mistaken'.

Such examples as have been quoted of soldiers and officers obtaining justice from a superior civil court were not common, perhaps, but they help in some degree to place courts martial in their proper perspective.

Any consideration of military law, however, must take into account the human material to which it is applied and the circumstances at the time. And it is significant that the humane Sir John Moore and the harsh Duke of Wellington, who declared bluntly that the only way to run an army was with 'a hand of iron', were obliged to resort to the same methods in similar circumstances.

As in all cases where an example is called for, the spectacle involved was as important as the expiation of the crime itself. A private of the 66th Foot (2nd Royal Berkshire) recorded this 'first impression of the stern duties of a soldier's life' during the Napoleonic Wars.

'A private of the 70th Regiment (then the Glasgow Lowland Regiment and later the 2nd East Surreys) had deserted from that corps and afterwards enlisted into several other regiments . . . sixteen different times he had received the bounty then stolen off. Being, however, caught at last he was brought to trial at Portsmouth and sentenced by general court martial to be shot.

'The 66th received a route to Portsmouth (from Winchester) to be present on the occasion and, as the execution would be a good hint to us young 'uns, there were four lads picked out of our corps to assist in this piece of duty, myself being one of the number chosen. Besides these men, four other soldiers from three other regiments were ordered on the firing party, making sixteen in all.

'The place of execution was Portsdown Hill, near Hillsea Barracks, and the different regiments assembled must have composed a force of about fifteen thousand men . . . The sight was very imposing and appeared to make a deep impression on all there. As for myself, I felt that I would have given a good round sum (had I possessed it) to have been in any situation rather than the one in which I now found myself; and when I looked into the faces of my companions, I saw, by the pallor and anxiety depicted on each countenance, the reflection of my own feelings. When all was ready we were moved to the front and the culprit brought out. He made a short speech to the parade, acknowledging the justice of his sentence and that drinking and evil company had brought the punishment upon him.

'He behaved himself firmly and well, and did not seem at all to flinch. After being blindfolded, he was desired to kneel down behind a coffin which was placed on the ground, and the drum-major of the Hillsea Depot, giving us an expressive glance, we immediately commenced loading. This was done in the deepest silence and the next moment we were primed and ready. There was a dreadful pause for a few moments and the drum-major, looking again towards us, gave us the signal before agreed upon (a flourish of his cane), and we levelled and fired. We had been previously strictly enjoined to be steady and take good aim, and the poor fellow, pierced by several balls, fell heavily upon his back. The drum-major gave another signal and four of our party immediately stepped up to the prostrate body, and placing the muzzles of their pieces to his head, fired, and put him out of his misery.'

Regiments were then ordered to march past in slow time and 'when each company came in line with the body, the word was given to "mark time" and then "eyes left" in order that we might all observe the terrible example.'[3]

Although the private of the 66th admitted frankly that it was the uniform which attracted him when he contrived to join the 95th Foot (Rifle Brigade) his intelligence and literacy made him an obvious candidate for this elite formation. At Shorncliffe camp the 43rd and 52nd Foot (1st and 2nd Ox and Bucks) and the 95th were the subject of a rare experiment in training, being encouraged instead of browbeaten, and required to think instead of obeying blindly. Athletics were promoted to combat drunkenness and vice. Badges were awarded for good behaviour and skill.

Under the supervision of Sir John Moore the men responded remarkably well and an officer was able to report that the 'cat' no longer had to be used 'and yet discipline is in the highest state of perfection'.

In the field it was a different story. Rifleman Harris, late of the 66th, was in the section of the army which Moore sent to

[3] *Recollections of Rifleman Harris.*

embark at Vigo when he retreated to Corunna with the bulk of his troops during the winter of 1808. To traverse Galicia's winding mountain roads in bad weather today presents problems even to motorists toasted by car heaters. A march along the same highways when they were stony tracks, unlit and blizzard-swept, defies imagination. The accomplishment of the troops who reached Vigo was in no small measure due to the leadership of Robert Craufurd, commanding the 1st Light Brigade. From the outset he was relentless. When two men were caught straggling during the early stages of the retreat he 'halted the brigade with a voice of thunder' and, holding a court martial on the spot awarded them one hundred lashes each.

A Rifleman who was heard to mutter angrily that it would have been more sensible to give them something to eat was sentenced to three hundred lashes. Night fell before the punishment could be carried out, but the following morning the grumbler was flogged, standing manfully with his arms folded in the absence of halberds not carried by sergeants in the 'Rifles'. Before the others could receive their complement of lashes, the enemy approached. Nevertheless at the next halt, despite the intercession of the commanding officer of the Rifles, a second man received seventy-five lashes and only then did Craufurd call quits.

Wrote Harris, 'Many who read this, especially in these peaceful times, may suppose this was a cruel and unnecessary severity under the dreadful and harassing circumstances of that retreat; but I who was there . . . a common soldier of the very regiment to which these men belonged, say it was necessary. No man but one formed of stuff like General Craufurd could have saved the brigade from perishing altogether, and if he flogged two he saved hundreds from death by his management.'

Standing with the rearguard, soaked like the rest of them, handing round a canteen of rum, even turning a blind eye to the surreptitious pilfering of a field of frozen turnips, Craufurd's example and influence upon morale was indelible and effective.

On the road taken by the main army disorder grew as it was realised that Sir John Moore did not intend to stand and fight. Bad staff work, a hostile population and the constant retreating from the French cavalry, sapped the spirit of the men who also laboured under an intolerable burden of equipment weighing nearly seventy pounds. At Bembibre, the centre of the local wine trade in a particular area of Galicia, all control vanished. The great vaults were plundered and the town was given over to an orgy on the last day of 1808. When the rear-guard arrived the next morning they tried in vain to rouse scores of drunks from their stupor. Some could not be wakened even by the bayonet and the 20th Foot (Lancashire Fusiliers) were left behind to stir any who could move to flee before the enemy arrived. It was a hopeless task and many drunks were abandoned to the swords of the French dragoons. A handful of gashed and mutilated soldiers who escaped were paraded by Moore later that day for the rest of the army to see. The ghastly spectacle had no effect. Villafranca suffered the same fate as Bembibre. Appalled by the disintegration of his army, Moore managed to rally them in the great square of the town where a dragoon who had struck an officer was ceremonially shot by men of his own squadron. In a speech, Moore appealed for better conduct saying 'none but unprincipled cowards would get drunk in the presence, nay in the very sight of the enemies of their country'. His plea fell on deaf ears. More houses were plundered that night and in retribution Paget, commanding the Reserve Division, tried the offenders by court martial and held a mass flogging.

Moore's men showed that they had plenty of fight left in them when they beat off their pursuers and embarked at Corunna. But the excesses of the retreat were not lost on Wellington when he took over the army in the Peninsula.

'I could not have believed it possible, had I not witnessed it,' wrote Moore shortly before his death, 'that a British Army could in so short a time have been so completely disorganised.'

*　　*　　*

The troops under his command, wrote Wellington to his brother William in September, 1810, were the worst that had ever been sent out from England. Despite his victories, which then included Busaco, Vimeiro, and Talavera, he was not at all satisfied with the conduct of either the troops or officers. The spectre of the breakdown of Moore's army on the march to Corunna was always lurking in the background. Plunder, drunkenness and desertion afflicted Wellington's army to an extent far beyond that of Marlborough or of William III. While with their regiments most men could be relied upon to behave decently. Once on their own, they seemed to take leave of their senses. Although Wellington was far from being an abstainer and in India had thoroughly berated a commissary for supplying inferior rum to the 33rd Regiment (Duke of Wellington's) he diagnosed drink as the cause of most of the evils among the rank and file.[4]

'No soldier can withstand the temptation of wine,' he wrote in November, 1810. 'This is constantly before their eyes in this country, and they are constantly intoxicated when absent from their regiments, and there is no crime which they do not commit to obtain money to purchase it, or if they cannot get money, to obtain it by force.'

Poor drafts from home, the excesses of stragglers on the peasantry and the wholesale desertion to the enemy of large numbers of Irish soldiers, gave Wellington much to ponder on. Had his officers been universally enthusiastic and expert, it would have made his task easier; but many junior officers took ample leave during the year to attend to their domestic affairs.[5] In the absence of close supervision it was simple to revert to brute force to maintain order. Sentences of 1,000 lashes were carried out more than fifty times during the war.

A startling example of the villainy of the troops was afforded Wellington when they stormed the fortress of Ciudad Rodrigo. Once inside, assault troops murdered a Portuguese sentry placed on the French liquor stores and fought as hard for possession of the rum casks as they had for the city. Some drowned after being pushed head first into the barrels. Others were burned to death incapable of saving themselves when the building caught fire.

Order was not restored until the following morning, 12 January, 1812. Three months later Wellington was again beside himself with rage at Badajoz when his soldiers, incensed by their casualties, ravaged the town mercilessly for seventy-two hours raping, robbing and killing.

In mid-summer, these same blackguards proceeded to beat the French in the open field at Salamanca and went on to besiege Burgos. The struggle commenced late in September

---

[4] *Supplementary Despatches and Memoranda*, edited by the 2nd Duke of Wellington.
[5] See Fortescue; Glover, *Wellington's Peninsular Victories*, and Longford, *The Years of the Sword*.

and dragged on through October, much of the time in bad weather. Then Wellington ordered a retreat and his worst fears were realised as the hungry, chilled regiments trudged back through the mud. Discipline crumbled and only the caution of the French spared the army more serious casualties. It was minus at least 5,000 soldiers, captured, straggled or deserted, when it reached winter quarters. Wellington poured out his feelings in a scathing letter which properly put the blame for the conduct of the troops upon their officers.

'It began by telling us we had suffered no privations,' wrote Captain John Kincaid of the Rifles, 'and though this was hard to be digested on an empty stomach, yet, taking it in its more liberal meaning, that our privations were not of an extent to justify any irregularities, which I readily admit; still many regiments were not guilty of any irregularities . . .'

The damning words were, '. . . this army has met with no disaster; it has suffered no privations, which but trifling attention on the part of the officers could not have prevented.' The only hardships Wellington would concede were those inflicted by the weather when it was 'most severe'.

Having seen his army turned into a rabble three times in a year, Wellington was unmoved by any indication of resentment. Mr Francis Seymour Larpent, a lawyer, was sent out to his headquarters as Judge Advocate General and immediately applied himself to the backlog of courts martial which had accumulated. Eight men were hanged, sixty were flogged 'severely' and a number of officers were cashiered. As an additional measure Wellington advised the Portuguese that if they prosecuted British soldiers under Portuguese law for civil offences he would not interfere. Some soldiers suffered deportation to Portuguese colonies as a consequence. By early July, 1813, he had persuaded Parliament to pass a law allowing courts of three officers to try troops on charges of offences against Portuguese property and persons. Other provisions allowed the death penalty to be inflicted for comparatively minor offences, and the number of officers required for a general court martial was reduced from nine to seven. Four squadrons of mounted military police made their appearance. Having devoted himself simultaneously to improving the pay, living conditions and hospital facilities for his troops and reducing the burden they carried on their backs, he might have expected concrete results.

The soldiers rewarded him by marching and manoeuvring admirably at the battle of Vittoria. Then they reverted to type and, before the action had finished, swarmed into the French baggage parks where to their glee they found chests containing the pay for King Joseph's beaten army. So great was the general chaos that French dragoons joined in, filling their pockets unhindered. Wellington reported with disgust amounting almost to despair:

'We started out with the army in the highest order, and up to the very day of the battle nothing could get one better, but that event has, as usual, annihilated all order and discipline.'

In his despatch a week after the battle Wellington estimated that deserters and stragglers still totalled double the number of battle casualties.

'It is quite impossible,' he continued, 'for me or any other man to command a British army under the existing circumstances. We have in the service the scum of the earth as common soldiers; and in late years we have been doing everything in our power both by law and publications to relax the discipline by which alone such men can be kept in order; and it is next to impossible to punish any officer for neglects of this description.'

Wellington had barely restored order when the fall of San Sebastian, after a siege in which the stormers again suffered heavily, unleashed a wave of unparalleled savagery on the townsfolk, the French garrison having retreated to the citadel. Only the destruction of the town by fire forced the blood-crazed troops to quit.

Anticipating further disorders once he reached French soil Wellington gave Sir Edward Pakenham orders to execute all offenders on the spot. The corpse of a Spanish muleteer dangled from the windows of a cottage from which he had stolen fruit. Just to make it plain what the crime was, the men of the Provost Guard stuck an apple in the gaping contorted mouth.[6] Two soldiers caught attempting to rape two village girls were hauled before a divisional staff just as Wellington himself arrived on the scene. He offered a soldier of the 51st (K.O.Y.L.I.) his life because of the bravery of the regiment that day, but only on condition that he immediately hanged the other prisoner who was in a Brunswick regiment. The Brunswicker was promptly suspended from a cork oak by his late partner in

[6] Hibbert (ed.), *The Wheatley Diary*.

crime. A sergeant in the 51st found no mercy, however, when found guilty of striking an officer in the execution of his duty. It was a stupid affair, arising out of a quarrel between two sergeants over some missing money, and the men expected their comrade to be reprieved because of his notable previous service, and the fact that he had been born into the regiment. Instead he was shot in front of the assembled 7th Division.[7]

Harsh though all these measures were, they did bring about some improvement in the behaviour of the troops heading into France and despite all that they suffered at his hands, the men were always ready to fight for Wellington. He took that for granted, although he also conceded that their courage might fail them on occasions and is reported to have said, 'All soldiers run away. It does not matter as long as their supports stand firm.' The men themselves observed a strict code of conduct. Sergeant Anton of the Black Watch records the case of a comrade at Toulouse who concealed the fact that he had been shot in the bottom with a spent bullet because he was ashamed to reveal that he had been struck from behind.[8]

Speaking of the necessity for a man to keep in the ranks during battlefield movements, Anton commented:

'It is on the united movement of the whole body that general success depends; and he that rushes forward is equally blamable with him who lags behind, though certainly the former may do so with less chance of censure, and no dread of shame. A man may drop behind in the field but this is a dreadful risk to his reputation, and even attended with immediate personal danger, while within the range of shot and shells; and woe to the man who does it, whether through fatigue, sudden sickness or fear.'

Rifleman Harris records how he established a high reputation with his comrades by telling another soldier that if he saw him flinching in the field he could shoot him out of hand.

'It is, indeed, singular how a man loses or gains caste with his comrades from his behaviour.'

As at Lauffeld in 1747, when the 21st Foot fired on panic-stricken Dutch cavalry fleeing from the French, the British troops expressed their feelings by firing on raw Dutch/Belgian troops retiring in confusion at Waterloo. Cowardice, or desertion in the face of the enemy, which amounts to the same offence,

[7] *The Diary of Private Wheeler.*
[8] Anton, *Retrospect of Military Life.*

did not appear as major problems affecting the British rank and file during the Napoleonic Wars. The courage of senior officers, however, could be called into question as in the case of General Whitelocke, who commanded the abortive expedition to South America in 1807. Although the court martial charges brought against him concerned the conduct of the operations at Buenos Aires, his unfortunate choice of a safe headquarters in the rear seems to have told against him more than anything and he was duly cashiered with ignominy. General Sir John Murray was lucky not to receive the same verdict when court martialled for abandoning the siege of Tarragona for doubtful reasons.

Officers of all ranks, in those days, were expected to be seen to be brave and generally were. Even in his famous condemnation after the retreat from Burgos, Wellington emphasised that his strictures were no reflection on the gallantry of his officers. Although, throughout the war, courts martial were kept busy trying officers on charges arising out of neglect of duty, disobedience or social offences, such as brawling and duelling, cases of misconduct in the field were rare. To some extent, however, this may have been due to the dual standard applying in the enforcement of discipline. Ensign Edmund Wheatley, an Englishman serving in a battalion of the King's German Legion, was merely kicked and abused when his colonel found him asleep while on duty in the Pyrenees. But when Wheatley discovered that one of his sentries had been murdered while two more lay in an alcoholic stupor, he buried the dead man secretly and reported him as having deserted to the enemy. Otherwise the two drunks would have been put to death for 'sleeping upon Duty before the enemy.'[9]

[9] *The Wheatley Diary.*

5

'Scum'—Wellington's Legacy

Unhappily, in the forty years after Waterloo, when Britain enjoyed peace in Europe, it was the Duke of Wellington's personality rather than the manner of his achievements that made the biggest impression on the nation. Either lionized as a hero or hated as a reactionary politician, the real legacy of his military genius was obscured by the mists of adulation and rancour. The Duke, who had assiduously applied himself to man-management when in the field, establishing secure bases, reliable supply systems, adequate medical facilities and proper pay for his troops, did little to drive these lessons home in peacetime. Never tired of repeating that his soldiers had been the scum of the earth, his attitude secured for the rank and file a place in the lowest strata of society. Although he commented that it was wonderful that the dregs of the nation should have been turned into 'the fine fellows they are', the scum tag stuck. Soldiers were housed in decaying, disease-ridden barracks, dressed like circus performers and drilled like dummies. Their fate rested in the hands of colonels who might be as absurd as Lord Cardigan who placed his men on street corners so that he could strut about London receiving their salutes. It was as if the reforms initiated by Sir John Moore had vanished with the last straggler frozen in the slush of Galicia's rutted roads.

In weaponry percussion caps eventually replaced the flints of the Brown Bess muskets, making them more reliable, but the armament was little different from the equipment of the Seven Years' War, while tactics fell to an abysmal low. Even Wellington's tried custom of posting his troops on reverse slopes and making them lie down to avoid casualties was forgotten. The gory killing match of Waterloo, with the grand finale of the victorious bayonet charge of the whole line,

43

bemused Britain's generals. The courage of the troops was used as a bludgeon during battles in India. Massed frontal assaults with the bayonet were a recurrent feature of the bloody Sikh wars of the 1840s. Always careful with the lives of his troops during the Peninsular War, the Duke of Wellington was so shaken by the infantry casualties which resulted from the crude tactics at Chillianwallah (January, 1849) that he talked of taking command of the army himself.

Wellington had been dead two years when in 1854, due to his own archaic views, the incompetence of his proteges, the neglect of the government and the indifference of the public, the military administration broke down completely in the Crimea. One positive result, thanks to a larger literate audience better served by newspapers, was a more sympathetic and favourable public attitude towards ordinary soldiers. Their role as protectors of the European community in India further established them in the regard of the nation. And as the long-needed reform of the army took place in the second half of the century, some of the harsher features of the Mutiny Act and the Articles of War were eased.

Flogging, except in time of war, was abolished in 1871 (thirty years previously colonels had been restricted to sentences of not more than fifty lashes). The buying and selling of commissions, with the attendant abuses, was ended. The Mutiny Act and the Articles of War were revised and embodied in the Army Discipline and Regulation Act of 1879, which, two years later, became the Army Act. From this code enshrined in the Manual of Military Law, supplemented by various instructions and orders, no aspect of a soldier's life was free. Taking into consideration the hard cases who formed a significant proportion of the 'other ranks' plus the spirit of the age, the Act seems to have worked remarkably well. With regiments able to look back upon two hundred years of tradition, the British Army developed still further its very special character. The battalion became its most important constituent, unit pride its strength. Despite the many small savage imperial wars, casualties on the whole, were light. Much of the tactical training, however, was obsolete.

For this the army had to thank the long reign of the Duke of Cambridge, Queen Victoria's cousin, as Commander-in-Chief. The Duke had behaved with distinction in the Crimea and his thinking constantly reflected his experience there. As the

44

Crimea was merely a less skilful extension of the Peninsular War, it is not surprising that close order drill *en masse* formed a feature of the Victorian martial scene up to the Boer War. No-one doubted that the men were brave and still could be relied upon to fight. But success was not universal. There had been an inexplicable panic at Chillianwallah in 1849 when the 9th Lancers, the 14th Light Dragoons and two native cavalry regiments had bolted although they had suffered no casualties. This was regarded as an unfortunate incident and was dealt with by an informal inquiry by the over-all cavalry commander on the spot without embarrassing recriminations.

Panic of a more explicable nature occurred during the British attempt on the Great Redan at Sevastopol on 8 September, 1855. In an attack resembling warfare sixty years later, British troops seized trenches following a bombardment. They held on for an hour suffering severely from counter-she'ling. When this was followed by a Russian mass attack with the bayonet the British gave way, their officers being carried with them in the flight. Although the regiments involved bore distinguished names they had been filled with raw troops who had until then spent most of their time in sedentary trench warfare.

In the Chamla Valley Expedition of 1863, British and Indian troops broke in terror when savage hordes attacked the garrisons of two hill positions. The attack was the last straw in a month of tension and strain caused by keeping watch against an enemy highly skilled in hill-craft and patrol work.

It was Majuba in 1881, however, which gave the Victorian army its greatest shock. Placed carelessly on an exposed hilltop, a detachment under Sir George Colley was attacked by a force of resolute Boers. One by one the red-coated soldiers, whose white cross belts made them even more conspicuous, were picked off. Sir George was hit by several bullets and killed. The hidden marksmen wriggled nearer and nearer. At some point the nerve of someone in the British firing line broke. The majority fled, throwing away their rifles. Only a few small parties, including a group of Gordon Highlanders under Hector McDonald, stood fast. Majuba was a word to be mentioned in hushed tones for years afterwards, a blot to be wiped out, a shameful affair. Only a few officers saw that it was the inevitable outcome of a clash between the rigid formation of the old and the flexible tactics of the new. It was one thing for solid ranks to face up to the fire of low performance

45

muskets which were seldom accurate beyond eighty yards, but another thing entirely to remain exposed to hidden snipers using high velocity weapons at five hundred yards and more.

Majuba, the panic at Sevastopol and the Chamla Valley affair have one important element in common. In each case the troops involved were a mixture of units. No single regiment was involved. The incidents illustrate the strength and weakness of the peculiar system by which Britain's soldiers formed a number of regiments instead of an army. Among their comrades, led by familiar officers, the men were capable of unselfish courage to an astonishing degree. In 1879 the 24th Foot (South Wales Borderers) fought shoulder to shoulder to the end against the Zulu hordes at Isandhlwana and the 66th Foot (2nd Royal Berkshire) had sacrificed three-quarters of their strength acting as rear-guard to a brigade of demoralised Indian regiments cut to pieces by the Afghans at Maiwand (1880). Perhaps even more impressive examples of the old discipline are to be seen aboard the troopships *Birkenhead* and *Sarah Sands*.

In the first case, fully-trained soldiers on their way to join regiments in South Africa in 1852, calmly put their wives and children in a handful of life-boats after the ship had been holed by a rock. Then they fell in and remained in their ranks as the *Birkenhead* went down knowing that to take advantage of the Captain's cry 'every man for himself' would lead to the boats being overwhelmed. Three years later, aboard the steamer *Sarah Sands*, the 54th Foot (2nd Dorset) paraded on deck after the blazing ship was abandoned by her foreign crew. Detachment after detachment stepped forward to fight the flames until they dropped exhausted, but in the end the soldiers gained the upper hand and helped to sail the ship to port which it reached fourteen days later. After these inspiring displays of devotion and after the courage in battle shown by regiments like the 24th and 66th, is it any wonder that Victorian England expected her soldiers to be extraordinarily brave?

It is a notable fact that where units were not weakened by raw reinforcements, split up or placed under unknown officers, they lived up to that high standard.

It has become fashionable, particularly on television in recent years, to sneer at the late Victorian army as being a force which owed its success to the fact that it used modern weapons against ill-armed and badly led natives. The truth is

46

that on the North-West Frontier the British soldiers' opponents were generally much more numerous, highly skilled in the use of their weapons and armed to the teeth. Tribal leaders, operating from secure bases, set tactical, supply and political problems which would have tried the patience of a martial saint. And while the denigrators point to the victory over the Mahdi's army at Omdurman as being 'easy', they conveniently ignore the trap which was very nearly sprung on the British there and could have resulted in a massacre in reverse. Only fifteen years earlier a well-armed Egyptian force, led by British officers, had lost more than 2,300 men killed in an encounter with the Sudanese spearmen.

The disasters of the Boer War have been magnified also. It is often forgotten that at the beginning of the war the Boers took the initiative with larger forces and superior artillery. And the incompetence of generals, whom the public expected to provide lightning victories to justify the self-generated propaganda, can hardly be visited on the troops. Panics occurred, in particular at Magersfontein and Waggon Hill, near Ladysmith, but there was never any suggestion that the reigmental tradition was suspect. The Boer War was not a walk-over simply because it takes time to subdue national forces operating over large and friendly areas. At any rate some of the innovations of the despised generals of that era have survived well into this century—Lord Roberts's 'scorched earth' policy and Kitchener's blockhouses have their counterparts in the 'search and destroy' operations and the fire bases of Vietnam.

What the darker side of the South African war has obscured is the remarkable adaptability of the British Army immediately afterwards. Within ten years of the defeat of the Boer the army had been completely re-equipped and reorganized. Even the War Office had been put on a sound footing. To change the character of the rank and file in that time would have been asking the impossible. Regular soldiers were still regarded by many as being at the lowest level of the social scale; drunken, wooden and unable to do anything without supervision. In fact, not only were many of them experienced and shrewd but much of the drill which was pounded into them was also intelligent, thus making the dullest of soldiers into efficient fighting men. When he took the field in 1914 the British infantryman was an expert in handling his personal weapon; the Short Magazine Lee-Enfield rifle, and was well-schooled

47

in minor battle tactics, put to the test in various parts of the Empire. The cavalry, despite their swords and lances, were as proficient in the use of machine-gun and rifle as the foot soldier. Man for man they were professionally superior to any of their counterparts in Continental armies. It hardly seemed necessary to remind these superlative regiments embarking for France that under Army Act, Part I, Section Six, a considerable number of offences had been added to the list for which soldiers on active service could be put to death.

★ ★ ★

The Manual of Military Law, a volume of 908 pages in a plain red binding, could be bought for 2/- from booksellers when the First World War began. The 1914 edition was the sixth of its kind and like the others had been added to and revised since the Duke of Cambridge (referred to in the original preface as His Royal Highness the Field-Marshal Commanding-in-Chief) stated in 1884 that he was pleased to approve of the work. Eminent lawyers, soldiers and statesmen had combined to produce a comprehensive code. Much of it was concerned with offences against the ordinary law of the land and there were sections dealing with the standing of neutrals, treatment of enemy property, the Hague Convention and many other aspects of 'civilized' warfare. Incidents in the Franco-Prussian War of 1870 were freely quoted together with examples from the Russo-Japanese War which had been fought only ten years previously. Earnest students could sympathize with the commander of a large body of Russian troops who ordered his bandsmen to play the Japanese national anthem as an indication of their wish to surrender after the Battle of Mukden, use of a white flag being impractical at night. Unfortunately the music was assumed by the suspicious Japanese to be a ruse to deceive them and they immediately increased the fire they had been directing on the Russians. In order to avoid such mistakes, the correct manner in which to surrender was given an almost embarrassing prominence in the book.

The terms of the capitulation of Port Arthur were given in full, along with the convention which led to a French army going into voluntary internment in Switzerland in 1871. In view of the subsequent development of aerial warfare the wording of the 'International Declaration Prohibiting the Discharge

48

of Projectiles and Explosives from Balloons', signed in October, 1907, now has a particularly quaint ring.

Bizarre though some of the details may seem, it must be remembered that Europe was emerging from a long period of peace and, at least for some, prosperity. Furthermore, if the British generals had been stuck in the mud of the Crimea until 1900 those of France and Germany were still obsessed with the conflict of 1870. No-one, certainly not the writers of the Manual of Military Law, had foreseen the developments which a global conflict was to bring upon them. Of one thing the British were certain, however, and that was the need to maintain strict order in a field army. Part 1 of the Army Act, which was devoted to 'Discipline' with the sub-title 'Crime and Punishment' made it quite clear that all offenders would be dealt with swiftly and rigorously.

The first seven offences listed carried the death penalty ('or such less punishment as is in this Act mentioned'). They applied to soldiers who:

Shamefully abandoned or surrendered a garrison, place or post to the enemy, or compelled another soldier to do so.

Shamefully cast away their arms, ammunition or tools in the presence of the enemy.

Treacherously corresponded with the enemy or 'through cowardice' sent a flag of truce to him.

Supplied the enemy with arms or ammunition or shielded an enemy who was not a prisoner.

Took service with the enemy having been made prisoner.

Knowingly, while on active service, committed any act calculated to imperil the success of His Majesty's forces or any part thereof.

Behaved in a cowardly manner or induced others to behave like cowards.

Notwithstanding the all-embracing clause dealing with acts 'calculated to imperil the success of His Majesty's forces', the act contained a further section which defined 'Offences punishable more severely on active service than at other times'. There were eleven of them for which offenders could be sentenced to death. A soldier might be executed for:

Leaving his commanding officer to go in search of plunder.

Leaving a post or patrol without orders.

Breaking into a military store.

Forcing an entry past a sentry or striking a sentry.

49

Impeding the provost-marshal and his military police or refusing to assist them when called upon.

Attacking anyone bringing up supplies or damaging property of the country in which he was serving.

Housebreaking for plundering purposes.

Deliberately discharging firearms, drawing swords, beating drums, making signals, using words, or by any means whatever to give a false alarm.

Treacherously giving passwords to unauthorized people.

Diverting to his own unit supplies meant for other formations.

Being asleep or drunk on sentry duty or leaving a sentry post without being properly relieved.

Four more offences which could incur the death sentence were listed under the heading 'Mutiny and insubordination'. In addition to these, it was declared to be a capital offence, while on active service, to disobey an order from an officer on duty, and to strike or threaten an officer on duty. Deserters and men who persuaded comrades to desert on active service were also in peril of their lives, as were soldiers guilty of treason.

Just to make it clear where a man stood in relation to military law an abbreviated version of the capital offences was pasted into the 'Small Book' which recruits were given on joining the army before 1914. It added the sombre warning with regard to desertion that the death penalty could be inflicted upon anyone who deserted while under orders to proceed on active service.

A count of the offences above will show twenty-five crimes for which a man might have to pay with his life. Some cases, such as the reference to plunder and attacks on supply columns, directly reflect the influence of the retreat from Burgos.

Having spelled out such behaviour as would reap condign punishment, the Manual of Military Law proceeded to illustrate in a supplement how charges should be framed. The first of 87 specimen charges deals with a soldier who throws down his rifle and decamps—a capital offence. The second is more explicit on the subject of cowardice.

It applies to an imaginary private 'charged with misbehaving before the enemy in such a manner as to show cowardice in that he ... during an attack ... and when under enemy fire, fell out of the ranks, under the pretence of being unable to march further'.

A third illustration accuses a fictional soldier of 'leaving the ranks on pretence of taking wounded men to the rear, in that he . . . when in the ranks, and during an attack . . . without orders . . . on pretence of taking to the rear Lieutenant ——, who was wounded, left the ranks'.

The specimen charges left little to the imagination. On the lesser offence of disobeying an order in barracks the action of a recalcitrant private has the ring of melodrama about it, 'in that he . . . when personally ordered by Captain —— to take up his rifle and fall in, did not do so, divesting himself at the same time of his waist belt, and saying "I'll soldier no more, you may do what you please".'

Quartermasters and honorary captains who sell hospital rugs, captains who embezzle mess funds, soldiers who blow off two fingers of their right hand to obtain their discharge, even men who tamper with medical treatment for syphilitic sores—presumably to delay their return to something they regarded as being even more unpleasant—all are covered. All 87 'illustrations' were to be translated into reality in some form during the war.

Indeed the planners had left so little to chance that they almost invited the implementation of their regulations. Everything down to the phrasing required for correctly recording court martial verdicts was clearly outlined. In the case of capital offenders the words '. . . the accused (No.–Rank–Name–Regiment) to suffer death by being shot' were even followed by the word 'hanged' in brackets, no doubt to allow for the 'exigencies of the service'. Whatever else the British Army may have been short of when it set its stout ammunition boots on France's pavé roads, it was supplied with ample instructions for enforcing the 'iron hand' which the Duke of Wellington had declared to be so vital for the better conduct of soldiers.

Courts martial had been giving the generals something of a headache just before the outbreak of the First World War. Sir Thomas Milvain, the Judge Advocate-General, had been applying himself too assiduously to the legal niceties involved and he had upset certain commanders. Captain Wyndham Childs then appeared on the scene.[1]

Captain Childs was an unusual soldier. Commissioned into a volunteer battalion of the Duke of Cornwall's Light Infantry he had served in Ceylon for part of the South African War

[1] His memoirs, *Episodes and Reflections*, were published by Cassell in 1930.

guarding Boer prisoners. Further service at Stellenbosch, an arid 'rest' camp in South Africa, was followed by a period during which, among other things, he was present during the Tonypandy Riots. Childs was a hybrid creature, being neither professional soldier, lawyer nor policeman and yet with a reputation for being able to combine all three roles. A gaunt, almost frail figure, with impeccable manners and considerable reserves of charm, he applied himself vigorously to his job as a staff captain under the Director of Personnel Services at the War Office, Sir Nevil Macready. The situation there was far from his liking as he explained in his memoirs.

'The position was that for some time an appalling number of courts martial had been quashed under the advice of the Judge Advocate-General on technical grounds which no soldier could appreciate. The general officers commanding were becoming increasingly perturbed at the effect of these quashings on the discipline of the troops.'

Carefully Childs got to work. He developed a system by which he and his chief attached their own memoranda to files in transit to Lord Haldane, the Secretary of State for War. When the documents returned along the usual channels of communication the suggestions and comments were removed and the Judge Advocate-General received them none the wiser. By the time Sir Thomas Milvain discovered what was going on the practice had become too well established to break.

Although Sir Thomas rushed off to complain to Haldane, a contented Childs was able to report that 'Uncle Richard' (as Haldane was apparently known) smoothed the matter over.

'As a result of our concentrated efforts' he recorded, 'the quashing of courts martial began to diminish in number, much to the satisfaction of the Adjutant-General and the General Officers Commanding-in-Chief.' In other words, cases were being decided with the views of senior army officers exerting a telling influence over the application of the law.

Captain Childs' exertions did not go unnoticed. A lieutenant in 1910, he was Deputy Assistant Adjutant-General when war broke out and when the British Expeditionary Force went to France, he went with them.

PART II

1914-18

'Bill . . . you're in a hell of a funk.'
'Yes, I am. If you were in as big a funk you'd run away'.

ANON

6

The Code is tested

Ninety-nine years after the Battle of Waterloo, the British Army returned to the Continent, a small but elite force with considerable experience of active service in other parts of the world. Five brigades of cavalry, four infantry divisions and four hundred guns were skilfully and secretly landed in France according to well-laid plans, on the nights of 12 and 13 August, 1914.

Field-Marshal Sir John French, whose energetic use of mounted troops had won him high praise during the Boer War, arrived at the Gare du Nord in Paris to take command. Under him were the Ist Corps headed by Sir Douglas Haig, who had been one of his staff officers in South Africa, and the IInd, led by General Sir Horace Smith-Dorrien, a survivor of the massacre at Isandhlwana. Their concentration area was Maubeuge. Within ten days they were in close combat.

On 23 August riflemen watched in amazement as the German infantry advanced in masses towards the little town of Mons. Concealed in shallow trenches on the other side of the Mons-Conde canal men who had spent years perfecting their musketry for long ranges opened fire at anything from five hundred to a thousand yards.

The slaughter went on throughout the day, in the green fields, in the grimy streets of the red brick mining villages and among the mountains of colliery slag. But during the late afternoon it was obvious that things were happening elsewhere. The battered regiments were ordered to fall back. As the British Expeditionary Force tried to disengage the following day, a bitter struggle brought still further casualties. Retreating in blazing heat over roads jammed with refugees and detachments of all arms of the service, the IInd Corps poured into another mining town called Le Cateau. An even bloodier battle ensued after Smith-Dorrien had decided that his men would stand a better chance of survival if they fought rather than fall back further in their exhausted condition. By the time they retreated again most regiments had now suffered more casualties in a matter of days than the enemy had inflicted on them in the course of their entire history.

Bleary-eyed from lack of sleep, faint from want of food and parched through the shortage of water, the finest professional soldiers in the world staggered down the dusty roads clinging to their rifles with one hand while the other clutched at general service wagons or the stirrup leathers of cavalrymen.

And yet, when the order was given to face about on 5 September and the manoeuvres called the battle of the Marne began, the B.E.F. cheerfully complied. By their prowess, endurance and steady behaviour the Regular Army of 1914 won admiration which is acknowledged publicly to this day. But their code was stern. And before long it was invoked. A soldier of the 1st Duke of Cornwall's Light Infantry was 'put back' for court martial on a charge of 'shamefully casting away his arms in the presence of the enemy' at Le Cateau.[1] He was alleged to have discarded his bayonet and pouches. For this crime there is little doubt that the man stood a fair chance of facing a firing squad.

Fortunately an officer was able to disclose what really happened. A barb had embedded itself in the soldier's webbing as he crawled through a fence. All efforts to free him failed including an attempt by the officer to cut through the webbing with a clasp knife. Only when bullets were sending spurts all round was the man told to wriggle out of his equipment—which he did. If the officer concerned had been killed during the fighting—and the D.C.L.I. had been heavily engaged—the soldier's life might have been in jeopardy.

The first official death sentence was carried out within the first six weeks of the outbreak of war. A British soldier who had hidden his uniform and put on civilian clothes had been caught by gendarmes and handed over. His execution speedily followed; perhaps too hastily. For the meticulous Childs, who took part in the retreat, explained:

'Under certain circumstances a Field General Court Martial may be convened on the spot and the record of proceedings made in a very brief form in a (field) pocket book. After the

[1] Wyrall, *The Duke of Cornwall's Light Infantry, 1914–1919.*

army became stabilised and entrenched, the proceedings became more formal.'[2]

As only one man is officially recorded as having been shot by sentence of court martial in the period 4 August to 30 September, 1914, this may well have been the case. But an authentic report exists of another execution carried out on 30 September, 1914, which sounds as though it was also of an informal nature.[3] A private of 'B' Company, the 1st Royal Berkshire Regiment, reported the fate of one of his comrades as follows:

'We were in reserve . . . on or about 22 September, 1914, each man in his own dug-out (a hollow scratched in the trench wall) when an enemy shell dropped in the trench, killing two men. I was standing in the road at the time. When the shell burst Private 'A' jumped out of his dug-out and I promptly jumped in. This occurred about 3.30 pm. At 5.30 pm the company fell in on the road, when Private 'A' reported himself to Sergeant-Major S——, who asked him why he ran from the trenches. 'A' stated that he was slightly wounded, whereas he was not.

'For this crime he was court martialled on 29 September, and executed on 30 September. Only his Company Sergeant Major was called to give evidence. I was the only man who saw what happened, and yet I was never called.

'The battalion was due to move into the line that night, and twelve volunteers were called for to carry picks and shovels.

'Now the men who carried tools at that time had the first chance of using them, so you see there were plenty of volunteers, but once on parade they realized that their job was to shoot poor 'A'. On his being brought out he broke away from the sergeant of the guard, and the firing party fired at him on the run, wounding him in the shoulder. They brought him back on a stretcher and the sergeant of the guard was ordered . . . to finish him off as he lay wounded.'

At the time of the case, the 1st Royal Berkshires were serving in the Ist Corps on the Aisne where the Germans had halted in their retirement from the Marne. Soon they were to move to Flanders with the rest of the British Expeditionary Force. In the meantime, in between fierce local attacks, the Regular regiments took stock of themselves and tried to digest the lessons of the retreat from Mons. Not all of the disciplinary

[2] Childs, op. cit.
[3] The investigations of Ernest Thurtle, M.P.

57

action ordered was severe. Saluting parades were ordered as it had come to the notice of Sir John French that there was some slackness due to a misunderstanding on the need for exchanging courtesies on active service. Sixty of the 2nd Royal Welch Fusiliers, of the independent 19th Brigade, who had become separated from their battalion during the retreat and joined other units, were sent off on route marches for two hours a day when in reserve to make sure they didn't stray again. Errant officers had to march with them.[4]

Two lieutenant-colonels found themselves in a much more serious situation. Haig's Ist Corps, comprised of the 1st and 2nd Divisions, and Smith-Dorrien's IInd Corps, made up of the 3rd and 5th, had been joined by the embryo IIIrd Corps under General Pulteney just after Mons. It was composed of a single division, the 4th, made up, like the others, of Regular line battalions. In the retreat following Le Cateau, in which the 4th Division were heavily involved, two companies of the 1st Royal Warwickshire Regiment were cut off. Major A. J. Poole, the senior officer, extricated them by marching at night and hiding during the day—an action that was never forgotten by one young officer, Lieutenant Bernard Law Montgomery.[5] The remainder of the Royal Warwicks and a large detachment of the 2nd Royal Dublin Fusiliers continued to retreat in the rear of the British and eventually straggled wearily into the main square of St Quentin.

Dirty and dispirited, the remnants of the two battalions collapsed onto the cobbles and lay exhausted while their Commanding Officers, Lieut-Colonel John Elkington of the Warwicks and Lieut-Colonel Arthur Mainwaring of the Dublins conferred. Just as worn as their men, they were looking for defensive positions when some excited civilians appeared, led by the mayor of St Quentin. The British, declared the mayor, could not fight in his town. There were women and children to be considered. A bombardment would mean the loss of many innocent lives. The soldiers must go. When it was explained that the men were too tired to march on the mayor became even more excited. Then he had a brainwave. The British could capitulate. Together they could prepare a formal surrender note and when the Germans arrived they could give in to them. The mayor was very persuasive. Almost in a daze the

[4] Richards, *Old Soldiers Never Die*.
[5] Montgomery, Field-Marshal Viscount, *Memoirs*.

colonels agreed. Rifles were piled and the soldiers slumped down waiting. Sullen, disorderly and insubordinate was how Major Tom Bridges found them when he trotted in at the head of a detachment of the 4th Dragoon Guards. His conversation with the mayor, who insisted 'It is all arranged', and the colonels took place in an unreal atmosphere in which he was almost persuaded that what had happened was in some way 'legally' correct. Perhaps he remembered the pages devoted to surrender in the Manual of Military Law. Then he realized the ridiculousness of the situation, appropriated the surrender document and got the troops on their feet. Even then some were reluctant to go.

'Our old man's surrendered to the Germans and we'll stick to him' shouted one irate private. 'And we don't want no bleedin' cavalry sticking their noses in.'[6] Others protested that they weren't fit to march. Bridges might have shot any laggards on the spot. Instead he commandeered carts for the acute exhaustion cases and, persuading one of the colonels to accompany him, marched the rest off to the music of a penny whistle played by his trumpeter and a toy drum which he banged himself. As his band of strays stopped every time he halted to let them go on their way, he was obliged to tramp with them until the main army was rejoined.

It was then his unpleasant duty to report what had happened. Elkington and Mainwaring were both charged under Part 1, Section 4 of the Army Act which dealt with soldiers who shamefully delivered up 'any garrison, place or post or guard' which it was their duty to defend. The maximum penalty for such a crime was death, but the court martial sentenced both men to be cashiered. Mainwaring, an officer of thirty years' service, faded from the scene, but Elkington, something of an eccentric, joined the French Foreign Legion and served throughout the war, winning two medals for gallantry and losing a leg.

It is probable that the unutterably weary colonels had drifted into a fantasy world and that their judgment rather than their nerve had gone. For strain at this period tested to the limit commanders at all levels, and Sir Douglas Haig was not exempt from it. His Ist Corps had not been involved in any heavy fighting at Mons. The brunt had been borne by Smith-Dorrien's troops. But at Landrecies on 25 August a

[6] Lieutenant-Colonel Arthur Osburn's account recorded in *Vain Glory* edited by Guy Chapman.

sharp evening attack assumed an importance out of all proportion in Haig's mind. He ordered secret papers to be burned.
Dramatically he spoke of selling his life dearly. When arrangements had been made to defend the town he and his staff
drove off into the night. Brigadier Charteris, later his intelligence officer, summed up the feeling at that time in the words,
'it was better than staying in Landrecies and having sooner or
later to surrender, which seemed the alternative'.

The threat to Landrecies was quickly disposed of but Haig
was by this time convinced that the whole of the 4th Brigade—
four Guards battalions—was in danger.[7] He reported the
following day, to the consternation of Sir John French, that the
position of Ist Corps was critical. Even Smith-Dorrien, hard-
pressed eight miles away at Le Cateau, had received an appeal
for help from Haig. It was a poor performance, even allowing
for the explanation put forward by some of Haig's partisans
that he had been suffering from severe constipation at the time.
One is inclined to wonder what would have happened to a
private soldier who put forward the state of his digestive
system as the reason for some temporary lapse.

Despite its occasional intensity the war of manoeuvre was
something for which the British professional army had been
trained and something at which it proved itself. But as primitive
trench war began on the Aisne, it became obvious that the
soldiers would have to accustom themselves to new conditions
in which the plentiful German artillery, and in particular the
5.9 howitzer, played a major part. At the time of the German
thrust through Flanders in October, 1914, neither the British,
who had moved to the area, nor the French or Belgians who
also took part in the First Battle of Ypres, could offer much in
the way of a reply.

Between 20 October and 11 November, massive German
forces tried to burst through the Allied line. Sometimes the
defenders were outnumbered by as much as seven to one,
sometimes only four to one. But whether the Germans came
in the dripping dawn or the flame-slashed night, British rifles
and machine-guns took a fearful toll. At the same time, fine old
regiments were shattered for the sake of holding a few battered
drainage ditches.

On 26 October Sir Douglas Haig, showing none of the signs
of strain that had led to the melodrama of Landrecies, trotted

[7] See Terraine, *Douglas Haig, The Educated Soldier.*

out to see for himself what was happening. He had heard that battalions of the 7th Division, in Rawlinson's new IVth Corps, were retreating in disorder through one of his own brigades and despatched a staff officer to see whether this was due to an infantry assault or 'whether they are leaving their trenches merely on account of shell fire'.

The condition of the dishevelled, wild-eyed infantry streaming past his report centre astounded him. It was sad, he reflected, that they had been 'reduced to inefficiency' because their commanders had sited the trenches on the forward slopes of undulations, where they were clearly visible to the enemy. In fact the men of the 7th Division had held out in a restricted salient for thirty-six hours under a deluge of 210 mm shells before falling back with their weapons choked with grit and mud.[8]

The 3rd Division, which had seen much of the heavy fighting at Mons and Le Cateau, also came in for severe criticism from Haig when he paid a visit to its headquarters. He noted a 'lack of fighting spirit' and seeing several 'shirkers' making their way to the rear comforted himself with the knowledge that in the Ist Corps (the 3rd Division was in the IInd) he made it a practice to order abandoned trenches to be re-occupied at once and court martialled 'all men who have funked in this way'. Unlike King George V, who visited France at the beginning of December, Haig was not under the impression that British soldiers were all naturally brave. Sitting between the King and the Prince of Wales at a dinner in St Omer he made a point of describing the plight of the soldiers he had seen retiring down the Menin Road having thrown away rifles and packs in absolute terror. A discussion about the propriety of awarding the Victoria Cross for the rescue of wounded men under fire reminded Haig that detachments of police had to be posted behind the battle area to make sure that wounded men were not helped from the line by more of their unhurt comrades than was necessary.[9]

In his comprehensive study of the period, Major-General Farrar-Hockley, as might be properly expected from a professional soldier, states with pride that 'with the exception of two individuals . . . during the period October–November,

[8] See Farrar-Hockley, *Death of an Army*.
[9] See Terraine, op. cit., also Blake (ed.) *The Private Papers of Douglas Haig 1914–19*.

there were no cases of cowardice or desertion or quitting a post under fire'. While this reflects the evidence of various unit reports, it is not borne out by the statement of the commander of the Ist Corps. And it conflicts with the statement made by a Member of Parliament in 1919 that, in the early winter of 1914, he sat on a court martial which sentenced five men to death, although he was unable to say whether they had been shot.[10]

In truth, the B.E.F. had achieved more than anyone had a right to expect, mainly with their rifles and against greatly superior numbers of men and guns. But by Christmas they had lost 85,000 men killed and wounded, all of them trained soldiers. After recalling Regular battalions from overseas and replacing them with Territorials, the Old Army could put eleven infantry and five cavalry divisions into the field at the end of 1914.

But the formations which had fought at Mons and Ypres were far from being the superb units of August. Sir John French complained bitterly that two battalions had been filled up with ancient reservists who had not fired their rifles since the Boer War. A Scottish regiment was finding difficulty in assimilating a draft which spoke only Gaelic. The major temporarily commanding the distinguished 1st Camerons looked despairingly at the meagre reinforcements sent to him and concluded 'most of them are useless'. They were 'not up to anything like the standard that the regiment requires'. Where they failed was in their discipline and training. 'The standards of the 79th', he wrote, 'are enough to make the late officers turn in their graves.'[11]

Another officer posted to a brigade of the worn 3rd Division was dismayed by what he found.

'They had cracked to a man. You could not send them back to base, yet they were in such a state that they would have willingly taken ten years' penal servitude to stay out of the line. In these circumstances it was only fear of death that kept them at their posts. It is the worst tragedy I have ever seen.'[12]

It became clear that although the Regular divisions would still take pride of place in the order of battle, the soldiers who would fight the battles of 1915 would include many who were not trained to the standard which had hitherto been required. Furthermore, all the combatants would be subjected to the

[10] Hansard: *Official Parliamentary Reports*.
[11] Craig-Brown Papers, quoted in *Army Quarterly*, Vol. 102, No. 1.
[12] Lieutenant-Colonel Lambert Ward, Army Act debate, March, 1927.

strain brought about by new tactics, new conditions and new weapons which would place an even greater burden on individuals. Among the descriptions of the casualties recorded, a new type of battle statistic had appeared. Four officers and four other ranks in the infantry and one cavalryman had been sent home classified as suffering from 'shell shock'.[13]

*   *   *

If Lord Kitchener, the Minister of War, had not taken part in the Franco-Prussian War as a volunteer in the army of Napoleon III Britain's forces might have been expanded in a more logical manner. It was during his period in France in the 1870's that Kitchener first came across the word Territorial. It applied to second-line divisions made up of men who had completed their compulsory military service and in some cases were approaching middle age. Their performance did not impress him. When the Territorial Force was created in Britain no-one made it clear to Kitchener that it was a completely different organization. Many people, Haig among them, saw in 1914 that the Territorial Force was an ideal channel for inducting and training the large numbers of recruits who were going to be needed. It had trained officers and N.C.O.s. It had equipment, albeit not of the latest design. And it had tremendous enthusiasm.

Kitchener would have none of it. Instead he made his famous appeal for volunteers for completely new armies which would serve for the duration, divisions composed of Special Service battalions. Had the excellent material available been trained and led by an adequate establishment of Regular soldiers and N.C.O.s this could have worked. But there were not enough Regulars to spare. Nor was the machinery available to deal with the avalanche of volunteers.

Before the war a man was required to be of good physique and free from mental and physical ailments in order to pass the necessary tests at the recruiting station. The Army could afford to be fussy. After the outbreak of war the rush to join up was so great that for a time the qualifications for entry were actually raised to give the authorities breathing space. But as casualties began to mount, the restriction was dropped. The minimum height of five feet eight inches was dropped to five feet five

[13] *Official History—Medical Services, Diseases of the War*, Vol. 2.

inches on 11 October. Thirty thousand soldiers were killed or wounded that month and on 5 November the standard was lowered to five feet three inches.

The Army had to call in general practitioners to help to cope with the rush and although many did their best it was unfamiliar work for most of them. Each doctor was paid two shillings and sixpence (12½p.) for every man he examined. One of them dealt with four hundred men a day for ten days.[14] What the Army got for its £500 we shall never know. Certainly they did not get a recruit whose mental suitability could be vouched for.

Many recruits were not being properly examined well into 1915. It was easy enough to dodge or circumvent the induction system. Sometimes a huge crowd of men would gather on a parade ground and an N.C.O. would cut out a section to become part of a regiment with a base at a particular town. But there might be men present who had gone through the preliminary examination and did not wish to be posted to that depot for personal or domestic reasons. So they simply gave their papers to bystanders who had not yet been through all the administrative and medical processes and queued up again.

While creaking veterans and a few professionals struggled manfully to turn the willing but awkward raw material into soldiers the British Expeditionary Force got on with the war. At Neuve Chapelle, on 10 March, the First Army[15] surprised the Germans with a short but intense bombardment which enabled them to breach the enemy line. The success was not exploited quickly enough and the gap was sealed. All attempts to advance later were crushed. The machine-gun had been established as lord of the battlefield.

The following month the Germans used poison gas for the first time in warfare. French colonial troops on the flanks of the apparently dormant Ypres salient reeled back in terror. Fortunately for the commanders, if not for themselves, the Canadian troops holding the area alongside the North Africans stuck to their trenches.

Counter-attacks by massed British battalions were a prominent feature of the bitter fighting that followed. The dead of the 10th Brigade lay thick, in neat lines, where they had been

[14] *Report of the War Office Committee of Enquiry into 'Shell Shock'.*
[15] The British had formed First (Haig) and Second (Smith-Dorrien) Armies at the end of 1914.

caught in enfilade. Among them sprawled the men of the 1st Royal Warwickshires and the 2nd Dublin Fusiliers. Some of them had been in the demoralized mob roused by Tom Bridges at St Quentin . . . perhaps even the soldier who said they didn't want 'no cavalry interfering'. The following day Sikhs, Pathans and Baluchis were drawn into the holocaust and consumed. So were three battalions of Northumberland Fusiliers, the first Territorials to see action as a brigade. They had been in France less than a week.

Furious fighting continued until the end of May. It was as if the lessons of the Boer War had been forgotten in the excitement and the generals had fallen back on their Crimean heritage. Nearly 60,000 men were killed or wounded to retain a salient which was simply a huge chopping block for the German artillery. To have pulled back to the straight defensive line of the Yser Canal would have saved lives and released troops for supporting the shorter front. But in the eyes of the public and many senior officers the corpses rotting in the dank grass of the Salient had made its cold clay sacred. It remained an abscess on the nerve of the British Army for four years.

The gas which had heralded the German attack was, strangely enough, not as great a menace as had been feared, although it was responsible, among other things, for an outbreak of self-inflicted wounds among the French Colonial troops.[16] But the development of weapons continued at a tremendous pace. Apart from the formidable 5·9s and minenwerfer which could blow whole platoons to glory, the defenders of Ypres also had to contend with giant missiles from a 17-inch naval gun which began to tear the city apart at the end of April, 1915. Bombs, which had hardly been seen in the hands of the infantry for 150 years, ousted the rifle as the principle weapon of the foot soldier. A gradual increase in the use of mines by both sides completed the picture of a total return to classic siege warfare, not unlike the battles outside Richmond towards the end of the American Civil War.

Into this menacing world marched the enthusiastic innocents of Kitchener's new armies, sent into the line by stages to learn the ropes from the old hands. It was against one of these new formations, the 14th Division, composed of light infantry and rifle regiments, that the Germans launched their latest weapon on the morning of 30 July, 1915, in the desolate,

[16] MacPhail, *Official History of the Canadian Forces 1914–19.*

cratered wasteland at Hooge. As pillars of oily black smoke marked the German advance, the 41st Brigade fell back in disorder before swirling gouts of 'liquid fire'. Two lines of trenches were lost. The gap was eventually sealed by other battalions of the same division who clung to a splintered copse known as Zouave Wood despite renewed flame-thrower assaults. But it was a near thing. An officer who helped to stop the enemy reported in a letter home:

'When they used liquid fire, some of 'C' Company (whose officers and N.C.O.s were all knocked out) broke from about thirty yards of front and began to fall back (small blame to them). The machine-gunners (under Sergeant Silver), who were just in the rear, yelled to them that if they did not go back to their line they would open fire on them and that the 6th Cornwalls were going to "bloody well stick it". So the few men of "C" Company reoccupied their line of trench.'[17]

The Cornwalls did stick it, as they were to on other occasions. But the experience had a telling effect on some of the survivors. Private Joseph Bolge, who joined the battalion just after the attack, recalls listening to a boy with blood-shot eyes, a dirty yellow face and hair which had gone white as a result of what he had been through. The haggard soldier could not get over the fact that when he and his comrades had tried to run away from the flames they had been driven back by the Company Sergeant Major with a revolver. The green troops were now coming face to face with stark reality.

In another Kitchener Division—the 18th—a sentry in the Northants did not hesitate to shoot down one of a party of East Surreys bolting from a listening post into which an equally terrified German had fallen while on patrol. The sentry was congratulated.

When a post of the Manchesters was surprised on 16 August losing one man killed, one wounded and one a prisoner, their brigadier commented, 'They must have been asleep. Survivors (three men had escaped) are being tried by Field General Court Martial.'[18]

If giving troops confidence in their leaders is one of the prime elements of good morale, little had been achieved in this direction by the end of 1915. Haig's attempt to repeat the

[17] Wyrall, *The Duke of Cornwall's Light Infantry 1914–19.*
[18] Unpublished diary of General Sir W. Heneker, by permission of David Heneker Esq.

surprise of Neuve Chapelle by another attack on Aubers Ridge in May, while the Ypres battle still raged, had proved sterile and expensive. The landing at Gallipoli had been a fine example of heroism, but the cost had been exorbitant. In France vicious trench warfare during the summer months erupted in September into a full scale offensive by the First Army in support of the French in the Champagne. But Loos, despite an early success, repeated the disappointment of Neuve Chapelle. Released from G.H.Q. reserve too late to exploit effectively the opportunities created, the 21st and 24th New Army Divisions evoked the pity of even the German machine-gunners who had ripped belt after belt into the khaki masses plodding forward behind mounted officers. The enemy ceased fire as the bewildered and exhausted survivors drifted from the scene. By some superhuman feat the British rallied to come on again, but the battle was over as far as prospects of success were concerned.[19]

Regardless of the shortage of grenades and shells and the slaughter wreaked in some New Army divisions before they had been 'blooded', confidence and optimism still abounded. Troops of the Kitchener divisions which had been broken in more gently were getting harder and more skilful. In Britain itself, careful censorship, shrewd propaganda and a wave of prosperity generated by the expanding war economy, diverted attention from more unpleasant things.

But with the steady flow of wounded returning home came disturbing tales and now that so many young volunteers were subject to the strictures of the Army Act, other tentative voices were raised. On 9 June a Member of Parliament asked if any executions had been carried out on British troops serving in France. He received a simple 'Yes' for an answer. This seems not to have registered, for on 1 July another member, Mr Chancellor, inquired 'whether any, and if so how many, death sentences have been imposed'. He was referred brusquely and unhelpfully to the answer of 9 June.

A week later, the Under-Secretary of State for War, Mr Harold J. Tennant, was asked what communication was made to the relatives of soldiers who were executed and how soon afterwards the death sentence had been carried out.[20]

'The next of kin are informed of the facts', he replied bleakly. 'This communication is made through the Records Office on

[19] See Alan Clark, *The Donkeys.*
[20] Hansard: *Official Parliamentary Report.*

receipt of the official report from the base.'

As far as Parliament was concerned, the subject remained closed for the rest of the year. Developments had been taking place, however, in which they might have claimed a legitimate interest. As Mr Tennant had confirmed, executions *were* taking place in France.

In the first days of 1915, the major who had brought the 1st Camerons out of the line at Ypres wrote, 'A private who had been sentenced to death by a Field General Court Martial was executed today by a firing squad'.[21] He was not the only one that year. In his unvarnished and simple narrative *With a Machine Gun to Cambrai*, George Coppard, of the 6th Queen's Royal West Surreys, states how soon after arriving in France in June, 1915, his battalion was formed up in a square and heard the colonel announce that now they were on a war footing 'the severest military laws would apply for any dereliction of duty, such as desertion, mutiny, leaving the trenches without permission, cowardice and sleeping on sentry duty. A conviction by court martial ... would carry the death sentence. The C.O. then directed the adjutant to read out the names of nearly a score of Tommies who had recently been sentenced to death by courts martial held at Hazebrouck. I was stupified as the adjutant droned out each man's name, rank, unit and number, followed in each case by the words "and the sentence was duly carried out".'

Officially, during the twelve months ending 30 September, 1915, forty-eight other ranks paid the supreme penalty after being tried by court martial. One was shot for murder; had he been in England he would have been hanged according to the law of the day. Two men were executed for quitting their posts. Five men faced firing squads for what was classed as cowardice. And forty went to their deaths for deserting in the face of the enemy.

Altogether 126 charges of cowardice were tried in this period and 380 for desertion on active service. Those found guilty but not executed may be assumed to have been condemned to death with their sentences commuted to jail or some other penalty.[22]

Many men who had been condemned but reprieved had the indefatigable Childs to thank for their situation. The pale, lean

[21] Craig-Brown Papers, *Army Quarterly*, Vol. 102, No. 1.
[22] See *The Statistics of the Military Effort of the British Empire during the Great War*.

figure of this unusual man takes on an almost sinister character as it glides through the shadowy periphery of the war. Whatever else was happening, at least he could be relied upon to be going about his melancholy business tirelessly and conscientiously. After the Retreat from Mons the illness of the Adjutant-General required one of his assistants to deal with the administrative details concerning casualties, reinforcements and staff. Childs, the other assistant, became responsible for courts martial and discipline. He paints a vivid picture of the post.

'It was my unpleasant duty to take to the Commander-in-Chief, for his confirmation, all court martial proceedings where a sentence of death or penal servitude had been passed. I came to the conclusion that Lord French [then still Sir John] was one of the most humane and big hearted men I had ever met.

"If I brought him the report of a court martial where I did not consider the sentence should be inflicted it did not take more than a few minutes to deal with it; but if there was any question of carrying out the death penalty, he used to make me read every word and every line of the proceedings. He would take a cigarette out of his case and pace up and down the room. If there were any possible grounds for reducing the sentence, he was always more than anxious to do so.'

Childs states that on one occasion he had to report a 'particularly difficult' court martial and took the papers with him to French's advance headquarters while the battle of Loos was actually in progress.

'Lord French said "Write down on a piece of paper your opinion and bring it to me tomorrow morning". We then went to see the wounded coming in, and I realized his extreme popularity among the troops. As he stood by the roadside there was not a man, no matter how badly wounded, who did not attempt to raise himself on his stretcher and cheer his chief. I went to the Chief next morning and handed him my slip of paper. He gave me one in exchange. On each slip was noted a decision not to inflict the death penalty.'[23]

The phrase 'where I did not consider the sentence should be inflicted' has an ominous ring to it. Behind the use of the personal pronoun is an undercurrent of power. Yet it would be unjust to see Childs as an unfeeling man, even though the manifestation of his humanity was sometimes frightening in its rationality. A carefree band of soldiers attracted his eye at St

[23] Childs, *Episodes and Reflections*.

Omer one day. They were whistling and singing as they marched through the streets, regardless of the escort who marched alongside with fixed bayonets. There were 120 men in all, enough to provide two platoons and most of them trained soldiers. Inquiries revealed that the reason for their merriment was their destination—a prison at the base. That night Childs prepared a draft for a Parliamentary Bill which, forwarded through the proper channels, became law. Henceforth, under the Suspended Sentences Act, a soldier might be awarded ten years' jail for an offence and still remain with his unit, knowing that it could be imposed at any time—even when peace had returned. The Act also allowed for the remittance of any sentence 'no matter how severe' for a period of good conduct or a deed of gallantry. Childs' view of capital punishment was summed up with icy simplicity:

'It is a fundamental principle that any penalty inflicted on the troops must be one that will not cause a shortage of men.'

With that proviso borne in mind, he felt that 'the power to inflict the death sentence must be invested in the Commander-in-Chief, otherwise I do not think that any soldier would take the responsibility of commanding a body of troops in war.'

Childs' view was fully supported by the various Commanders-in-Chief during the war. In applying their powers they had no evidence to indicate that it would adversely affect their popularity with the troops. Field-Marshal Lord Roberts, who had begun his service during the Indian Mutiny and died of pneumonia while visiting France in November, 1914, had been steadfastly in favour of the death penalty and still retained the affectionate nickname 'Bobs'.

Nearly all the senior officers had served under Roberts at some time and most of them had been in South Africa when the old man, whose patriarchal appearance belied his toughness, warned the Boers that farms and houses would be burned down in the vicinity of any telegraph or railway lines damaged by guerrillas. A proclamation by 'Bobs' authorizing the use of prominent citizens as hostages on the engines of trains in troubled areas was withdrawn after only eight days, but it had its effect. In Roberts, commissioned a year before the Duke of Wellington died, the doctrine of the 'iron hand' had a devoted practitioner.

Paradoxically, one of the soldiers who had been most closely associated with Roberts throughout his career, General Sir

Ian Hamilton, was also one of the most progressive, an enlightened and humane man. But even he felt constrained to employ the ultimate sanction as the Dardanelles campaign ran its sterile and bloody course. Hamilton, who had had one arm permanently crippled at Majuba in 1881, found himself facing increasing difficulties in maintaining morale on the Peninsula, every inch of which was within range of the enemy's guns.

Like all serving soldiers, the troops sailing for Gallipoli had been warned what to expect if they failed in their duty and even the Royal Army Medical Corps were not exempted. On 4 August, Sergeant I. W. Austin of the 1/1st Welch Casualty Clearing Station noted in his diary as the troopship left Port Said:

'. . . we sailed in the evening about 5 and this time it is said for a destination where we are to come into contact with the grim realities of warfare. We know not yet where—we have had warnings from the O.C. as to what to expect; had impressed on us the demands of duty and discipline and the severity of punishment. It is the forerunner of experiences which we have been expecting since we appended our signatures to the attestation forms but now the hour has come, and our imagination starts conjecturing many things. All we hope is that we shall have the health and strength and grim determination to carry out faithfully and with a sacred purpose the duties allotted to us.'[24]

Two weeks later Sergeant Austin and his Welsh comrades were toiling without rest until dark in tents through which shrapnel occasionally ripped. On 22 August four hundred cases passed through . . . 'numerous legs and fingers being amputated—bullets extracted and various wounds attended to. Ghastly sights but work of surgeons clever. Big percentage of sick, chiefly from dysentery and diarrhoea. Effectiveness of treatment limited to tents and marquees could not be erected owing to closeness of shell firing. The dead are buried on a little hill right behind our office tent which is far from being such as one would find in the Cardiff City Hall or County Hall. It is a little structure of mackintoshes held up by a few poles with an open stretcher on one side to keep away the wind. . . . Flies are about by the million (no exaggeration) attracted by foodstuff and blood.'

As he wrote, Turkish shells dropped twenty yards away.

[24] Extract from an unpublished diary, quoted by permission of John Austin Esq.

The little, sand-blown cluster of canvas shelters is a portrait in miniature of the agony of Gallipoli. Through it go Indian mule drivers, hit by the shrapnel in the notorious gullies; an acknowledged hero of the 8th Welch Regiment denies that he did all the things attributed to him; a 'very obstreperous' wounded Royal Welch Fusilier from Llanberis is calmed by Sergeant Austin speaking Welsh to him and on 20 October 'several men with self-inflicted wounds and one sick case of a boy of 19 sentenced to death by court martial and commuted to five years' penal servitude.'

In November devastating gales and icy winds sent dozens of frost-bite and exhaustion cases through the clearing station and Austin reported 'English and Turkish soldiers on parapets looking at each other minus rifles'.

Despite reference to the young soldier reprieved after being sentenced to death, three men were shot on the beaches of Gallipoli by sentence of court martial, one of them a sergeant in the 13th Division who refused an officer's order to take out a patrol on what he thought was a futile expedition.[25] There might have been five more if Hamilton had not been the type of man he was. At one point he had confirmed the death sentence on five of the Worcestershire Regiment. They were within a few hours of being executed when the general went up to watch an attack. He was so impressed by the gallantry of the troops involved that he gave instructions immediately that the condemned men were to be reprieved and the sentences commuted to penal servitude.[26]

In an effort to stimulate the spirits of the troops he published details of the case in routine orders. But the rigours of Gallipoli continued to take their toll. No-one was immune. As early as 26 May special instructions were issued with regard to the prevalence of self-inflicted wounds. They were repeated again in July and each succeeding month. The 1st Australian Division was notably affected and the 2nd Australian Division had twenty cases in October. In November, the month of storms, the Deputy Adjutant-General of the Mediterranean Expeditionary Force stated that there were so many offenders that they would have to be treated at the front and not evacuated to hospitals on the island bases which served Gallipoli.[27]

[25] Testimony of ex-Sergeant S. W. Blythman, now living in Australia.
[26] Parliamentary statement by Ernest Thurtle, April, 1925.
[27] *Official History of the Australian Army Medical Services*, Vol. 3.

Disease, constant danger, poor rations, and a depressing existence among cemeteries containing the remains of their friends, were responsible perhaps even more than the enemy for driving to despair a handful of the courageous men who had stormed and held the beaches. But at the end of 1915, there was no need to issue any further admonitory orders to the troops at Gallipoli. On 4 December, Sergeant Austin, whose clearing station had been dealing with an endless stream of frost-bite, exposure and exhaustion cases, reported that the fickle weather had turned more like mid-summer than mid-winter. On 12 December, after noting almost casually that shell bursts not far away must be caused by a new Turkish 12-inch gun, the good sergeant, who had found inspiration in divine services throughout the campaign, recorded in his diary: 'Talks of evacuation and an early return prevalent. Hopes raised and visions of home.'

On 19 December, under the noses of the Turks and despite their new 12-inch gun, the Peninsula was abandoned without a life being lost. In their relief, the troops did not consider the fresh ordeals that lay ahead of them in France.

★   ★   ★

In one of the many vicious little battles that persisted after the battle of Loos, James Norman Hall, an American serving as a private with a New Army battalion of the Royal Fusiliers, witnessed a furious struggle for a sandbag barricade in which box after box of grenades was expended, lighting the night with lurid flashes. A soldier with bandaged eyes was led back by another with a shattered arm. Behind them hobbled a man displaying unfeigned delight at the wound which would act as a passport home. There were others.

'One lad, his nerve gone, pushed his way frantically down the trench. He had 'funked it'. He was hysterical with fright and crying in a dry, shaking voice . . .

'It's too 'orrible. I can't stand it! Blow you to 'ell they do! Look at me! I'm slathered in blood! I can't stand it! There ain't no man can stand it!'

'He met with scant courtesy. A trench during an attack is no place for the fainthearted. An unsympathetic Tommy kicked him savagely.

'Go and 'ide yerself, you bloody little coward!'[28]

Although 1915 had been a taxing and terrible year, a lot more men would seek desperately for places to hide themselves before another year had passed, bringing with it even greater horrors.

[8] Hall, *One of Kitchener's Mob.*

7

Case of the East End Boy

The truce which had been observed informally by the soldiers on both sides at Christmas, 1914, was not repeated when the season of peace and goodwill came round again. Sir Douglas Haig, who had taken over from Sir John French as Commander-in-Chief on 19 December, ordered two officers of the Scots Guards to be court martialled for defying specific orders and allowing their men to fraternize with the enemy. Although Sir Nevil Macready, the Adjutant-General, tried to avoid the issue by raising some obscure question of the need for having the King's permission, he was over-ruled. The Army Act must be applied to Guards officers in the same way as to any other officers who might do wrong on active service, Haig declared. Towards the end of January one officer was acquitted but the Commander-in-Chief confirmed the sentence on the other, Sir Ian Colquhoun. Sir Ian was to be reprimanded but because of his distinguished service the sentence was remitted.[1] Discipline had been re-asserted. It was a strange incident which seemed to absorb Haig's interest unduly at a time when more relevant matters might have demanded undivided attention.

Intense mine warfare had developed as an aftermath to the battle of Loos. The pits dotting the area of the First Army gave ample proof of the suitability of the terrain. Heavily involved in this exacting form of warfare were the volunteers of the 12th Division of Kitchener's Army.

Their emblem was the Ace of Spades but in the winter of 1915–16 they came to regard it as a ruddy shovel. The 12th had arrived in France on 1 June and, after a spell in quiet sectors, had fought for twenty-one days in the Loos area losing more than 3,000 men. Later they had occupied the flooded meadowland at Festubert where the front was held by

[1] See Blake (ed.), *The Private Papers of Douglas Haig.*

75

sandbag 'islands' which could not be relieved by day.

Despite the issue of gumboots and whale oil for rubbing sodden feet, plus the setting up of soup kitchens behind the line, scores of men went down with trench foot and other illnesses. One of those who stuck it was a young Jew who came from the East End of London and had enlisted in the 11th Middlesex Regiment in September, 1914. 'Aby' was the despair of his parents. If he had been a scholar, or gone into business, or trained for a profession they would have regarded him as a credit to their name. To be a soldier was almost shameful. And Aby was their only son.

The 12th Division was holding the line over Christmas. On 21 December, the enemy blew a mine near Givenchy, but it did no harm. Another caused 25 casualties on 23 December. During the 24th a furious battle raged over the crater and both sides showered rifle grenades on each other.

On 29 December four bombers of the Royal Sussex were manning a small T-shaped sap on the lip of a crater when the Germans exploded yet another mine and partially buried them. Doggedly the section struggled from the earth and drove the enemy back. A furious exchange of shelling followed and spread along the front.[2] During the general turmoil Aby was hurt. Two weeks later his father received notification from the Infantry Office at Hounslow:

'Sir, I regret to inform you that Private——, 11th Battalion Middlesex Regiment, G.S., is ill at 38th Field Ambulance, France, suffering from wounds and shock (mine explosion).'

His mother, to whom he had written in an earlier letter the pathetically frank confession 'I do not like the trenches', immediately wrote back. A rambling reply arrived, dated 24 January.

'Dear Mother, You don't know how I was longing for a letter from you. I would like to know what the War Office said was the matter with me. I am very sorry I did not write before now, but we were in the trenches on Christmas Day and had a lot to do. Also I was sent to hospital. I am feeling a little better now, so don't get upset. Don't send any letters to the company as I won't get them. Also you cannot write any letters to the hospital as I won't get them. I am sending you this photo of one of the officers who was killed. He was very

[2] Rutter, O. (ed.) *History of the Seventh (Service) Battalion, The Royal Sussex Regiment, 1914–1919.* The Times Publishing Co. 1934.

good to us. Frame it for a keepsake.'[3]

The 12th Division came out of the line on 19 January and went into reserve. During this period Sir Douglas Haig and General Joffre, the French Commander-in-Chief, inspected the 36th Infantry Brigade to which the 11th Middlesex belonged. Three weeks later the formation was back in action for some of the stiffest fighting of the war, when the British made a determined attempt to seize the group of giant sludge-filled pockmarks known as the Hohenzollern Craters, plus three trenches known as The Chord, Little Willie and Big Willie. The Germans, suspecting an attack, tried to forestall it. On 13 February three massive explosions caused eighty casualties in the 11th Middlesex but as the Germans rushed forward hurling stick-bombs they were met by a storm of fire and driven back. The Corps Commander sent the 11th a special message of appreciation.

For the rest of the month, in snow, sleet and rain, the sodden atmosphere was frequently rent with a dull glare as one side or the other detonated mines. Germans and British then raced to occupy the resulting cavity. Grenades were the most common weapon used and their splinters ripped into the unprotected backs of troops trying to set up machine-guns on the lips of craters. Body after body, wounded and dead alike, slithered down the muddy slopes into the stinking, smoking pools that formed at the bottom. In some of these vicious battles, great deeds were performed.

Lance-Corporal William Cotter of the 6th Buffs, with a leg blown off at the knee, and wounded in both arms, dragged himself to one crater and took charge of shaken troops there. For two hours he directed their fire and encouraged them to hold out. Fourteen hours later he was carried to the rear. He lived long enough to hear he had been recommended for the Victoria Cross, which was awarded posthumously.[4] It was a great event in the history of the Division. But when Private Aby —— heard of it, he was under arrest. On 23 February, ten days after the Germans had blown a mine under the 11th Middlesex, he wrote to his mother:

'I have sent you a letter that I have received the parcel. I am well and hoping all of you are quite well. Dear mother, we were in the trenches and I was ill, so I went out and they

---

[3] See Pankhurst, *The Home Front;* also quoted by Chapman in *Vain Glory.*
[4] See Scott and Brumwell, *History of the 12th Division.*

took me and put me in prison, and I am in a bit of trouble now and won't get any money for a long time. I will have to go in front of a court. I will try my best to get out of it. But dear mother, try to send some money. I will let you know in my next how I get on. Give my best love to father and Kath. From your loving son, Aby.'

The next letter which arrived concerning Aby was not from France. It came from Hounslow. Dated 18 April it said:

'I am directed to inform you that a report has been received from the War Office to the effect that No. ——, 11th Battalion Middlesex Regiment G.S., was sentenced after trial by court martial to suffer death by being shot, and his sentence was duly executed on 20 March, 1916.

I am Sir,

Your obedient Servant,

P. G. Hindley,

2nd Lieut. for Col. I. C. Infantry Records.'[5]

The Army List for the period shows a 2nd Lieut. P. G. Hindley as working in Infantry Records, Hounslow.

According to a member of No. 5 platoon, 'B' Company, of the 11th Middlesex, Aby was shot at dawn at Sailly La Bourse. 'He was known to the whole company as a bundle of nerves. He ran away from the trench known as Vigo Street after it had been bombarded for six days and nights, and we had suffered heavy casualties.'[6]

It was not the first time that Sailly La Bourse had been the scene of an execution. George Coppard, whose battalion was also in the 12th Division, recalled a memorable guard duty there.[7]

'It was early November and the nights were dark and cold. Flashes of light from the Hohenzollern Redoubt five kilometres east, lit the sky. I could hear the deep roar of minnie bursts as I paced up and down the miners' cottages in which my companions were sleeping. At first light . . . a party of a dozen men approached my post, and turned off into the Annequin Road where there was a disused coal mine. Later I heard a volley. On that day a rumour went round that two Tommies had been executed that morning. Rumours of that kind were generally based on fact.'

The day after the frightened Jewish boy from the East End

[5] Quoted by Pankhurst and Chapman.
[6] Information collected by Ernest Thurtle.
[7] *With a Machine Gun to Cambrai.*

made his last journey, quite likely to the same disused coal mine, the Under-Secretary of State for War, Mr Tennant, was fielding an awkward ball in the Commons.[8] On 27 January, against considerable opposition, the Military Service Bill had become law. As from midnight, 1 March, all bachelors who had not joined the army already were reckoned to have been automatically enlisted for the period of the war. It was just one step on the road to conscription. Boards were instituted to hear appeals. What Mr Tennant found embarrassing was the questioner who wished to know if he was aware that the Market Bosworth Tribunal had exempted all hunt servants of the Atherstone Hunt as being employed in an indispensable occupation.

It was a nasty one, but Mr Tennant, the Liberal Member for Berwickshire, dealt with it bravely.

'I have little doubt that the Tribunal dealt with the matter carefully and conscientiously' he declared, adding cautiously that he had no direct information on the matter.

At the beginning of 1916, however, the Commons were showing signs of posing much more troublesome questions.

Mr Philip Snowden, the renowned Socialist member for Blackburn, started the ball rolling late in January when he wanted to know simply how many soldiers had been shot for desertion and other military offences since the outbreak of war.

Mr Tennant carefully played the matter down. He stated specifically that no British soldier had been shot in the United Kingdom. As far as the forces overseas were concerned, he did not consider it to be in the public interest to give details, 'but I will ask my honourable Friend if he will be good enough not to believe that the number has been considerable.'

It was a tortuous way of saying 'not very many'.

Not everyone was satisfied with it. A month later Mr Tennant faced another inquiry which showed how ignorant even Parliament was about the conduct of courts martial:

'How many hours elapsed between the dismissal of an appeal by the Court of Criminal Appeal or the confirmation of a death sentence, whichever the case might be, and the execution of a condemned soldier?'

'I find the approximate average interval has been five days'

[8] The following extracts from Parliamentary Debates are all quoted from *Hansard*.

was the reply. Mr Tennant did not take the trouble to explain that the Court of Criminal appeal was not involved. Appeals, he knew, were a subject to be avoided.

On 8 March a question with even uglier implications was fired at him by Mr Thomas Lundon, an Irish Nationalist M.P. He wanted to know if it was true that post-cards were used to notify parents that their sons had been sentenced to death and shot. Would steps be taken, he asked, to notify parents of the death of their sons without reference to courts martial or otherwise? Mr Tennant expressed surprise.

'I am not aware that deaths taking place in the circumstances mentioned have been notified by open post-card' he said. 'Record Offices are provided with forms on which to notify deaths. As regards the last part of the question, it has been decided that as, in these cases, the relatives were bound to know sooner or later the circumstances of death, it was better that they should be informed at once.'

Once again there was a certain amount of evasion—he had not specifically denied that post-cards had been used.

Later that month when challenged to state the number of soldiers under twenty years old who had been shot he grew openly testy.

'Just as it is not in the public interest that a question like that should be asked, so it is not in the public interest that it should be answered' he snapped at Mr Outhwaite, a perverse Tasmanian who for some strange reason represented Hanley and was a member of Mr Tennant's own party.

Then, in May, the case of the East End soldier of the Middlesex Regiment came to light. Miss E. Sylvia Pankhurst, the formidable socialist and radical, was told that five families in the East End of London had received letters saying that their sons had been shot and went to investigate. Four of the families seem to have had second thoughts, but she found the fifth in a poor street off the Whitechapel Road. A sorrowing mother showed her the boy's last letters. Miss Pankhurst, then thirty-five years old, got to work.[9]

On 4 May, Mr F. W. Jowett, another socialist stalwart, took the opportunity to ask Tennant a series of questions relating to the boy. He wanted to know if the Under-Secretary would lay on the Table of the House:

the record of the court martial;

[9] Pankhurst, *The Home Front*.

the names of the officers constituting the court martial and the name of the officer or officers who confirmed the sentence.

He also wanted to know if Tennant would indicate whether the private referred to was defended by counsel, solicitor, or prisoner's friend.

Mr Tennant: 'It is regretted that it is not possible to comment upon the sentence of courts martial approved by the Commander-in-Chief.'

Mr Snowden: 'Are we to understand from that reply, that it is or is not a fact that this boy, only nineteen years of age, was shot?'

The answer to this question was too curt—almost callous.

Mr Tennant: 'I don't know what his age was but undoubtedly he was shot.'

Mr Outhwaite moved in quickly and indignantly: 'Is the Right Honourable Gentleman aware that sentence of death was passed within a month of this boy leaving hospital where he had been for a nervous breakdown caused through wounds due to a mine explosion? Is it customary to shoot boys in such circumstances?'

Mr Tennant showed definite signs of being rattled.

'I was not aware of that fact. . . . If there was any desertion . . .'

Mr Outhwaite carried on relentlessly.

'If I show the Right Honourable Gentleman the letters I have received on this subject, will he take this matter into consideration?'

There was no reply. The treatment of deserters remained, as it had been since August, 1914, shrouded in mystery. Mr Tennant did nothing to illumine the House. But the conscience of many Members was disturbed. During the first eighteen months of hostilities, the parents or relatives of men who had been executed had remained silent. A sense of shame, heightened by the patriotic fervour of the period, kept them silent. And the military authorities, anxious to promote recruiting, were hardly likely to broadcast the more severe penalties inflicted on soldiers for breaches of discipline. Scores of boys of sixteen and seventeen had contrived to get themselves into uniform and many more were not officially adults. On 10 May, 1916, Mr Jowett wanted the government to give an undertaking that the death sentence would not be applied to soldiers under twenty-one except where an offence under the civil

81

criminal code would merit the same punishment. He went further and asked that no soldier, whatever his age, should be shot if he had been wounded previously—unless he committed murder. But Mr Tennant would concede nothing.

Another Member, Mr Farrell, Nationalist Member for North Longford, then raised a specific case, involving a Private Hope who had been shot the previous spring. Was it true that no hint had been given to Hope during the entire proceedings that he was in mortal danger? Could the Secretary of State for War enlighten the House on the allegation that it was not until an hour before his execution that Hope was informed that he was to die?

According to Mr Farrell, Hope had previously given gallant service in the trenches and had proved that he was neither a coward nor a shirker. Had this been brought before the court martial? Furthermore, he would like to know whether the man had been defended and whether the sentence had been confirmed according to the regulations laid down.

Mr Tennant was well prepared. If it was Private T. Hope of the 2nd Leinster Regiment who was referred to, he had been tried by a field general court martial on 14 February, 1915, on a charge of desertion and other minor charges. The evidence showed that he had been missing from the trenches from 23 December, 1914, until 9 February, 1915, when he was arrested.

'It is well known to all soldiers that desertion in the face of the enemy is liable to be punishable by death. Private Hope was informed of his sentence more than twelve hours before it was carried out. The sentence was passed on 14 February, and was most carefully reviewed before it was confirmed by the Commander-in-Chief on 27 February.'

It was obvious, Mr Tennant continued, that counsel could not be employed in the field. Hope had called no evidence as to his previous conduct and none was before the court martial. He added in answer to a further question:

'When a man has been sentenced to death and all the possible means of obtaining a reprieve have been exhausted, to defer the execution unduly does not appear to be at all desirable in the interests of the condemned.'

No more was heard of Private Hope whose regiment had distinguished itself in the battles near La Bassée in the autumn of 1914.

Further attempts to gain the figures of executions were made later that month, but without success. Mr Tennant did reveal, however, that separation allowances to wives, widowed mothers, etc., were paid for twenty-six weeks after notification of death. He refused a plea to have all death sentences sent to England for confirmation.

Towards the end of the month, Mr Jowett adopted a new tack. He wanted to know if any men had been summarily shot without the benefit of a court martial and whether the names of the officers ordering the executions were kept at the War Office for reference.

Stonily Mr Tennant replied, 'There is no power to inflict a death sentence for a military offence except after conviction by court martial. The rest of the question, therefore, does not arise.'

The intransigent attitude adopted by Mr Tennant may be explained by the fact that he was probably aware that preparations were in hand for major operations in France. It was no time for faintheartedness. Certainly the commander of the 9th Royal Irish Rifles took a stern view of any signs of weakness.

Lieutenant-Colonel F. P. Crozier, member of an old service family and veteran of campaigns against the Boers and dissident tribesmen in West Africa, took the view that 'funk in itself is nothing. When unchained it becomes a military menace, and for that men die at the hands of their comrades.'[10] On active service at Kano, in Northern Nigeria, he had superintended the execution of an African soldier who had murdered and robbed a trader in the market. Having some experience of native marksmanship he solved the problem of an unreliable firing squad by having the condemned man shot at close range with a Maxim machine-gun.[11] Colonel Crozier was definitely not a man to be trifled with. Endowed with a heavy sense of humour he allowed himself to be taken to a recruiting centre by a woman who offered him white feathers as he strolled in civilian clothes through Coventry Street, London, at the beginning of the war.

His humour had an unfortunate effect when it entailed the participation of a young officer in his battalion. Crozier thought it would be a fine idea to send the man out with a notice to hang on the enemy wire stating that their wives and children were being starved by the British blockade. It was a tense and highly dangerous excursion and stretched the nerves of the

[10] Crozier, *A Brass Hat in No-Man's Land.*
[11] Crozier in an article in the *Sunday Express*, 13 May, 1928.

young man to the limit. Later that day, when the Germans laid down a heavy mortar bombardment, Crozier was shocked to see a wild-eyed figure bolting up a communication trench, scrambling past him without stopping. It was the officer who had hung the notice on the wire. He was found some hours later in a disused French dug-out. Immediately Crozier arranged a court martial which found the officer guilty of charges of cowardice and desertion in the face of the enemy.

About the same time an absentee, whom Crozier named as Private Crocker, was caught behind the lines by the military police. He too was court martialled and found guilty of desertion. Soon afterwards Crozier received an order to release the officer from 'arrest and all consequences'. As Crozier refused to have the freed man back in his battalion he was posted elsewhere. At the same time the authorities wanted to know if he wished the death sentence to be carried out in the case of Crocker. Unhesitatingly he sent off the reply, 'In view of certain circumstances I recommend the shooting be carried out'. The court martial sentence and confirmation were read out before the prisoner and the whole battalion which Crozier then led back to billets, drums beating.

'We all feel bad but we carry out our wartime pose,' was his description of the occasion.

Crozier gave the padre permission to visit Crocker but advised him not to be too long-winded and later sent his company commander for a farewell chat. Otherwise Crocker was left alone with his guard, a bottle of whisky and a pint of rum. Having assured himself that the condemned man would have a comfortable billet for his last night on earth, the colonel then superintended the next step.

In the back garden of a ruined villa a post was set well into the frosty ground. Into this were driven a number of hooks so that the ropes binding the man to the stake would not slip. Crozier regarded the hooks with a certain amount of professional pride . . . 'we always do things properly in the Rifles!' Finally he selected a junior officer to take charge of the execution, warning him that in the dawn light, when cold and nervous, even the best marksmen sometimes miss. So the youngster would have to be prepared with his revolver to complete the job should it be bungled. Just to make sure that the officer did not seek refuge in drink that night and appear with a hangover in the morning Crozier insisted on him joining him at dinner. No doubt it gave the veteran an opportunity of regaling the subaltern with his experiences of other grim events in West Africa.

The next morning, in the winter darkness the 9th Irish Rifles formed up by companies and marched along the road which ran beside the villa. They halted in front of the park wall. On the other side stood the post waiting for its victim. The military police had a difficult job with Crocker. He had drunk most of the whisky and all of the rum and it was like trying to truss an alcoholic jelly. Finally they carried his unconscious body out into the morning air and hung it from the hooks Crozier had so thoughtfully provided.

From his position on his horse in front of the battalion on the other side of the wall, Crozier could see everything, the firing party, the padre, the medical officer and the subaltern standing with his revolver drawn and loaded as ordered. No orders were to be given on the side of the wall where the execution was being carried out. By arrangement Crozier would call his men to attention when the officer in charge of the squad raised a white handkerchief. At the same time the execution squad would raise their rifles to the present. As the officer dropped his arm they would fire. Everything went according to plan. As the handkerchief rose the Rifles obeyed their colonel's command and crunched to attention. When the arm fell the volley roared out. Then Crozier saw the medical officer hurry over to the limp figure and turn.

'Alas, as I had expected, although only a few yards from the doomed man, several bullets missed their mark.'

The young officer used his drawn revolver immediately.

With a roll of drums the band of the 9th Irish Rifles struck up and in quick time to a merry march the battalion followed its leader back to breakfast, leaving Crocker's own company to bury him. Colonel Crozier had given instructions that the dead man was to go into the 'Died on active service' return so that his dependants could claim a pension. He was most annoyed to learn that the authorities had notified the next-of-kin, to avoid just that eventuality.

The arrival of the official notification in the Belfast street where Crocker lived may have caused a mild sensation. But his solitary death would be quickly forgotten in the welter of other dreaded letters soon to arrive. For the Battle of the Somme was about to open.

8

No mercy for an Officer

Guns were to be the key to success. In the pleasant woods along the River Ancre, dozens of metal monsters were hauled into position so that their black mouths gaped towards the white ribbons of trenches cut into the chalk by the Germans.

Haig's immediate plan was to crush the German defences with a devastating bombardment after which elements of sixteen British divisions, half of them New Army formations, would advance over the ruins and enable the reserves to 'go through'. Five French divisions would co-operate on the right of the twenty-five miles of front to be attacked. Apart from the obvious results of inflicting a major defeat on the German field army the offensive was intended to relieve pressure on the French at Verdun where the battle begun in February was raging furiously.

It was not thought necessary to conceal the vast effort being made in the rear of the British lines. The Germans looked on and continued to strengthen the defences on which they had been working for eighteen months. Every village was turned into a fortress.

Unaware of the full strength of the opposition facing them, the British troops looked forward to their task with optimism, in particular the Kitchener divisions, the men who had answered the first call for volunteers. Where the old army relied on regimental tradition many of the new battalions had a strength born of their provincial origins, of the factories and industries they had left. The Regular divisions, although they had assimilated many recruits far below the standard of the 1914 B.E.F., contained enough returned wounded and long-service officers to maintain their professional superiority. Nowhere was the optimism greater than at G.H.Q.

The British artillery preparation began on 23 June. Before

long the woods were stripped of their leaves and palls of dust rose with the blast and recoil of the massed batteries. Six 15-inch, eleven 12-inch, sixty 9·2-inch, sixty-four 8-inch and one hundred and four 6-inch howitzers shook the earth with their ranting and bellowing. Shells weighing up to eight hundred-weight plunged on the German positions over a considerable depth. Crossroads six miles behind the line were blasted by the 290 lb. shells of the 8-inch guns.

It went on for a week at the end of which the 18-pounder field batteries concentrated fire on the German barbed wire. At 7 am on a fine sunny morning the drum fire on the German front line lifted and the British infantry advanced, walking forward with nearly eighty pounds of ammunition and equipment on their backs. Many of the entanglements were still uncut and the Germans emerged from their warrens to riddle the attackers with machine-gun bullets. Nearly 20,000 British soldiers were killed and 40,000 wounded by nightfall on 1 July. The German loss was trivial by comparison. On the right of the line one of the few successes of the day was notched up by the 30th Division. They fought their way forward and overran the defences of Montauban. The 21st Division, which had suffered so heavily at Loos, also clung grimly to the ground it gained. But the assault failed to rupture the defences and, in furious attempts to burst through, the deluge of shells grew thicker and thicker, the target areas smaller and smaller and the German counter-barrages heavier and heavier. Into this inferno the units of the divisions used in the initial assault were sent time and again. As the summer wore on and these shattered units were reduced to skeletons, others took their place. Intolerable noise abused their ears, unspeakable sights affronted their eyes, and death in hideous forms threatened on all sides. But for five months the British soldiers inched their way forward against the toughest imaginable opposition.

Gradually a large bulge in the enemy lines was created with a maximum depth of slightly more than six miles. Inside this pulverized area the battalions of the B.E.F. lived and worked and assembled before each attack. They were expended ruthlessly.

Proven reinforcement methods had to be dispensed with in order to keep regiments up to strength. Drafts were sent to fill depleted battalions regardless of their origin.

Disillusioned soldiers met some of them at the base depots

with cries of 'More for the slaughter house'. Returning wounded particularly resented being sent to units where they were among strangers, in regiments with alien traditions and different regional background. To a man, the soldiers who fought the battle of the Somme had been born into the reign of Queen Victoria and brought up with a romantic vision of the army as men in scarlet jackets who fought short sharp battles under the blazing sun. The Somme was the longest continuous battle fought by the British Army up to that time and the appalling circumstances had a visible effect. As early as the afternoon of 1 July a crowd of shaken Ulstermen had fallen back from trenches they had seized near Thiepval. They were given water and food and led back. A German counter-attack sent the 8th and 9th Royal Irish Rifles surging to the rear in headlong flight. Lieutenant-Colonel Crozier saw them push aside a subaltern and rush on shouting that 'it was all up'. Even the young officer's drawn revolver failed to halt them. Then he fired. A British soldier fell dead and the rest of the fugitives allowed themselves to be rallied.[1]

A medical officer serving with a field ambulance recalled later: 'The division was kept in until practically everyone was done up, and then one saw men streaming down. There was nothing wrong with them except that they were absolutely fagged out and could not go over the top again. They had been over about eleven times in a fortnight and simply could not do it again.'[2]

The trial and execution of the private in the 18th Manchesters described at the beginning of this book took place about this time.

Incessant gunfire and rain which turned the battlefield into an unspeakable morass in October and November affected even the hardiest spirits. Captain Hubert Essame, waiting with the 2nd Northamptonshires to go over the top, heard one of his men say suddenly, 'It's no good. I can't take it any more' and saw him put the muzzle of the rifle to his mouth and fire.[3]

Colonel G. S. Stubbs, who commanded the 1st Suffolk Regiment, describing the effect of concentrations of high explosive, said it seemed to drain him of all his stamina, a

[1] Crozier, *A Brass Hat in No-Man's Land*.
[2] Dr W. Johnson, Physician, Royal Southern Hospital, Liverpool, in evidence to 'Shell Shock' Inquiry, 1922.
[3] Personal recollections of Major General Essame.

condition which lasted for several hours and generally until he'd had a long sleep. Other men reacted differently. A senior medical officer declared later that 'during the battle of the Somme a large number of men deserted from the line on the claim that they had shell shock.' Lieutenant-Colonel G. Scott-Jackson a Northumberland Fusilier officer, said his men had arrived on the Somme in September and, after heavy fighting, remained for a long period in bad trenches. It was at this period that 'shell shock' set in. During 1915 he had refused to recognize such a thing. Officers or men pleading such a condition were returned to the line. Towards the end of 1916, however, the number of shell shock cases progressively increased.

'I noticed that when we'd had a rough time in the trenches it was not the day we came out that the men had shell shock, but it was the day we were going back into the line that most of the cases occurred.'[4]

A Royal Army Medical Corps officer has described one particularly bad case. His post was in a crumbling German dug-out not far from brigade headquarters which were housed in a more substantial hole in the ground. Shells of every size and description were shaking the earth all around. Suddenly three dishevelled signallers appeared half-carrying, half-dragging a staff officer about thirty years old. They shouted something about 'general's orders' and disappeared back into the maelstrom. Unable to find a wound, the R.A.M.C. man could only stare at the officer who lay on his face gibbering and grovelling. Then 'a hurricane of whizz-bangs' burst around the dug-out sending smoking clods of earth rolling into the entrance. Possessed by new paroxysms of terror, the man began to dig furiously at the mud walls slobbering, moaning and oblivious of the stretcher bearers who huddled together looking on in amazement at the behaviour of this red-tabbed apparition.

All attempts to calm the man failed. Promises of a long rest and return to base fell on deaf ears. Brandy was knocked aside. In the end three men overpowered him and risked their lives to drag the incoherent, babbling wreck to an ambulance hidden in an old gun-pit 150 yards from the dug-out. 'Extreme terror had driven him back through a thousand generations to some pre-human form of life' in the opinion of the medical officer.

[4] Evidence to 'Shell Shock' Inquiry, 1922.

'But when one thinks how we treated this staff officer, and how, on the other hand, some poor, half-educated, blubbering plough-boy, whose nerves had likewise given way . . . was sent back to face the enemy or be shot for cowardice . . .' that could never be regarded as justice.[5]

Haig's final attacks on the Somme were made in chilling rain. On 13 November, seven divisions struck against German strongholds in the valley of the Ancre which had been objectives on 1 July but still held out. In the centre lay Beaumont Hamel, the target of the 51st Highland Division. On its flank lay the ruined village of Beaucourt, also immensely strong. It was to be seized by the 63rd (Royal Naval) Division. Formed from seamen who were surplus to sea duty requirements at the beginning of the war and made up with large drafts of North Country miners, the 63rd Division had seen heavy fighting at Antwerp in 1914, Gallipoli in 1915 and after arriving on the Somme had spent a depressing month, first in tents pitched on a sea of slime and then in trenches 'planned by a short-sighted fool and destroyed by a watchful enemy'.[6] According to their historian, 'there were virtually no dug-outs; the communication trenches, which ran across a conspicuous ridge, were under constant fire; in the firing and support lines men could only stand or freeze in the mud; there was no room to walk or to lie down, and digging, in the face of the enemy, was impossible.'

To make matters worse, General Paris, the divisional commander, who had been with them since they were raised, had been wounded. His replacement, Major-General C. D. Shute, interfered on a large scale with the naval traditions which had been observed in the division since its formation. One of the three brigades was made up of army battalions and its commander, a Regular, commented after joining at the end of October: '. . . the whole show is in a chaotic state and without cohesion. I think my brigade is the best, for the others are sailors and Marines jumbled together and nobody knows anything.'

He also noted gloomily that a patrol had taken two hours to cover 300 yards because of deep mud and having narrowly escaped a sudden bombardment while visiting the front line wrote: 'The noise of our own and the enemy's guns (was) so bad one had to shout when speaking.'[7]

[5] Osburn, *Unwilling Passenger*.
[6] Jerrold, *The Royal Naval Division*.
[7] General Heneker's diary.

At 5.45 am on the 13th, while it was still very dark, the 63rd Division attacked in a thick mist. Two lines of trenches were pierced and hundreds of prisoners taken. But a German redoubt between the first and second lines survived the British barrage unscathed and opened a devastating fire on the attackers. Fighting raged throughout the day and all night but on the 14th a Naval Division lieutenant led a small group of tanks against the redoubt and six hundred men surrendered. A big New Zealander, Lieutenant-Colonel Bernard Freyberg, who had been wounded twice while leading Hood Battalion deep into the German defences, rallied scattered detachments of his own and five other battalions and captured Beaucourt with 800 prisoners. He also sustained a third wound.

The citation given with the Victoria Cross awarded to him included the sentence: 'The personality, valour and utter contempt of danger on the part of this single officer enabled the lodgement in the most advanced objective of the Corps to be permanently held'.

As Freyberg was being evacuated from the battlefield, and as the stretcher-bearers sought for survivors among the heaps of dead, Temporary Sub-Lieutenant Edwin Dyett, R.N.R., was discovered in a ruined house behind the lines. On the 13th he and another officer, both of whom had been left in reserve, were ordered forward to rejoin their unit which had lost its colonel and most of its officers near the deadly redoubt. An explanation of his presence elsewhere than in the captured trenches was immediately required of Dyett.

The problem of what to do with officers whose nerves had gone, or whose powers of endurance had broken down temporarily, was a difficult one. Incompetent officers could be and were sent home by the score . . . corps, divisional and brigade commanders were dismissed without compunction. The position of regimental officers was different. By tradition and fact they were father figures, no matter how young, to the men of their battalions. In the case of the Regular army they had always been better educated than their men, and the same applied generally in the early war years. To uphold the authority of these junior leaders in a vastly expanded army was essential. Crozier's treatment of the subaltern in the Royal Irish Rifles who was posted elsewhere after a lapse in the trenches, has already been described. Others, with perhaps less excuse, received similar treatment.

An officer of the Royal Welch Fusiliers was sent home as being 'inefficient', in the eyes of this particular Regular battalion's medical officer, 'the inefficiency was that he simply rolled into any odd corner as soon as a shell came over'. The officer was sent out to France again and retired home a second time. On his third tour of duty he disappeared for an hour while his company was waiting to cross some bridges under shell fire. The doctor, a Boer war veteran, refused to treat him but reported him as a disciplinary case. But the result was simply to get the man transferred to a labour unit.[8]

The Medical Officer in question had more sympathy for another officer who had spent some time at the front. This man was all right until he came under machine-gun fire; then, without being able to help it, would find himself running like the wind down the nearest communication trench. He too went to a labour company.

Up to the winter of 1916 no officer had been shot for a disciplinary offence. Quite a number had been cashiered but none had been executed. Why Temporary Sub-Lieutenant Dyett should have been made an example of cannot be stated for certain. But his fate may have something to do with a comment made by a staff officer after the war. He described the Battle of the Ancre in 1916 as 'the only battle in which I had direct evidence that British troops deserted in considerable numbers to the enemy. I believe this was due to the low nervous condition produced by the appalling surroundings of the battlefield.'[9]

A further clue may be gained from an entry in Haig's private diary. On Wednesday, 6 December, 1916, he records the fact that the Adjutant-General brought to him the court martial proceedings of a young officer sentenced to be shot. After confirming them he noted that it was the first time since he became Commander-in-Chief that the death sentence had been actually inflicted on an officer.[10] In his view desertion in the case of an officer was even more serious than in other ranks and he thought it important that the ordinary soldiers should realize that their officers were subject to the same law.

As Dyett had not then even been tried, and as only two other officers were shot during the war (one not a disciplinary case as

[8] Evidence before 'Shell Shock' Inquiry, 1922.
[9] Lieutenant-Colonel J. F. C. Fuller before 'Shell Shock' Inquiry.
[10] Public Records Office.

such, but for murder) it would seem that the morale of some of the troops was giving cause for concern at this time.

In Dyett's case, his undoubted offence was committed on 13 November, 1916. But the decision to court martial him was not taken until the end of the following month. A new commanding officer had arrived in place of the one killed at Beaucourt and, before going to superior authority, he had to satisfy himself that the charge could not be dealt with at his level. The result was that Dyett remained under arrest with Nelson Battalion when the 63rd Division went into rest billets near Rue on the coast near Le Tréport.

The trial took place on Boxing Day. In the War Diary of the Nelson Battalion it is recorded simply as 'December 26th Champneuf, Court-Martial of Sub-Lieutenant Dyett at Battalion H.Q.'

To understand the events that followed it is necessary to revert to the clauses of the Army Act and the rules for procedure. According to Section 52 every member of every court martial had to be administered the oath as follows:

'You ... do swear, that you will well and truly try the accused before the court according to the evidence, and that you will duly administer justice according to the Army Act now in force, without partiality, favour, or affection, and you do further swear that you will not divulge the sentence of the court until it is duly confirmed, and you do further swear that you will not on any account at any time whatsoever disclose or discover the vote or opinion of any particular member of this court martial unless thereunto required in due course of law. So help you GOD.'

The army interpreted the phrase *'not to divulge the sentence of the court until it is duly confirmed'* as meaning to apply to the accused. Thus when the evidence had been heard at the trial at Champneuf, Dyett was marched out and the court went into close session. Then the court called for evidence of character. Had he been acquitted, Dyett would have been released there and then. When the president of the court asked for details of his service he knew he had been found guilty. The sentence, however, was not disclosed. Dyett was returned to his quarters under close arrest. The papers in his case then passed through channels laid down by Colonel Childs.

At the beginning of the war, when a soldier was sentenced to death, all that was sent to the Adjutant-General who had to bring the case to the Commander-in-Chief was:

The nature of the charge.

Evidence concerning the offence.

Evidence as to character—merely a copy of a man's conduct sheet, showing how many times he had been awarded C.B. or punished for minor offences.[11]

There was no assessment of his use as a fighting soldier and Childs had realized the weakness of this system when he had to consider papers concerning a soldier of his own regiment. Knowing the man as a 'harum scarum' type, Childs wrote to the commanding officer involved and inquired whether he thought the death penalty should be carried out. Back came a reply saying that the man was a good soldier who had simply got drunk. As a result of this the death sentence was commuted. Childs then set to work to establish a new procedure. Under it, when a man was condemned to death by a court martial, a number of reports had to be filed:

(i) From the soldier's company commander and commanding officer as to his character.

(ii) From the commanding officer an opinion as to whether the death sentence should be carried out.

(iii) From a medical officer describing the soldier's nervous condition.

(iv) From the commanders of the brigade, division, corps and army in which the battalion was serving, each stating whether or not they considered it was necessary to make an example of the individual under sentence.[12]

Dyett was tried and found guilty on 26 December. Although he did not know it, he had been sentenced to death and the court had recommended him to mercy. The papers were sent off to superior authority forthwith. In the meantime, the life of Nelson battalion went on as usual. There was considerable sympathy for Dyett and[13] to pass away the time he was given the task of censoring the letters of the men. On 4 January as he was playing cards with other members of the mess a tight-lipped officer entered carrying a large blue envelope. Calling for the attention of the assembled company he read out the verdict that had been passed at the court martial ending with the familiar words that the sentence had been confirmed by the

[11] Childs, *Episodes and Reflections.*

[12] *Medical History of the War,* Vol. II.

[13] Comment from a former corporal in his brigade.

Commander-in-Chief and would be carried out the following morning at dawn.

On Friday, 5 January, Dyett was shot by men of his own battalion.

Somewhere along the line of senior officers to whom the papers went, someone, perhaps more than one person, had decided that it was necessary to remind at least part of the British army that stern penalties awaited those who failed in their duty. It was unlikely to be Commander Nelson who had just taken over the unit bearing his name. He was the only naval officer left at the head of a battalion in the 189th Brigade. But there were others along the way who might have had reasons for tightening up discipline—Brigadier L. F. Philips, Major-General Shute, Lieutenant-General E. A. Fanshaw, commanding the Vth Corps or Sir Hubert Gough, commanding the Fifth Army, in which the 63rd Division was serving. Finally the papers had to go before the Commander-in-Chief.

On 28 December, Sir Douglas Haig had received some welcome news. A King's Messenger arrived with a letter from His Majesty appointing him Field-Marshal. The award of the prized baton cannot have failed to raise a warm glow of appreciation. But it did nothing to ameliorate his response to the request that an example must be made of Temporary Sub-Lieutenant Edwin E. A. Dyett, for the good of the service. The boy was only 21 years old. His youth was the ground on which the plea for mercy had been made. But it was not his fate to remain merely another statistic in the files of the Adjutant-General. The Field-Marshal was to hear of him again.

9

Doctors versus 'Shell Shock'

On a gloomy day in December, 1916, a Royal Army Medical Corps colonel squelched across a soggy field to a hut where four morose soldiers sat unhappily on their beds. There was no privacy. There was little in the way of facilities. Yet this was to be the new treatment centre for cases of nervous disorder in the whole of the Third Army.[1] Along with a number of other 'shell shock specialists' the colonel had been sent to take charge of one of a number of special treatment centres which had been opened due to the mass of psycho-neurosis casualties on the Somme. After two years of trying to turn a blind eye to the existence of such a complaint the military authorities had been forced to act, blasted out of their obtuse attitudes by hard facts. During the early months of the war, unless a man was actually seen to have been buried or hurled forcibly to the earth by an explosion, he was expected to carry on. As early as 1904, the Russians had employed doctors to deal with cases of insanity arising out of the fighting in Manchuria.[2] During 1915 the French had set up special hospitals and so had the Germans who reserved five per cent. of hospital beds for such cases. British generals at that time regarded the creation of such treatment centres for apparently unwounded men as mere havens for malingerers.

A man who pleaded 'shell shock' as an excuse for desertion was thrust before doctors who were expected to place him either in the category of being insane and, therefore, destined for a lunatic asylum, or a shirker more likely to finish up in front of a firing squad.[3] And for a time it looked as though the generals might be able to point to statistics to prove their

[1] Miller, *The Neuroses in War.*
[2] Farrar, *American Journal of Insanity,* Baltimore 1917.
[3] Myers, *Shell Shock 1914–18.*

96

point. Up to the middle of 1915 only 150 soldiers had been recorded as battle casualties loosely termed 'shell shock'. Then came the Battle of Loos, in the churned up misery of the coalfields of Artois. By the end of the year, 1,200 new cases had been registered.[4]

At Gallipoli a considerable number of cases had also been noted. One doctor treated a hundred men for 'war shock' including twenty Anzacs.[5] Hypnosis was one of the methods used to restore these patients to duty. It was used on a nineteen-year-old Australian sniper whose sight had been affected from an unusual set of circumstances. He had been firing from a loophole when an enemy bullet struck the stock of his rifle. After a pause the Aussie resumed his position. Five rounds later another Turkish bullet struck the rim of the loophole and splashed sand into his face. For an hour the gap was closed, then the sniper carefully opened it again. But this time, no matter how hard he tried, he was unable to see the sights of his Lee-Enfield. All sorts of accusations could have resulted from this apparent unwillingness to play an active part in the fighting, but a careful examination revealed a shocked condition. The action of the eyes was a subconscious reaction in the interests of self-preservation. It took hypnotic suggestion to enable the soldier to be returned to duty.[6]

Whether it was fair to use it to send another Gallipoli case back to the front is a matter for conjecture. Many people might have thought that a twenty-three-year-old Irishman, who had never been concerned with anything more exciting than plumbing until the outbreak of war, had done his bit. He had been in a post held by a weak platoon when they were attacked by two hundred Turks. Although he and a sergeant led a charge which drove off the enemy, he received fifteen bayonet wounds. Eight of them were slashes and seven penetrated his body. A month later, although the wounds were healing, his right hand was set in a claw-like grip.

'In bayonet fighting you must clutch your rifle very firmly and never let it go' he explained repeatedly to a sympathetic medical officer. 'You must be on your guard all the time.'

Subconsciously he was fighting for his life still and his hand did not relax until he had undergone hypnosis.

[4] *Medical History of the War*, Vol. 2.
[5] Eder, *War Shock*.
[6] Eder, op. cit.

In the first six months of 1916, including the costly and vicious Battle of the Craters and the strenuous mine warfare, the number of officially recognized psycho-neurosis casualties rose to more than 3,000. Although this had been disturbing, the stream of casualties classified as suffering from nervous disorders brought about by their war service, grew to a positively alarming figure during the six months after the Battle of the Somme opened. By the end of December, 1916, it totalled 847 officers and 16,138 men, the equivalent of a whole division.[7] The generals were forced to acknowledge the existence of this new enemy and take steps to combat its ravages. In August the first special treatment centre opened. By the spring of 1917 five centres were operational in France and Belgium. Due to the absence of special arrangements many of the men who collapsed with symptoms of nervous diseases during the Somme fighting had been evacuated to England from which the likelihood of their return was not very great, certainly not to be accomplished without considerable trouble. Now the centres would deal with them first.

To these were to be sent all soldiers who 'without any visible wound, became non-effective from the effects of British or enemy weapons in action'. The definition was laid down by the Adjutant-General.

At first the treatment centres, designated 'N.Y.D.-N.' Hospitals—the initials standing for 'Not Yet Diagnosed—Nervous'—were primitive affairs, reflecting the distaste and suspicion with which the staff viewed them. The Third Army hut, described at the beginning of this chapter, afforded patients no privacy whatsoever. There was neither a separate room for clinical treatment nor a private cubicle for interviewing patients. It was left to the medical officers on the spot to beg, bully and persuade the authorities to provide better facilities. The Third Army centre quickly grew to two huts with thirty beds, two clinical and two interview rooms. Later it expanded to the extent that it could and did handle up to five hundred cases.[8]

One of the major contributions the new centres made to the established system of evacuating wounded was to take some of the pressure off the harassed medical staff dealing with surgical cases. The British arrangements were undoubtedly the best found on the Western Front and, as such, made a

[7] *Medical History of the War*, Vol. 2.
[8] Miller, *The Neuroses in War*.

significant contribution to morale.[9] It was confidence in receiving speedy treatment which led men to hope for a 'Blighty' wound. First of all the cases were dealt with by a doctor working in a front-line dug-out or even a shell-hole. There the splints were fixed, arteries were tied up and patients received anti-tetanus and pain-killing injections. Details of the treatment were written down and orderlies placed this record in a water-proof envelope which they tied to the clothing of the patient. Sometimes, to make doubly sure, they would scribble information on the patient's forehead with an indelible pencil.

The next stop was an advanced dressing station, perhaps in the gas-proof cellar of a ruined church, where more attention could be given and emergency operations carried out. Still further from the front lay the field ambulance, with convoys of vehicles, motor and horse-drawn. There teams of a dozen or so doctors re-examined the patients in marquees before loading them for transfer to a casualty clearing station where operations were conducted non-stop during periods of intense fighting. For example, one casualty clearing station with sixteen surgeons, once dealt with 1,400 patients in thirty-six hours. Under the remorseless attacking policy of Haig, there was always more than enough for doctors to do.

It was a task requiring the strength of the hardiest and yet some of the doctors were almost straight from college. A young Yorkshireman who had passed through grammar school and university and qualified at Leeds, opened his first medical practice in Wakefield in 1914. By the spring of 1915 he was in France and a year later he was the Medical Officer of an infantry battalion. Some idea of what he faced may be gauged from these accounts of two days at the Aid Post of the 4th Duke of Wellington's Regiment:

July 20: 'He might have been in a hospital far from the scene for all the excitement he showed . . . many a man owed his life to the skill and care lavished on him . . . but the casualties of those first days of the Somme were so appalling that the medical staffs were quite inadequate to deal with them. Hour after hour the battalion worked to clear the wounded but fresh cases streamed in far more quickly than earlier ones could be evacuated. And all this time, into the midst of that deadly valley, the 5·9s screamed taking their remorseless toll of human life and limb.'

[9] See Woods-Hutchinson, *The Doctor in War*.

September 3: 'The Aid Post became frightfully congested, not only with the battalion's own men, but with crowds from other units; and it is no exaggeration to say that the dead lay around in heaps.'[10]

Under such terrible pressures, doctors did not have time to give a thorough examination to a man who did not show blood. Sometimes harassed beyond caring the doctors scribbled 'G.A.K.' on the label ['God Alone Knows'] and despatched the patient to the rear. Now they could at least write down 'N.Y.D.N.' with the knowledge that the man would get a proper examination and, most important, not take up beds sorely needed for surgical cases. After two years the British Army had at last brought itself to admit that a man without visible wounds could be a war casualty and that the failure of a man in battle was not automatically to be ascribed to 'cold feet', 'funk' or plain 'cowardice', all of which had been associated with the term 'shell shock'.

According to scientific definition, when a bomb or a shell detonates, 'the solid explosive is converted into gases which initially are confined in the casing at a pressure that has been variously estimated as between 100 and 650 tons per square inch. As a result of this pressure the casing is blown to pieces and the gases escape and by their expansion produce a blast wave in the surrounding area'.[11]

Although there are few references in the medical literature of the 1914–18 war to the fact that the shock waves mentioned above can cause internal injuries without inflicting surface wounds, the weird and often fatal effects of blast had been noted on many occasions. A source of much more concern was the apparent effect on the mind or nerves of a man subjected to prolonged exposure to heavy detonations.

'Shell shock' had been noted in the British Army during the nineteenth century. An officer in the Royal Engineers who blew in the gates of the fortress of Ghuznee on the North-West Frontier in 1839 was so dazed by the explosion that he gave the stormers completely wrong directions. No-one held him responsible for his actions. His condition was recognized even though he exhibited no wounds. Nearly twenty years later doctors were intrigued by the experiences of a drunken Irish soldier who was accidentally blown up with a rebel fort at

[10] Bales, *History of the 1/4th Duke of Wellington's (W.R.) Regiment 1914–1919*.
[11] Green and Covel in *Medical History of the Second World War*.

Lucknow and survived apparently unscathed.[12] In the Boer War a number of men were classified as insane 'due in part, at least, to failure to recognize the real nature of severe neuroses, similar to those grouped under the term "shell shock".'[13]

The psychiatrists and psychologists who staffed the N.Y.D.N. hospitals had, therefore, little to go on. And considering the pressures to which they were subjected, their achievements are all the more remarkable. Their conclusion, basically, was that there was no such thing as emotional shell shock, although internal injuries and concussion were obvious by-products of an explosion. The nervous diseases and neuroses from which soldiers suffered were exactly the same as the complaints experienced in civilian life. Their manifestation in the army was due to the stresses under which soldiers laboured. The danger of death, increased responsibilities, sexual deprivation, separation from their families and guilt over killing were all contributory factors.

Sometimes a man exhibited bravery because he had become indifferent to his surroundings, due to the monotony of life in the trenches and a general decrease in mental activity. Others, who might have broken down because of the lack of intellectual activity, the same scenery and uniforms and the repetition of the ugly scene of trench warfare, were prevented from doing so because the constant threat of danger absorbed their attention.[14]

A large proportion of soldiers sent to N.Y.D.N. centres were in fact simple exhaustion cases, worn out by lack of rest and proper food.[15] Fresh troops, in action for the first time, were liable to break down if they had not been adequately trained. So were battle-tested troops after a period of prolonged trench warfare. The vulnerability of married men over forty was noticed by some doctors. Others felt that young, single men were affected more by lack of rest.

Officers, with their greater degree of responsibility, had a higher proportion of breakdowns than other ranks.[16] Specialists, such as machine-gunners, tank crews, Royal Engineers

---

12 Fortescue in a written statement to the 'Shell Shock' Inquiry.

13 Comment in *The Medical Department of the U.S. Army in the World War*, Vol. 10, p.499. There is also a reference to the Spanish American War.

14 See Bartlett, *Psychology and the Soldier*, and Miller, *The Neuroses in War*.

15 *Medical History of the War*, Vol. 2.

16 Miller states categorically that the vast majority of patients with anxiety states were officers. The U.S. official history says neurasthenia was five times more common in officers than men.

and other troops with tasks involving concentrated strain, also figured high on the list of those who broke down.

In the first months of the war an N.C.O. in a Regular battalion who developed 'an irresistible fear of danger, associated with causes of terror and anxiety at the front, leading up to desertion from the post of duty or reckless behaviour' was eventually shot as a persistent deserter, although his pre-war conduct had been excellent.[17] Cases of this nature now had a reasonable chance of being given a thorough examination. Indeed, the longer the N.Y.D.N. centres operated the more it became obvious that the incidence of malingerers among patients was almost negligible.[18] Many tended to exaggerate their symptoms, such as the trembling of a limb, but almost all were genuinely ill. Out of a thousand cases in which soldiers pleaded 'shell shock', one doctor could find only twenty-eight cases of malingering. Most of them pretended loss of memory and all of them confessed to him in the end.[19]

The prime concern of the medical authorities at the special centres was, of necessity, to prevent a repetition of the Somme fiasco when so many of the 'shell shock' cases were evacuated to England. Once there, the inducement to stay at home was almost irresistble. Fortunately, the treatment given behind the lines, often within sound of the guns, generally proved enough to satisfy the requirements of generals and doctors. A large number of patients responded to treatment and were returned to their units while those who were definitely unsuitable could be removed from the scene for good and the gap could be filled by a replacement. One early example occurred in the winter of 1916. A raiding party was seen creeping over no-man's-land in bright moonlight. As they slithered back into the trenches a German mortar shell pitched among them. Five were killed, three wounded and eleven men stunned and evacuated suffering from 'shell shock'. A delirious private kept on shouting 'Kill all men with white faces tonight'—the raiders had blacked their own with cork—and 'Bomb them! Bomb them!' Before the opening of the centres all eleven men might have been sent back to base. As it was, after forty-eight hours rest and treatment they were back on duty in the front line.[20]

[17] Evidence of Squadron-leader W. Tyrell, D.S.O. MC., to 'Shell Shock' Inquiry, 1922.
[18] *Medical History of the War*, Vol. 2.
[19] W. B. Brown, Consultant Neurologist, Fourth and Fifth Armies.
[20] Miller, *The Neuroses in War*.

Men who had been subjected to long periods of exposure to bad conditions, and had regularly seen comrades mutilated, were a more difficult problem. Sometimes, having repressed their feelings for months, they would be unnerved by a trivial incident, a comparatively minor explosion or slight graze. Their self-control then went completely.

Even so, a significant number of these men were reclaimed for general service, although in the case of men who were naturally physically and mentally below average this was unusual.

'There was also a class of men', says the *Medical History of the War*, 'who were once sturdy soldiers but had been broken by wounds, sickness and their length of service in the battle line. With a nervous laugh they would say they no longer felt sure of themselves and dreaded a possible breakdown in front of their comrades. To these men great sympathy was due.'

Yet another strata of military society passed through N.Y.D.N. hospitals in the third year of the war—men who had been found, perhaps dazed, behind the lines, or guilty of some other breach of discipline which led to them being accused of cowardice or desertion. Some of these individuals were quickly seen to be suffering from clearly identifiable mental illnesses, and registered as sick. It was in cases where a man showed only slight symptoms—perhaps a man who had done his best to fight against his emotions—that considerable difficulties arose. According to Army orders, 'when a man accused of desertion . . . pleaded that he was suffering or had suffered from shell shock, he was to be admitted to the special army N.Y.D.N. centre for a period of observation'. These forlorn figures were kept there for at least a month, being regularly examined and interviewed, being watched by special orderlies day and night, so that a report could be sent to army headquarters for consideration in connection with the man's fate.

The duty was onerous and distasteful. As the Canadian war historian states:

'Under cover of vague and mysterious symptoms, the malingerer found refuge and impressed a stigma on those who were suffering from a real malady. The medical officer was bewildered in his attempt to hold the balance between injustice to the individual and disregard for the needs of the service. Especially was he haunted with a dreadful fear when he was called upon to certify that a man was "fit" to undergo punishment for a "crime" and most especially when it was his duty to be present alone with the minister or priest to certify that the award of a court martial for cowardice in the face of the enemy . . . had been finally bestowed. This attendance at executions was the most painful . . . of the medical officer's many duties.'[21]

Colonel W. B. Brown stated:

'After my first two or three courts martial, I found I was practically in every case giving evidence in favour of the man. The reason was that I felt that his state of mind in the line, when he was under heavy shell fire, was not the same as his state of mind when he was at the base or somewhere between the base and the line.'

With the passing of the dreary winter of 1916 and the dawning of the spring of 1917 the British army took fresh heart as the enemy retreated to the fortified position known as the Hindenburg Line. The waterlogged craters and pulverized villages of the Somme were left behind—although the Ypres Salient remained as loathsome as ever.

Nearly every person has a pet fear. Some people cannot bear to handle birds. Others have a feeling of revulsion at the sight of snakes or mice. For some it may be a simple fear of the dark. So it was with the soldiers. Some did not mind one weapon yet feared another. A soldier in the 1st Gordon Highlanders who had been blown up by a shell earlier in the war was filled with terror whenever he was exposed to heavy artillery after he rejoined his unit.[22] The case of the officer who ran uncontrollably from machine-gun fire has already been mentioned. By 1917 a man could add to these menaces, gas, of either the cloud or shell variety, flame throwers, bombing aircraft and the inevitable nerve-wracking mining. Yet, somehow, they learned to live with them. Toughened by their experiences, proficient with their weapons, and aware that the Germans were only human too, the British army reached a peak in the early months of the third year of battle. Haig himself noted the confident bearing of the highlanders in the 15th Scottish (New Army) Division who had taken part in the battles of Loos and the Somme. He found words of praise even for the much-tried 3rd Division of which he had spoken so scathingly at First Ypres. Although the British Imperial Armies had suffered more than a million casualties they were

---

[21] MacPhail, *History of the Canadian Forces* 1914–19.
[22] Evidence before the 'Shell Shock' Inquiry, 1922.

stronger than they had ever been in men and guns. On 9 April they proved just how formidable they were.

Emerging from the mediaeval sewers, tunnels and cellars under the shell-damaged city of Arras, Sir Edmund Allenby's Third Army took the Germans by surprise and almost broke through. Vimy Ridge was seized by the Canadians and the British 4th Division penetrated deep into the third lines of defence. Failure to make the best of the opportunity, the worsening in the weather which made it difficult to move the guns forward, and the swift reaction of the Germans brought the attack to a halt. It took days to haul up the heavy artillery through the slush. The 30th Division which had been committed on the first day of the Somme were in the forefront of the battle on 9 April. They were sent in again on 23 April.

At 3·25 am on St George's Day the steady rain of shells which had been falling on the German positions became a deluge. Twenty minutes later, in a sickly yellow dawn, the numbed infantry clambered obediently from their shell holes and shallow assault trenches on a front of nine miles. As they did so the German barrage crashed down and an unprecedented hail of machine-gun fire ripped into them. A screen of snipers picked off Lewis gun teams as the light improved. In the heart of the hurricane were the 18th Manchesters. After the battle had deteriorated into a slogging match for 'limited objectives' what was left of the battalion was withdrawn to recuperate. While behind the lines, they were paraded once more in a hollow square to hear that two of their comrades had been sentenced to death for desertion.

They were men who had gone over the top on 1 July and on 9 April. On 23 April they had been reported as missing. Military police had detained them aboard an American ship loading cargo for England at Rouen. Both were in civilian clothes.

The prisoners were popular with the battalion. They had chummed up after volunteering in 1914 and become inseparable. After the attack on 9 April, the older of the two had received news that his wife was seriously ill. He had applied for compassionate leave but, probably because of the casualties the battalion had suffered and because every man was needed for 23 April, he had been refused. It was then that he decided to make his own way home. Unable to stand the thought of going into action without his friend, the younger man went with him.

In the few hours left before the sentence was due to be carried out the Roman Catholic chaplain and the Church of England padre combined their efforts in a desperate attempt to save the doomed men. They were present the following morning when, seconds before the volley was fired, the older man turned to his friend and said simply and calmly: 'Well, good-bye, Albert.'

The event left the 18th Manchesters—and the other Pals battalions in the brigade—sickened and resentful, although they did not show this openly.[23] Elsewhere, other soldiers were not hiding their feelings so manfully. Open mutiny had broken out in the French army.

[23] First-hand account from an ex-private in the 18th Manchesters.

10

The French Mutiny

Political agitators were blamed at the time of the French
mutinies and their propaganda was quoted frequently to
prove the point. But only one man was responsible for talking
the troops into open rebellion. That was the Commander-in-
Chief, General Robert George Nivelle. The general pioneered
the technique of telling the troops everything—which has
since been adopted successfully by other military leaders,
when used with discretion.

Nivelle, who began the war as a colonel, distinguished himself in Alsace in 1914 and by the end of 1916 had risen to
command the French Second Army at Verdun. In October,
1916, he gave France the success she had been longing for ever
since the Germans had launched their great offensive the
previous February. He recaptured Fort Douaumont. It had
been reduced to a battered unrecognizable ruin and its case-
mates had been pierced in places by huge howitzer shells. The
earth around it was churned to a poisoned mush littered with
decaying human fragments. But Douaumont's cracked and
blackened corridors, foul smelling and dripping with con-
densation, were the richest prize in France. The loss of the
fort had been the greatest single blow to national pride during
the war and Nivelle avenged it handsomely. First of all he
duped the Germans into unmasking their guns by making a
feint attack with artillery. Then, having neutralized the opposing guns, he launched his divisions in overwhelming strength.
He had promised them that this time they would be able to
walk over the enemy defences with their rifles slung. They'd
all heard these stories before but in this case it had actually
happened. Nivelle's prestige was enormous. When the time
came to replace 'Papa' Joffre at the head of the French Army,
the victor of Douaumont was selected. The dour Pétain, whose

skill and determination had made the Germans pay so dearly at Verdun and saved the city in its darkest days, was passed over.

Nivelle's plans for an offensive in 1917 were based on the supposition that the Germans would remain exposed in the great salient they held at the end of the Somme offensive. The French would attack one shoulder, the British the other. He was sure that he had the secret of victory and he managed to convince the British cabinet too—mainly because, having an English mother, he could speak her language. The withdrawal of the German army to the Hindenburg Line posed a new problem. By shortening their line, the enemy were able to switch reserves to the front between Soissons and Rheims which was threatened by Nivelle. The superiority of force on which he counted to launch an attack 'of violence, of brutality and of rapidity' was dwindling. Senior officers urged a change of plan. But Nivelle would hear none of it. He continued to talk of speed and surprise, of 'the rapid and sudden eruption of our infantry'. He stated sternly that 'No consideration should intervene of a nature to weaken the *élan* of the attack'.

Surprise, however, was already impossible. In order to imbue his troops with the knowledge that would lend zest to their operations and help to develop that *élan*, detailed plans of the attack were circulated down to company commander level. By 3 March the scope of the attack was exposed to the Germans in a captured document. At the beginning of April the battle instructions of the French Fifth Army were captured by Bavarian raiders. In particular the Germans noted that the French intended to obscure their exact point of attack by dispensing with 'jumping off' trenches.

A considerable portion of the position to be stormed consisted of limestone hills, dotted with quarries and tunnels where the defenders could shelter in safety. Even though the bombardment lasted fourteen days, intensified during the last five to fever pitch, it was ineffective. Unprotected by assembly trenches the French infantry were forced into the open by the German retaliation. The weather was bitter. Snow lay on the ground in places.

On a damp, cold morning at 6 am crack Colonial battalions in khaki and the regiments of Metropolitan France in *horizan bleu* were cut to pieces as they worked their way forward in the face of nest after nest of machine-guns on the rocky slopes of the Chemin des Dames and the plateaux north of the Aisne. They were still fighting their way slowly forward at nightfall but had advanced only a mile or so the next day. Drifting smoke from sixty heavy Schneider and St Chamond tanks which had been reduced to blazing hulks by the German artillery added to the gloom cast by the low clouds and mist. This time there had been no walk-over with slung rifles. All the talk, all the promises, all the printed orders, had brought nothing.

Among the many things that went wrong were the medical arrangements. Their inadequacy is pathetic testimony to Nivelle's belief in his own grandiose plans. Clearing stations were overwhelmed as 100,000 wounded flooded back during the first ten days. The French suffered heavier casualties on different occasions and under different circumstances—the incredible carnage of the initial frontier clashes, in the Champagne in 1915 and at Verdun. But then some factor had intervened to prevent morale cracking. In 1914 patriotism was at a premium, in 1915 the casualties were treated in the area immediately behind the front, at Verdun . . . that was Verdun. But on the Aisne there was nothing to mitigate the disastrous losses, including 30,000 corpses on the bullet-swept slopes. The wounded had to be evacuated as quickly as possible wherever beds and doctors were available. As the hospital trains pulled into towns all over France the word spread. Nivelle had failed with terrible losses. In the army, the sense of betrayal was almost unbearable. The offensive which had begun with great hope continued for a time but the heart had gone out of it.

Some reports say the first mutiny occurred on 16 April, the day the offensive began. Seventeen men of the 108th Infantry Regiment deserted their posts. It is probable, however, that this could have happened regardless of the outcome of the day. More serious signs of discontent began behind the lines, in the rest camps to which shattered divisions were withdrawn. Communist agitators, inspired by the success of the Russian Revolution, helped to fan the flames. Towards the end of April, 200 men of the 20th Infantry Regiment took to the woods for the day when they heard they had been ordered back to the front, but rejoined later. On 3 May printed notices appeared in the camp of the 2nd Colonial Division. They stated: 'Death to war criminals! Down with war! Why should we starve on five sous a day while our brothers in munition factories earn 20 francs a day.'

With the arrival of reinforcements to fill the ranks of divisions which had suffered heavy casualties, dissension spread. There was little sign of disobedience in the front line now that the offensive had come to a halt, but in the rear demonstations occurred daily. Sixty armed men of the 18th Infantry Regiment refused to board lorries waiting to take them back to the line and marched to the railway station at Fère-en-Tardenois saying they were going to take the next train to Paris. They finally gave in to a force of gendarmes. Rumours that Annamite workers in Paris had run amok, raping and looting, set off another wave of unrest. The crack 5th Infantry Division held protest meetings for more than a week. In the 77th Division groups of men from élite light infantry regiments hid in the woods and had to be disarmed.

A general sent to report on the condition of the Sixth Army stated that it required rest and, if the offensive was continued, 'we run the risk of seeing our men refuse to leave the trenches'. Another officer, investigating the morale of a division in reserve, wrote to his superiors: 'It is an army without faith.' Intelligence agents were of the opinion that the army did not wish to start a revolution, but if one was being organized 'it will wish to take part in it'.

The French government reacted to the situation with efficiency bred from fear. First of all they clamped tight security restrictions on the area most affected. Secondly, despite his protests, they removed Nivelle and replaced him with Pétain who had shown at Verdun that he had the confidence of the ordinary soldier. Finally they prepared to concede some of the demands of the mutineers, particularly in respect of leave.

Figures of the number of units which became involved are still not clear. Pedroncini, who made an intensive study of the subject, gives the number of regiments in which mutinies occurred as 121 infantry of the line, 23 light infantry, seven colonial infantry, one Territorial and seven artillery. The Belgian historian, General Wanty, makes the count 113 infantry regiments, 22 light infantry, two of colonials and twelve of artillery. Most authorities agree that more than 60 divisions were affected, Pedroncini making the figure as high as 68 out of the total French strength of 112 divisions.

Lloyd George, the British Prime Minister, may have been nearer the mark than he realized when he said that Pétain's role in 1917 was 'that of a head nurse in a home for cases of shell shock'.[1] For therapy was applied liberally. Pétain restored the leave entitlement of seven days every four months, improved rations, introduced cut-price co-operatives and ordered the building of proper rest camps. So much for the carrot. The extent to which the stick was applied remains a mystery to this day. And perhaps no-one will ever know how many men were shot as a warning to others.

Official records, according to Pedroncini, show that 554 men were tried and sentenced to death for offences committed after 16 April, 1917. Of these he states that only 43 men are known to have been executed. Doubts remained in the case of 23 more. The rest of the sentences were commuted, a considerable number of men being sent to penal colonies. More than 2,000 other mutineers received punishments of varying degrees and many of these were sent abroad to serve them. Even at this distance in time the efficiency of the security of 1917 remains effective. In 1937 the Australian Official History of the War reported the number of sentences as 150, of whom it states 23 were shot. Wanty's 1967 account says 200 men were condemned of whom 'about twenty' were executed. John Williams in *The Ides of May* published in the same year, says that of 412 death sentences 56 were carried out. Whatever the truth may be, it is certain that the French high command firmly believed in the use of the firing squad to restore order.

An official French publication laid it down thus: 'Men composing an army must be placed in this dilemma; they must either do their duty, bearing all the fatigue and danger it entails in the hope of returning, or else be seized by the court martial from which they can return only to die.'[2]

Major-General Sir Edward Spears, chief British liaison officer at French headquarters, had seen this principle applied on the Aisne early in 1914. He was standing with General de Maud'huy when twelve soldiers under an N.C.O. came round the corner of a street with a prisoner escorted by two gendarmes. Their mission was obvious. While Spears looked, de Maud'huy halted the party. Wrote Spears:[3]

'He asked what he, the prisoner, had been condemned for. It was for abandoning his post. The General then began to

[1] Lloyd-George, *War Memoirs.*
[2] Quoted by Ernest Thurtle in *Time's Winged Chariot.*
[3] *Liaison 1914.*

talk to the man. He quite simply explained discipline to him. Abandoning your post was letting down your pals, more, it was letting down your country that looked to you to defend her. He spoke of the necessity of example, how some could do their duty without prompting, but others, less strong, had to know and understand the supreme cost of failure. He told the condemned man his crime was not venial, and that he must die as an example, so that others should not fail. Surprisingly the wretch nodded his head. The burden of infamy was lifted from his shoulders.'

De Maud'huy and the doomed soldier shook hands and the party marched on to carry out their orders within earshot of Spears.

Such noble sentiment was little in evidence in the summer of 1917. Some generals called for decimation—the execution of one in ten mutineers in selected units. Others wanted to turn artillery and machine-guns on them.

In particular, General Duchêne, the domineering commander of the Tenth Army which was seriously affected by the mutinies, was vociferous in his demands for extreme measures and repression. When it was rumoured that he had ordered recalcitrant soldiers to be walled up in the caves where they had taken refuge no-one doubted the tale, although it was not true. He was so stupid and brutal anything could be expected of him. Such disciplinary action as Duchêne proposed was unacceptable, fortunately, to either Nivelle or Pétain. But both of them sought special powers to enable them to suppress propaganda and agitators. Premier Painlevé demurred at first. He was a conscientious and humane man who was known to walk the streets at night trying to think of good reasons why a condemned soldier should be spared.[4] He had appeared on Pétain's doorstep at 6 am to argue for a man's life. By 8 June, however, even Painlevé conceded that the situation required unusual steps. He gave Pétain the right to inflict an immediate death penalty should 'the necessities of discipline require it'. Up to then, every condemned man had the right of appeal to the President of the Republic. Painlevé's action, in the form of a decree, meant that he would advise the President, M. Poincaré, not to exercise his right. This state of affairs remained in force until the decree of 8 June was rescinded on 13 July. Seven summary executions are known to have taken

[4] Sir Edward Spears in conversation with the author.

place during that time. But it is more likely that during this period the army took the opportunity to inflict more through the medium of the dreaded courts martial. These tribunals, consisting of three officers, could seize and try an offender and execute him on the spot. According to General Spears there could be no appeal, no recriminations and the wave of fear created by these courts had a salutary effect upon the rank and file. Certainly by the time the decree giving Pétain a free hand was cancelled the situation had improved beyond all recognition. By August, Pétain could claim that order had been restored.

Draconian measures were by no means new to the French Army. Clausel, who conducted the retreat from Vittoria in 1813, admitted shooting fifty soldiers who had thrown away their arms. By 1914, the French had not advanced much beyond the Napoleonic age. Gaols were still combed to form battalions of criminals—including murderers and thieves. The Joyeux, as they were called, stood the chance of remission if they managed to survive the unpleasant tasks allotted to them. Their insignia was the Ace of Spades which led to the British 12th Division receiving a cautious reception when it moved into billets on occasions. Some of the peasants seeing their identical sign thought the British were going a little too far.

While engaged in battle the Joyeux were given to pursuing their calling. One of them, who had taken part in three attacks in one day, complained to his company commander: 'Only eleven and a half sous, mon capitaine! It's not good enough.' Some of the Joyeux were tragic creatures. One kept murmuring to the nurse as he lay dying, 'I didn't really mean to kill the woman, ma soeur.'[5]

A lesser penalty held over French soldiers was posting to his regiment's own punishment company. These remained part of the unit but got all the dirty jobs, wiring in no-man's-land, burying the dead, taking up gas cylinders and so forth. There was no trial for soldiers in these cases. A man was sent there on the orders of his colonel and did not come back until the colonel said he could. It was a system that worked well on occasions but fell down badly if the colonel was not a good judge of character. It certainly did nothing to help a soldier who might have a personal problem.

Unlike soldiers, officers in punishment companies and penal

[5] Sir Edward Spears.

battalions were volunteers who could count on accelerated promotion if they survived. In a way this emphasises the difference between the French and British. At the beginning of the war, British officers were, by comparison with the other ranks, better educated, wealthier and brought up to believe that they were natural leaders. In order to assert their authority, French officers had to create artificial social barriers, not always an easy thing under the scrutiny of a suspicious Republican government. When the mutiny broke out, this difference was accentuated. Not one officer joined it.

The last serious flickering of mutiny in France appeared in September, 1917. A brigade of Russian troops deposed their officers and set up soviets in their camp at La Courtine in the Massif Central. The Russians were part of a force which had been sent to France the previous year as a gesture. Armed with French weapons they had taken part in various actions before news of the revolution in Russia reached them. Perhaps influenced by the fact that the Russian soldiers were setting up committees and indulging in dangerous practices, the French had selected a formidable task for them in the Nivelle offensive. Six thousand were killed or wounded in a desperate effort to seize the notoriously strong Fort Brimont on 16 April. The survivors were sent by rail to La Courtine where they issued a statement which began 'We have been told that we have been sent to France to pay for French munitions . . .'[6]

Although one brigade pledged loyalty to the Allies, the other remained defiant. Towards the end of September the unaffected brigade surrounded their Red comrades. At a distance behind the 'loyal' Russians a ring of French troops were deployed. Six field guns were used to reduce the rebels and fighting lasted three days. The ringleaders were executed and their followers were sent, like French mutineers, to penal colonies in Africa and Indo-China.

By coincidence, the army of the Russian provisional government led by Kerensky also had its problems in the summer of 1917. Major-General Sir Alfred Knox, who was in Galicia when the so-called Kerensky offensive started, observed:

'There was really no fighting at all on the part of the Russians. A few officers went forward, accompanied by a few non-commissioned officers, and here and there an odd man or two. But there was really no fighting and the number of

[6] Churchill, *The World Crisis*.

casualties was infinitesimal. I interviewed General Gutor . . . and I asked him what measures it was necessary to take to restore the fighting efficiency of the Russian army. The first thing he said was:

"You must press furiously to restore the death penalty. You must press Kerensky to restore the death penalty."

Since assuming power Kerensky had refused to sign one death warrant, taking the view that he wished the troops to realize that things had changed since the Czar had been deposed. Later, when Kornilov took over from Kerensky, the death penalty was reintroduced, with no discernible results. The Bolsheviks retained it and used it with much greater effect.

* * *

The Russian Army was down, the French were still reeling and the Italians were showing signs of flagging. America was in the war but her men were not yet in the field. Of all the Allies, only the British were in a condition to strike a serious blow after the spring of 1917. They did so on 10 June as the last flickers of the Arras battle were dying out. Nineteen enormous mines were exploded under the Messines Ridge which dominated the east flank of the Ypres Salient. Although General Plumer, who commanded the Second Army and was responsible for the operation, let slip the chance to exploit his victory, the battle was not allowed to drag on. All efforts were directed towards preparing for the next great offensive scheduled to take place at Ypres in July. The tardiness of the French who were to support the left of the British Fifth Army caused delays —their soldiers had to have the rest and leave promised by Pétain after the mutinies—and the assault was put off until the 31st of the month. During the weeks immediately preceding 'Z-Day' the enemy produced yet another surprise—mustard gas, delivered in shells which splashed the earth with a dark yellow liquid. Evaporating with a slight smell of garlic it was hard to detect. If inhaled it caused severe inflammation of the lungs, generally fatal. One of its more sinister properties was the delayed onset of the symptoms, victims often appearing perfectly normal a few hours after breathing the gas. But men did not have to breathe the gas to become victims. Many men suffered severe blistering and casualties among kilted regiments were particularly high. Shuffling files of temporarily blinded soldiers became a new feature of casualty clearing stations. Decontamination centres had to be improvised to deal with troops whose clothing had absorbed the deadly fumes.

From less than 1,000 gas casualties in the B.E.F. in June 1917, the number had risen to an average of eight thousand a month by the end of the year. Thanks to the use of respirators the death rate never exceeded 3·4 per cent, but the man-power drain was considerable. Mustard gas—dichlorethyl sulphide—was yet another strain on the hard-pressed morale of the individual soldier. It did not make the Third Battle of Ypres any easier.

The operation was one in which Sir Douglas Haig had complete faith. His objectives were:

To clear the Belgian coast so U-boats could not use its ports;

To pin down enemy concentrations which might otherwise attack the doubtful French armies;

To break through and turn the German flank so that his whole line could be rolled up.

The opening attack was made by divisions which had seen heavy fighting during the previous twelve months and immediately it ran into trouble. Numerous concrete pill-boxes, concealed in the tangled debris of woods, broke up the advancing waves. Rain, which began on Z-Day, filled the craters and prevented the artillery and supports from moving forward in the days that followed. Although the troops, many of them conscripts, battled stubbornly onwards, the summer rains had washed out all hope of a breakthrough in August. A hot spell in September transformed the Salient into a baked moonscape and better progress was made on the firmer ground, but storms in October turned the desolate battle zone into a swamp in which unwounded men, horses and guns were swallowed.

The commanders themselves became jumpy and unsure. Gough, whose Fifth Army was shouldering the main burden, asked Haig to call off the offensive in August. Testily, Sir Douglas reduced the scope of Gough's operations and transferred the main attack to the more malleable Plumer.

The 30th Division remained an unlucky formation. Put in yet again on the first day of a 'Big Push'—the others being 1 July, 9 April and 23 April—they achieved little in the face of fierce opposition. It had been suggested that they had not recovered from their earlier experiences and should be relieved.

This proposal was turned down on the grounds that it would take too long. On 31 July the Lancashire men had more than 3,000 casualties and morale slumped. The only Londoner in the 18th Manchesters, a hard case from the East End, told his sergeant that he couldn't stand it any more and that he was going to shoot himself. The sergeant, who was equally fed up, told him: 'You can do what you like as long as you don't do it in my sector.'

The soldier squelched off and a few minutes later a man from the neighbouring platoon stumbled into the position to say: 'That Cockney chap of yours has just shot himself.'[7]

One Manchester man became so indifferent to his fate that when all attempts to bring in a wounded comrade had failed he simply stood up on the tumbled sandbags that formed the trench and walked over to him. The Germans did not bother to fire as he carried his friend to safety.

At a particularly grim moment, a corporal and a platoon sergeant made a vow to shoot each other simultaneously to end their misery. Only the unexpected arrival of relief prevented them keeping their pact.

Service in the Ypres Salient had been wearing on the nerves at any time but the strain became intolerable with the advent of mustard gas and the unprecedented hurricane of high explosives which answered each attempt by the British to drag themselves nearer the twin bastions of the Houthulst Forest and the ruins of Passchendaele.

'There was a feeling of tension. Notwithstanding the work, the men had previously sung going up to the trenches and coming back; but they gave it up. They gave up all social business; they were getting into a state of nervous exhaustion.'

This assessment was made by the medical officer of the 4th Black Watch, serving in the 39th Division which had spent fourteen months in all at Ypres.

He wrote to his divisional chiefs requesting that his letter be passed on to Army headquarters. He could not be responsible for the men of his battalion if they were kept in the Salient any longer. The plea was heeded and the medical officer noted that the move to another part of the front made such an improvement in the condition of the men that they were 'unrecognizable as the same battalion'.[8]

7 Eyewitness account.
8 Evidence before the 'Shell Shock' Inquiry, 1922.

From another medical officer, who broke down and had to be evacuated, comes a moving glimpse of the soul-racking ordeal. Four times he had seen his battalion re-formed after suffering heavy casualties. During one of the battles of Third Ypres they took their objective without great loss and were digging in when the enemy opened up a fearsome barrage as a prelude to a counter-attack. Together with the rest of the officers the M.O. was crouched in a trench when a heavy shell killed and wounded everyone present except himself. He escaped with his eyebrows singed and took over control of the battalion. After being buried in a dug-out, extricated and revived with a stiff Scotch, he eventually handed over to a relieving battalion, many of whom were in tears at the sight of the desolation and carnage. Then, having collected three young subalterns and three hundred men, he led them out of action. As dawn was breaking he marched the mud-spattered little band down the road on which they had set out at full strength only a short time before. At the cross roads stood a shadowy figure. The quartermaster had brought up the senior officers' horses. When the 'Q' reported, the M.O. could only shake his head speech-lessly and stare at the waiting animals. Then he broke down with uncontrollable sobs. There were the horses, but there were no officers to ride them. They were all dead.

Said the M.O.; 'The sight of them finished me.'

There seemed no limit to the horrors of battle. Reinforce-ments thrust in to fill the ranks of the battered divisions died in futile attacks without ever getting to know their officers or their officers them.

Faceless and hopeless, battalions struggled one after the other through a bullet-lashed quagmire and melted into the slime. Reliefs sometimes degenerated into disorderly flight on the part of the relieved.

From the very beginning, when hopes were highest, strict precautions had been taken to maintain discipline. A number of orders were issued stating that any men found behind battalion headquarters after zero hour would face a field general court martial. As the situation worsened some units began to eye their neighbours with more and more suspicion. The Guards Division objected strongly to the prospect of going into the line with a certain battalion on their flank. They felt certain it would let them down. Their commander said they would extend their front and take over the position with one of their own units but they did not want the suspect battalion near them.[9]

Lieutenant-Colonel Viscount Gort had to deal with 'The Case of the Artful Grenadier'. This soldier had gone over the top on the Somme where he had been slightly wounded. Just before the next attack he had skilfully evaded the battalion aid post, where he was well known, and reported to the advanced dressing station where he successfully feigned illness. He was court martialled for desertion in the face of the enemy but the evidence of his visit to the dressing station secured his acquittal. He had been found to have a 'slight temperature'. When the Guards attacked on 31 July at Ypres the Artful Grenadier ducked out once more and got away with it. Afterwards Gort had the soldier brought before him. They talked in the Orderly Room man to man and Gort put the soldier on his honour to go over with his company in the next attack. To his delight the man did so, but soon afterwards he reverted to his old trick of dodging. Ironically a sniper relieved Gort of this problem while the battalion was holding the line during a particularly quiet spell. Inquiries revealed that the Artful Granadier had been a tramp in civilian life and had never done a day's work in his life before joining the army. Gort thought him 'a clever man'.[10]

An officer of the 13th Royal Fusiliers used a trick similar to the Artful Grenadier's in order to dodge taking part in a forlorn assault on a group of concrete machine-gun posts near the Menin Road. He reported to the adjutant with a note just before the attack to say that he was being sent to the rear as sick because his 'bowels had not moved for four days'. The note had been signed by the medical officer of a neighbouring battalion. When the adjutant asked why he had gone to a strange unit the officer made the excuse that he could not find the Fusiliers' own M.O. Although it was obvious that he had avoided someone who knew his reputation as a dodger, there was nothing that could be done under the circumstances. A subaltern was sent up to replace the 'sick' officer and was killed during the battle. Feeling ran very high in the battalion and the case was referred to divisional headquarters. Major-General H. Bruce Williams evidently did not believe in courts martial for he sent for the officer and without any trial arranged for him to be returned to the ranks, forwarding a confidential report to

9 Evidence before the 'Shell Shock' Inquiry, 1922.
10 Evidence before the 'Shell Shock' Inquiry, 1922.

higher authority. Another officer in the same battalion whose sheer inefficiency had nearly got his company wiped out, was reduced to the ranks at the same time.[11]

Not all faint-hearts and incompetents were so lucky. On 28 November, as the British infantry hung on grimly to the gas-drenched marsh they had wrested from the enemy, Mr Snowden asked the new Under-Secretary of State for War, Mr Macpherson, if he was aware that out of twenty-five executions confirmed by Sir Douglas Haig 'in part of the month of October' only one of the soldiers was defended. Was there any other army where such an administration of military law was tolerated?

The outraged Under-Secretary spluttered: 'I cannot accept the Member's statement.'

But he did not deny it either then or later.

[11] Chapman, *A Passionate Prodigality.*

11

Parliament's Challenge

It was not until the Third Battle of Ypres was almost over that the Commons returned to their quest for facts about the way in which military law was administered. Mr Snowden began at the end of October by bringing up the case of a nameless soldier to whom he referred as Private No. A/6730, of the 2nd Royal Scots Fusiliers. He wanted to know if the incident of desertion for which the Fusilier had been shot had happened on 29 August. On that day, as the battalion was on its way up to the trenches, a shell burst close to the man and he had 'walked out of the ranks'. This was to be expected, Mr Snowden said, as the soldier, who was only 21, had been invalided home five months earlier with 'shell shock' and had just rejoined his unit.

Mr Macpherson replied that he was 'not prepared to interfere with the discretion of the Field-Marshal Commanding-in-Chief, who only confirms the proceedings in cases of this character after the fullest consideration.'

This did not satisfy Mr Snowden. He wanted to know what were the rights of an accused man to obtain help in his own defence. The reply was a disturbing one.

'It is not the duty of any officer to defend an officer or man charged before a court-martial.'

Mr Macpherson then hastened to explain. Although a prisoner had no statutory right to be represented, this assistance was granted 'wherever possible'. If a person charged with a grave offence had difficulty in finding an officer for the purpose 'on application by the accused, endeavours would be made to find a suitable officer'.

'On application by the accused' is a stony phrase. Anyone familiar with the workings of a magistrates' court will be aware of the monumental ignorance of legal proceedings displayed by many offenders who come up for trial. In the days before radio and television the lack of knowledge must have been even greater.

Not long after Mr Snowden had raised the ghost of Private A/6730, the question of the way in which the next of kin were informed that their sons, fathers, husbands or brothers had been shot, was raised again by Mr Hogge, Liberal Member for Edinburgh East.

'Is the honourable Gentleman aware that they are informed by a very brutal letter?'

He also pointed out that the names of executed men were not included in the return of those 'Killed in Action'. At a time when casualty lists were an essential part of everyday reading this made it very difficult for families to explain why their own particular sorrow had not been publicly proclaimed. And in those days, when curtains were drawn to mark a bereavement and formalities were observed by the humblest folk, such an omission stood out. If they did wish to conceal the fact that one of their family had died at the hands of his comrades, this made it even more difficult.

A few days later Mr Hogge put another question asking whether the Government were able to announce any new practice in announcing the deaths of men shot at the front by order of courts martial. It was answered by the Leader of the House, Mr Bonar Law.

'It had been arranged that in future the communications made to the dependants of soldiers shot at the front should merely state that they have died on service.'

The question of whether pensions would be granted was still being considered.

The pensions question was very much to the point. Two days later Mr Hayes Fisher, President of the Local Government Board, was obliged to admit that Boards of Guardians, the bodies which administered Parish Relief, had been passing resolutions calling for the Government to pay pensions to dependents of men who had been executed and thus relieve the local authorities of the necessity of supporting them.[1]

Many members felt distinctly uncomfortable at his reply. The thought of the widows of executed soldiers having to plead for public assistance was nothing less than a national scandal. Especially as no-one in authority was prepared to allow the public to know the details of the cases. In vain did Mr Snowden

[1] *Hansard*

try to obtain permission for the relatives of victims to inspect the documents of courts martial. About this time, too, a Member of Parliament at last took the trouble to study the Army Act. Snowden asked pointedly if the Under-Secretary was aware that the relatives of a person convicted by court martial could take criminal proceedings against the members and the confirming officers. He stressed that this was the only means available to secure 'a re-investigation of the circumstances which may have led to a soldier being wrongly executed'. Diplomatically, Mr Macpherson fended off the first part of the question. It raised difficult questions of law, he said, 'upon which it would be unwise to express any opinion in the absence of the facts of any particular case'. As to obtaining a re-investigation 'the proper and constitutional remedy of any relative is to petition His Majesty'.

Under such a barrage the Government decided to take some of the sting out of their tormentors' questions. They put up Sir Robert McCalmont, the Unionist Member for Antrim East, to seek information that would enable the official answers to allay suspicion. Sir Robert was a young brigadier-general who had served in the Boer War with the Royal Warwickshires before joining the Irish Guards when that regiment was formed in 1900. At the outbreak of war he had raised the 12th Royal Irish Rifles before taking over command of the 1st Battalion of his own regiment. He was a fire-eater but hardly a skilled diplomat. His first question elicited the reaffirmation of an earlier statement that although soldiers accused of a grave offence had no right to a legal adviser, in practice, attempts were always made to obtain 'a suitable officer'. The manner of the dialogue was not altogether reassuring. Three days later General McCalmont boldly spelled out what he meant by the term 'grave'. He specifically mentioned the death penalty. If soldiers on trial for their lives were not offered legal assistance automatically, he wanted the Government to 'suggest that Commanders-in-Chief should issue instructions that, subject to the exigencies of the service, this should be arranged'. A favourable reaction was implied.

General McCalmont took it upon himself to intervene when other Members wanted to know if it was possible for a man suffering from 'shell shock' to be executed. According to the gallant brigadier, exhaustive reports were called for after a man was condemned and it was 'practically impossible for a man to be executed who had suffered from shell shock because the fact that he has so suffered is certain to be included in his report'.

If Mr Macpherson was hopeful that this would stem the flow of questions, he was disappointed. Mr N. Pemberton Billing, the Member for East Herts, who had served in the Boer War and completed two years in the Royal Naval Air Service, fired another pointed question at the beginning of December. What, he wanted to know, was the highest rank of any officer who had been court martialled for cowardice in the face of the enemy and the highest rank of any officer on whom the death penalty had been inflicted? No reply!

Mr Billing then sought information on the system of announcing the results of courts martial. Although the war was more than three years old the Commons still seemed to be uncertain of this. Did such parades still take place and, if so, were the names, numbers and ranks of the executed men read out? If this were the case would the government take steps to discontinue the practice?

Mr Macpherson replied shortly: 'The answer to the first two parts of the question is in the affirmative; and to the last in the negative.'

Undeterred, Mr Billing continued to press for more details forcing from Mr Macpherson the statement:

'My honourable Friend will recollect that there has been a War Cabinet decision that the relatives of these soldiers shall be informed that the soldier so punished will be placed in the casualty list as having been killed.'

The answer appeared to be illogical to Mr Billing who pointed out that publicity in France led to rumours being circulated in England and it might be just as well to publish the facts at home.

This time there was no reply. Mr Macpherson's statement about the War Cabinet's decision had not made it plain whether they had decided to tell their next-of-kin the truth about such soldiers, while at the same time including them in the 'Killed in action' lists, or whether the fate of condemned men was to be made known to the British Army as a whole, while being concealed from their closest relatives.

Perhaps Mr Macpherson was counting on the amazing docility of the relatives of the executed men—few spoke out in protest. The propaganda was perhaps too much for them.

Unrestricted submarine warfare, the sinking of the *Lusitania*, Zeppelin raids and the general emphasis on 'Hun frightfulness' had created a situation where a father and mother might think twice before speaking up on behalf of a son who had apparently let down his comrades in the trenches. And if the Army's senior officers were sceptical about the validity of nervous diseases caused by war services, the public at large were even more ignorant.

All the same, considering the activity of the firing squads between 1 October, 1916 and 30 September, 1917, the period covered by the Adjutant-General's report, it is surprising that there was not a greater outcry.

Seventy-eight men had been shot for desertion; five executed for cowardice; three for murder; two men each for the offences of mutiny, striking a superior, quitting their posts, casting their arms away and sleeping at their posts, a total of ninety-six in all.[2]

Despite the considerable number of death sentences carried out, there is evidence to show that court martial could be sympathetically inclined towards prisoners and, depending on the unit, a court might be positively biased in their favour. Details exist of three cases in the 2/5th Lancashire Fusiliers of the 55th Division arising out of the battle of the Menin Road which commenced on 20 September.[3]

The inclusion of the 55th Division in the assault formations was in itself open to criticism. The West Lancashire Territorials, who had seen heavy fighting on the Somme the previous year, had formed part of the original attacking force on 31 July. Although they had penetrated the German defences many of the enemy pill boxes and much of the wire had been missed by the artillery and the most bitter fighting ensued. The attackers found themselves assailed not only by numerous machine-guns but by 77 mm shells fired at close range from field guns in concrete emplacements. Low-flying aircraft sprayed them with bullets. Up to their knees in mud and water, the Lancashire men clung to their gains and drove off waves of Germans plodding towards them through drenching rain. The casualties of the division amounted to 135 officers and 3,720 men killed and wounded before they were pulled out of the line.

[2] *Statistics of the Military Effort of the British Empire.*
[3] Unpublished papers of Major-General J. C. Latter, deposited with the Imperial War Museum.

In the weeks that followed, reinforcements were slow to arrive. Training proceeded for the next battle but 1,000 men arrived too late to be assimilated into their units and were left out. They could consider themselves fortunate. The tapes laid down to guide the assault troops on 20 September were seen by the enemy who opened a withering fire at zero hour. Although the 55th once again seized and held various pill boxes their losses amounted to just under 2,000 men. Little wonder that a Company Sergeant Major in the 2/5th Lancashire Fusiliers gave a broad hint to a medical orderly when they went into a quiet sector that he would be grateful for an injection in the knee that would render him unfit for further service. Court martial proceedings were opened after the orderly reported the incident, but subsequently the Sergeant Major was acquitted and went on to gain a commission.[4] Two other cases were more serious.

A private who vanished while the battalion was under shell fire near the notorious Goldfish Chateau, was arrested by Military Police at Cassel, headquarters of the Second Army. On being returned to his unit he was court martialled, on a charge of desertion. According to the Army Act, a field general court martial could be held by any three officers with more than one year's service and in this case an experienced major sat as president. An officer with legal training in civilian life sat in as 'courts martial officer' to advise on points of law, a practice which was growing although by no means mandatory. The Prosecutor in the case was a young officer who later became a major-general. Another young officer, M——, acted as 'prisoner's friend' helping him to put his case. The Prosecutor records:

'I could see M—— was rather at a loss as to his line of defence and he failed to see it even when the prisoner made a very good point for himself in his evidence by saying that he did not intend to desert but was merely trying to make his way to the 6th Lancashire Fusiliers where he had a brother and in which he himself had served. Still M—— showed no glimmer of consciousness as to the chance he had; so I leant across to him and pointed out that this amounted to a plea of not guilty to desertion but guilty of absence without leave.'

The line of defence suggested by the Prosecutor was immediately seized upon, the plea of guilty to the lesser offence

4 The Latter papers.

126

was accepted and the prisoner was sentenced to three years' jail, later reduced to two years and suspended.[5]

In the other case a sergeant was accused of cowardice on the third day of the Menin Road battle. An officer checking the amount of small arms ammunition available to hand over to a relieving battalion found the sergeant and three men in a trench near a pill box behind the line known as Hindu Cottage. They were doing nothing and could not give a satisfactory explanation as to their movements since Z-Day.

All four were brought down from the trenches under arrest. The battalion commander then dealt with the privates at regimental level, awarding them 28 days' field punishment No. 1—which meant being tied to a fixed object for at least two hours a day but was infinitely preferable to being shot at dawn. Having disposed of their cases, the C.O. was then in a position to call the men to give evidence against the sergeant at his court martial.

The defence was based on the plea that the sergeant had been 'took bad' just before the attack and had informed his officer—not available to testify as he had become a casualty along with the rest of the platoon. It looked as though all would be well for the prisoner until he was asked if he knew where the front line was—he had been found some distance behind it. Unhappily the question was put by M——, the 'prisoner's friend'. The same young officer who had fulfilled the role of Prosecutor in the previous case wrote later that he knew very well that the sergeant was aware of the location of the front line but . . .

'I gasped for I knew that if he admitted that he did, it would be all up with him.' Fortunately, hardly were the words out of M——'s mouth than the courts martial officer said:

'I don't think I should ask that question if I were you.'

The sergeant was acquitted although, according to the Prosecutor, 'the man's whole demeanour when brought to battalion H.Q. and his previous record proved the charge.'

The cases of the fusilier accused of desertion and the sergeant on the cowardice charge were tried in October, 1917, at the village of Aizecourt-le-Bas and demonstrate the tremendous element of chance involved. Had the court martial officer confined himself to legal matters in the second case, the prisoner would certainly have been found guilty. If the Prose-

[5] The Latter Papers.
[6] The Latter Papers.

cutor had not reversed roles temporarily in the first case, the same might have happened. At its best the system is shown to be haphazard and open to irregularities, hardly the ideal basis on which to try a man for his life. Nevertheless, the cases quoted show that officers with legal knowledge were exerting their influence on the military process of law. Much rougher justice was being dealt out in the heat of the battle.

Just as Haig concluded the Battle of the Somme with a powerful thrust at Beaumont Hamel, so he approved plans for a final stroke against the enemy after the high hopes of the summer had been submerged into the slough of Passchendaele. Sir Julian Byng's Third Army, using 476 tanks, broke through the Hindenburg Line on 20 November and took 10,000 prisoners and more than one hundred guns. Stunned by his own success, Byng was unable to develop it. The reserves which might have been used to exploit the situation had been swallowed up at Ypres or rushed to Italy to bolster the Italians after their collapse at Caporetto. The Germans responded rapidly and a furious battle raged for the possession of the key position of Bourlon Wood in which the 40th Division played a major role.

The 40th were one of the last divisions raised for Kitchener's New Army and did not arrive in France until June, 1916. For more than a year they were used to hold the line and did not take an important part in any of the major battles. In attacking the wood with the help of tanks they did extremely well. Then the infantry were faced with the problem of holding what they had won. A hectic struggle ensued, in the forefront of which were the Welsh battalions of the 119th Brigade under Brigadier Crozier, promoted after his service with the Ulster Division. Men of all four battalions mingled in a firing line dug amid a tangle of tree stumps and shattered branches. Dismounted cavalrymen who included many pre-1914 Regulars joined them, earning a respectful mention in enemy battle reports for the excellence of their musketry. A perspiring machine-gun company arrived, setting up their weapons in shell-holes to bolster the defence. Detachments of highlanders scrambled through the German fire to lend their support. At the height of this savage infantry battle, part of the line gave way. According to Crozier:

'A few men with flagging energy and less staying power than the rest, lost their heads and some of them their lives as a consequence. They fled from danger, only to encompass disaster. A revolver emptied into "the brown" accounted for five; a Lewis gun fired into the panic-stricken mass put many on the grass and undergrowth.'

An officer who made his way back with a slight wound was pounced on and 'forced, with others, up the hill again, there to die.'[7] Crozier, conscious that 'in one battle a colonel shot another colonel in order that a situation might be restored',[8] was not surprised when one of his own commanding officers shot several infantrymen from another brigade 'to save the situation'. The ruthlessness of all the colonels and all the Croziers was unable, however, to achieve the capture of Bourlon Hill and its forest of blackened stumps. But Haig was determined to seize this stronghold which overlooked the city of Cambrai. He ordered Byng to take personal control from Lieutenant-General Woollcombe whose IVth Corps was responsible for the attacks and on 27 November arrived in person to watch the attack in which the Guards (whose commander had objected to the plan) also took part.[9] When it failed the Cambrai offensive was over. Three days later the Germans took Byng by surprise and recaptured much of the ground lost on 20 November, plus more than 100 British guns and 6,000 prisoners. Squadrons of low-flying fighters gave the German attack an extra cutting edge.

Once again the British divisions had been left in a dangerous salient and without exception were weakened from heavy losses at Cambrai or 'Third Ypres'. Observers who watched the thousands of men retiring wearily over the fields compared them to a race crowd leaving the hill at Epsom. Others reported signs of panic, some soldiers retiring without rifles and others showing a reluctance to use them.

Transport blocked the roads; the commander of the 29th Division was almost captured in his headquarters and irate artillerymen discovered that the infantry of the 20th Division had left them alone to face the enemy. Many howitzers, including weapons captured on 20 November, were abandoned and destroyed, but as the fighting line receded resistance stiffened. With the deep trenches and captured portions of the Hindenburg Line to fall back on, the tired troops of the Third Army took a heavy toll of their equally worn enemy. Fierce

[7] Crozier, *A Brass Hat in No-Man's-Land.*
[8] Crozier, *Sunday Express*, May, 1928.
[9] Edmonds, *Official History*, 1917.

counter-attacks by the Guards Division and dismounted cavalry drove the Germans from some of their gains and the battle died of the mutual exhaustion of both sides. Churlishly Byng, who denied that he had been surprised, blamed the defeat on the poor training of junior officers and N.C.O.s and particularly the 'lack of staunchness' of the machine-gun corps. Haig, damning with faint praise, pointed out that retreating troops had masked the field of fire of machine-guns in some cases. He supported Byng's view and took responsibility for ordering the fighting at Bourlon which had placed a strain on the Third Army. Three senior officers in England who studied Haig's report, endorsed the criticism of certain infantry and machine-gun units, and General Smuts, an 'independent' member of the War Cabinet, expressed the view that 'no one down to and including corps commanders was to blame'. The government accepted this assessment and also declared lack of training as one of the causes for the collapse of certain units.

A Court of Inquiry was opened at the order of Sir Douglas Haig and sat at Hesdin towards the end of January. But it was an unsatisfactory affair. Neither Byng nor the two corps commanders most involved gave evidence. The conclusions let the responsibility for the collapse lie where it had been carefully placed—on the shoulders of the troops, and on two divisions in particular, the 12th and the 20th. And yet these same formations had played a major part in giving Haig the victory which caused the church bells to be rung in triumph in England only ten days before the German counter-attack.

*　　*　　*

With the enforced respite of winter, the exhausted combatants licked their wounds. In four intense periods of battle, at Arras Messines, Ypres and Cambrai, both Germans and British had lost heavily. Along with most of the invaluable professionals and enthusiastic amateurs, the spirit of 1914 had vanished. Morale on both sides was low. The need for more men became critical. For the Germans, who had called up the 1919 class, the race was on to transfer divisions from defeated Russia to the Western Front before the Americans arrived in large numbers. Just as urgently the Allies tried to find reinforcements for their spent divisions before the enemy attacked. Following steps already taken by the French and Germans, the British reduced the number of battalions in a brigade from four to three in order to maintain the number of divisions. Increased fire-power, in the shape of extra Lewis guns, was expected to make up for the deficiency in riflemen. No regular battalions were disbanded, the choice being restricted first to New Army battalions and then to second-line Territorials. The 11th Middlesex disappeared from the 12th Division and the Nelson Battalion from the Royal Naval Division.

Thousands of troops were available in England, but a large proportion of these were boys of eighteen and a half, and Lloyd George was pledged not to send them overseas. Apart from that, he no longer had any faith in Sir Douglas Haig. Throughout the autumn the Commander-in-Chief had justified the heavy losses in Flanders with reports that German morale was broken and that their divisions were being shattered one after the other. 30 November had given a rude shock to the government.

Dominion governments had similar man-power problems. Sir Robert Borden, the Canadian Prime Minister, in a desperate bid to push through conscription, passed an Act which gave the vote to close women relatives of men and women, living or dead, who had served in the Forces outside Canada. He also dis-franchized Conscientious Objectors and all aliens who had become Canadian citizens after 1902. Having gained re-election by these dubious means, he duly passed the conscription Bill in the spring of 1918. Thereupon 20,000 men immediately took to the forests of Quebec and the wilds of Ontario. Fifteen thousand of them were still on the run when the Armistice was signed.[10]

In England more than 6,000 men defied the Military Service Acts on ground of conscience during the war and were arrested. Rigorous attempts to break their spirits failed. At Reading Gaol the 'Conshies' were fed from pails. R. Palme Dutt, an Oxford classical scholar who was later to become a leading Communist, was held in Hut 16a of the Royal Herbert Hospital, Woolwich, with soldiers suffering from venereal disease . . . and in poor sanitary conditions which afforded little protection from infection.

Nearly one hundred conscientious objectors including four-teen New Zealanders and twenty-five Canadians were taken to France and court martialled. Thirty-four of them were paraded

[10] MacPhail, *Official History of the Canadian Forces.*

to hear an officer read out sentences from a large form on which the word 'Death' had been printed in red and underlined twice. All the sentences were commuted to ten years' gaol. One man, in England, who experienced a similar trial, was placed against the wall of Winchester Prison, blindfolded, and heard the order to fire given before he was told he had been 'pardoned'. Another who broke down and agreed to join the army cut his throat in a fit of remorse.[11]

In the search for more men in the winter of 1917, the medical services were required to play their part. A proportion of returned wounded could be counted on, and in this respect the N.Y.D.N. centres proved their value. There was no alarming permanent loss of 'shell shock' victims after the Third Battle of Ypres as there had been during the Somme fighting. Of 5,000 men treated at the centres most concerned, more than 4,000 were returned to duty, the majority going back to fighting units, others being transferred to less arduous posts.

Even the V.D. hospitals yielded 4,000 convalescents to act as stretcher-bearers in casualty clearing stations. In dealing with the problem of V.D. the army had shown considerable common sense early in the war by allowing troops to visit streets which contained known brothels. Such establishments were medically supervised and as a result the infection rate fell dramatically. Of 171,000 men known to have visited houses in a particular street in Le Havre within a year only 243 contracted any form of disease. The result was that, although the equivalent of a division was always out of action from this cause, the V.D. figure was kept down at a period when the army expanded rapidly.[12] Had it not been for the Dean of Lincoln, it might have remained low. But in 1918, when the manpower search was at its height, a question was asked in Parliament in respect of a brothel at Cayeux-sur-Mer. There, troops from resting units were given camp passes which made it clear that certain streets were in bounds at specific hours. This invoked the wrath of the Dean. On 20 February the following letter appeared in *The Times*:

'In your issue of this morning it is stated by Mr Macpherson (the Under-Secretary of State for War) that the question of brothels in France is "one entirely for the civil authorities and therefore we cannot take any action". This is not true; it is

[11] See Pankhurst, *The Home Front*, and Ward Boulton, *Objection Overruled*.
[12] *Official Medical History of the War*, Vol. 2.

known at the War Office to be not true. There is much they can do; they can avoid encouraging the men to visit these places by entries on camp leave cards which give the hours when they are not out of bounds for British soldiers.

'They can take a leaf out of American Army custom and not stultify discipline and moral appeals as had been thus done.

'The honour and morality of our public policy is being besmirched by this silent consent to the action of men who are in favour of the entirely discredited policy of the C.D. Acts.

'The chaplains know and hear enough to make me ask: Why do they not resign in a body? What are the headmasters doing whose young boys are going out to temptation in French areas?'

The letter, signed 'T. C. Fry, the Deanery, Lincoln,' put Mr Macpherson in a difficult position. On the one side the army was in no doubt that the retention of *maisons tolerées* was essential to avoid sending up the 'casualty' rate from V.D. at a time when every man was needed. On the other, thousands of youngsters were now in khaki. And although for the most part they were stationed in Britain, there seemed little doubt that in this seemingly interminable war they would end up in France and the arms of some scarlet woman at some time. The Church in Britain did not like the idea at all.

Mr Macpherson tackled the problem bravely. In answer to Parliamentary questions he explained that the army could not 'ride roughshod over institutions which were accepted as part and parcel of the life of the country'.

This was greeted with firm cries of 'Hear, hear!'

Mr Macpherson went on to explain that where the situation required it, British officers went 'very quietly' to the mayor of the town involved and joint action was taken 'without hurting the sentiments of the French people or casting any slur on an institution they thought proper to retain in their midst'.

Having gone so far, Mr Macpherson threw caution to the winds and declared that he was not at all sure, 'human nature being what it is', that it was such a bad thing to have certain houses in which women were registered.[13]

In the ruminative silence which followed this statement, a pompous Member wished to know if the Right Honourable Gentleman was aware that unregistered women were most numerous in the neighbourhood of registered brothels. Dryly

[13] Debate on the Army Estimates, February, 1918.

Mr Macpherson replied that *he* was not, leaving the questioner to face dozens of curious stares and raised eye-brows.

Within a few days of the debate the King visited Rochester Row Military Hospital, Woolwich, and inspected the V.D. wards, later expressing his sympathy 'with the practical efforts now in progress to combat this national danger'.[14] But the controversy raged on and in April the clergy had their way. *Maisons tolerées* were put completely out of bounds. Immediately the V.D. rate began to increase. It was, after all, the hardest self-inflicted wound for the army to detect.

The energy of the Church in dealing with this threat to the moral welfare of young British soldiers was in marked contrast to their silence on a subject on which the Chaplains to the Forces were also well informed. The case of Sub-Lieutenant Dyett was raised in considerable detail on 20 February, thirteen months after his death. It received a passing mention in *The Times* but did not draw any letter from the Dean. It did not tempt so much as a single curate into print.

[14] Report in *The Times*, 26 February, 1918.

12

John Bull's Revelation

The Dyett case was raised by Mr Philip Morrell, the Liberal Member for South Oxfordshire. Holding up a copy of the popular weekly paper *John Bull* he drew attention to the main article signed by the editor, Mr Horatio Bottomley, which was entitled 'Shot at Dawn'.

Striking a reasonable note, Mr. Morrell accepted that the shooting of soldiers as an example might be justifiable.

'It is a stern, terribly stern necessity that this should be so,' he said, 'but we are bound to see that the conditions under which these trials take place are as fair as possible.'

He was particularly concerned that relatives could not inspect the court martial papers and also that Dyett had been shot despite the recommendation to mercy. He read a passage from the article in *John Bull*:

'The accused was young. It was dark when he lost his way in seeking to find British headquarters. There was great disorder, and hundreds of men were retiring at the time. From what he said and wrote, the poor boy evidently thought that the worst that would befall him would be the loss of his commission.'

If the contents of the article were not true, said Mr Morell, then the author should be prosecuted.

'If it is true, I think it goes to show, like many other facts which have come to my knowledge, that there is a case for investigation as to the method of procedure in these courts martial.'

Mr Morrell had been educated at Eton and Balliol. His tone was reasonable. The Under Secretary said with some relief that before he expressed an opinion he would like 'to have all the facts investigated, because one finds that very often those cases —not from any unpatriotic spirit—are dealt with in a way which often leaves a good deal of room for doubt in the minds of ordinary men.'

The voice of Mr J. H. Thomas, the formidable Member for Derby, brought him up sharply.

'Will the honourable Member enable some of the Members of this House to see the evidence of the court martial in this case?'

"That', said Mr Macpherson, 'raises a very technical point—namely that no man is allowed to see the proceedings of a court martial and see what the facts really are in the case without the consent of the person who has been tried by court martial, and the extraordinary technical difficulty arises that if the man is dead, unfortunately, that consent cannot be given.'

Mr Macpherson promised, however, to study the proceedings himself and explain further to the house 'if I can, consistently with my duty and with the law'.

He then went on to deal with the oft raised question of providing 'prisoner's friends' to give legal advice and assistance to men on trial for an offence which might carry the death penalty. That very day, he said, he had made it his business to call on the Director of Personal Services (none other than the industrious Childs, now a General).

'Fortunately for the House, he had at his disposal an Assistant Provost-Marshal from France—a very gallant officer, Captain Montgomery—and he got him to write down what he actually did in his own division.'

Captain Montgomery's description of the system as applied to the 36th (Ulster) Division was for him to ask soldiers what witnesses they wished to call in their defence and if they wished a particular officer to act as prisoner's friend.

'I have always found that the officer asked for by the accused has been allowed to act for him by his Commanding officer, unless the exigencies of the service forbid it, and in this case the accused has been so informed, and he has been given the opportunity of asking for someone else or the name of another suitable officer suggested.'

There were, he added, usually 'plenty of officers in battalions with legal training who were only too glad to act, and in fact, rather enjoyed the job.'

Why infantry battalions should contain an abundance of lawyers capable of defending a man on a capital charge was not explained. Nor was it made clear what happened if most of the officers were killed or wounded—a common occurrence. Some doubts did strike Mr Macpherson. He announced that although he wished to cast no disrespect, 'far from it', on the 'gallant soldiers and officers who are in charge of courts martial' he was arranging for the publication of 'a definite Army Order reminding all commanding officers and the various distinguished officers concerned what the proper procedure should be in the case of a court martial, in case any doubt may arise as to the justice of the sentence that has been passed.'

The object of this order was 'above all, to remind the court martial officer that it is his duty to place every fact that is in favour of the accused before the court.'

He then read out part of the order:

'If the accused desires to make his own selection of a friend subject to military law, whether of commissioned rank or not, the request should be granted.

'The friend of the accused shall be notified, and a copy of the evidence given to him in sufficient time to enable him to give due consideration to the case and to consult with the accused. The attendance of a friend of the accused in no way relieves the court of its responsibility for safeguarding the interests of the accused and eliciting all the facts which may tell in his favour.'

Any hope that Mr Macpherson might have entertained that he had put the House at rest was promptly dispelled.

'Has the instruction previously been issued?' asked Mr Thomas.

Exasperated, the Under-Secretary replied that it had always 'been the rule'. Indeed it had been the practice. The reason for the new Order was to relieve public opinion of a very serious burden of doubt which had been cast upon it.

The mind of one Member, a Major Davies, remained unrelieved nevertheless. Until machinery had been put in motion to make properly qualified officers available at, say, corps level where they could act on behalf of the accused men 'this matter will not be put on a satisfactory basis'.

He went on:

'Personally, I had some experience of courts martial in France. We all know that occasionally fact, and material facts, are not brought out. It does not always follow, though the court may have done their best to give a proper decision, that such is the case; it must necessarily arise in some few cases that their decisions are not exactly what they ought to be.

137

'I contend that as a criminal in this country has a right to counsel, and to expert legal advice on his behalf, that we surely ought to allow some measure of protection and of justice to our gallant fellows in the field.'

On this note the discussion came to an end, at least for a few days. But on 14 March the case was raised again. Major Davies spearheaded the attack by asking specifically 'whether the officer who was to defend this officer (Dyett) did not see him until half an hour before the trial?'

Mr Macpherson: 'My information is that it is not true that the officer who was to defend the accused did not see him until half an hour before the trial. I understand he was with him from eleven to three o'clock two days before the trial. I may say that he is an officer with legal qualifications.'

Mr James Alexander Pringle, Unionist Member for Fermanagh, then joined issue, driving home some highly relevant points as befitted a barrister of some eminence.

First, that Sub-Lieutenant Dyett, a 1915 volunteer who had seen considerable active service, had been aware that his nerve was going and had asked, as a Royal Naval Reserve officer, to be returned to sea duty only a month before the attack of 13 November, 1916. His Commanding Officer had persuaded him to withdraw the application on the grounds that nearly all soldiers went through periods of strain and generally got over it. Because of this Dyett had been left in reserve.

The implication was plain. Had Dyett's commanding officer not been killed in the attack, it was hardly likely that he would have pushed through a court martial.

Secondly Mr Pringle claimed that not only did the officer appointed as prisoner's friend have very little time in which to prepare the case—four hours on Christmas Eve—but he did not receive the summary of evidence on which the case was based until half an hour before the court sat.

Mr Pringle felt very strongly that where a man's life was at stake he should have legal assistance not only at the trial but also when statements, which might be incriminating, were taken during preliminary inquiries.

He also made a new and important point. Dyett, he stated, had been found behind the line 'by another officer who happened to be his one and only enemy in the army, and it was largely, if not entirely, upon the evidence of this one man that this boy officer was condemned to death and ultimately shot.'

Stressing that for ten days Dyett had been kept in ignorance of the fact that he had been condemned to death and that the sentence had been carried out only eight hours after he was informed, Mr Pringle pleaded for soldiers to be given the right to appeal—a practice which was allowed in the French Army.

'This right of appeal is possessed by the lowest and meanest criminal in the country,' he declared. 'It is denied to men who have freely and voluntarily joined the Forces to fight the battle of their country and who, in a moment of nervous breakdown may have committed offences against military law.'

On the subject of the refusal of the War Office to allow relatives access to court martial papers he was most scathing. According to 'this piece of red tape, the minutes of evidence are not available to anybody but the accused, who is now dead.'

It was a formidable condemnation and Mr Macpherson did not made a good showing in reply. He argued lamely that it was in the prisoner's interests not to have legal advice when statements were taken:

'This way of collecting evidence has for a long time been the established practice in the army and I understand it is a practice which meets with general favour among both officers and men.'

He was even less convincing when refuting the allegation that the prisoner's friend had access to the summary of evidence only half an hour before the trial.

In Mr Macpherson's eyes, if a rule was laid down in 'regulations' then, *ipso facto*, it must have been obeyed.

'It is the established practice that the moment a summary of evidence is taken, a copy of it is by order handed to the accused person,' he declared, adding almost indignantly, 'I for one cannot understand why, if, as is admitted now, two days before the trial the accused and the accused's friend were in long consultation for four hours (on the Christmas Eve), the accused did not produce a copy of that summary of evidence which he was bound in law to have.'

Mr Pringle interrupted quickly to ask, 'Is there any evidence that he did have it?'

Mr Macpherson was momentarily shaken.

'I do not know anything about this, but I am almost certain that he had, because I believe it is the law that the accused person must have it.'

Having recovered himself, he went on reassuringly: 'In any

case, he must have known the evidence against him.'

Soothingly, he pointed out that, like Mr Pringle, he was also a lawyer and that if he were called on to defend a man on such a grave charge he would first of all ask whether he had the summary of evidence.

Mr Pringle was not pacified. He was in no doubt about what had occurred. No less a person than the prisoner's friend had told him that Dyett had not had a copy of the summary of evidence and that one was obtained only half an hour before the trial.

Somewhat illogically the Under-Secretary brushed this off, saying that, even so, he could not see how any blame could be attached to the War Office or the Commander-in-Chief. Hastily he proceeded to deal with the availability of the court martial record. Giving right of access only to prisoners seemed to him to be a sound rule 'because any person might at any time, and for the most flimsy reasons, ask the Judge Advocate-General, who is the custodian of all proceedings, to hand over the proceedings of a court martial to him. I think that would be intolerable.'

Then Mr Macpherson let slip one of the real reasons for his intransigence.

'In the Dublin cases, I took that line, and I went further.'

In other words, if the court martial proceedings were to be available to interested parties, the relatives of rebels shot during the Irish rising of Easter, 1916, might be in a position to ask awkward questions or to threaten the lives of witnesses who had testified.

'It is a technical point, and some might call it a lawyer's point,' he explained, 'but I said that because he [a prisoner sentenced by court martial] is dead there is no person alive who can compel the Judge Advocate-General to produce the proceedings. I for one, until the law is altered, will not produce the proceedings in this case.'

Now in his stride, Mr Macpherson brushed aside an assertion by Mr Pringle that if a person was told the result of his trial only eight hours before the time set for his irrevocable execution the chance of anyone finding out the ground on which he had been condemned was 'practically eliminated'.

Switching adroitly to the subject of the possibility of a 'shell shocked' soldier being sentenced to death, Mr Macpherson produced what he obviously thought was a trump-card, a communication from the Commander-in-Chief. He quoted the following passage from Sir Douglas Haig's letter:

'When a man has been sentenced to death, if at any time any doubt has been raised as to his responsibility for his actions, or if the suggestion has been advanced that he has suffered from neurasthenia or shell shock, orders are issued for him to be examined by a medical board which expresses an opinion as to his sanity, and as to whether he should be held responsible for his actions. One of the members of this board is always a medical officer of neurological experience. The sentence of death is not carried out in the case of such a man unless the medical board express the opinion that he is held to be responsible for his actions.'

Before the Commons had digested this mouthful, the Under-Secretary flashed a shrewd thrust at the consciences of his listeners. In Dyett's case, he said, all the military commanders had done was to administer an Act given to them by Parliament. 'Unfortunately' an officer had suffered the death penalty. 'I would ask the House further to believe that he suffers it having been carefully and humanely tried by the only laws which the military had provided for them, laws humanely administered and justly given effect to.'

In as much as Mr Macpherson was stating facts, this reproach was justified. The House went on to debate the activities of the Committee on Oil Production. But as they left for home that night many Members must have sensed the presence of an accusing ghost in the shadows. As they climbed into their comfortable beds they must have wondered about the unanswered question of the role played by the person described as the dead boy's 'only enemy'. And as the light went out they may have reflected on how *they* would have felt if they had been told only a few hours earlier that they had been sentenced to die at dawn. Honest men would admit to themselves that if the generals were guilty, then so were they.

In the Commons a month later Mr King tried once again to change the controversial regulations that allowed a man to be kept in ignorance of the fact that he had been sentenced to death. Mr Pringle attempted to secure the release of court martial proceedings and said that Dyett's father had sought to obtain them in vain. A blunt letter from the Army Council had informed him that the evidence could be made available only to the accused and as the accused was now dead, nobody could obtain it from the War Office.

Neither of these efforts to change the law met with any success. But on 17 April, Mr Macpherson himself moved the insertion of a proviso in the oath taken by members of courts martial. In future they would swear to maintain total secrecy 'except so far as it may be permitted by instructions from the Army Council for the purpose of communicating the sentence to the accused'.

It would be interesting to know what Mr Macpherson's reaction would have been if he had known that only three days earlier a British officer had ordered the summary despatch of a considerable body of troops of his own side and that it had been carried out without hesitation.

* * *

Smashing through weak defences with a highly sophisticated and immensely powerful bombardment, the Germans hurled back a large proportion of the British Army in ten days of savage fighting in March, 1918. Reinforced by eighty divisions made available by the collapse of Russia, they reached the outskirts of Amiens and almost split the British and French before they were held. Dangerous though this thrust had been, the second step in an all-out effort to smash the British Army was even more deadly. On 9 April a tremendous barrage swept away four demoralized Portuguese brigades. Many of these unfortunate troops stole the bicycles of the XIth Corps cyclist battalion to make their escape and others abandoned their boots. In some areas the British troops reacted as they had done at Lauffeld and at Waterloo when they fired on retiring Dutch and Belgians. The Portuguese were reported to have 'got in the line of fire of their allies' machine-guns with unfortunate results to themselves'.[1] Nevertheless the Germans surged over the Flanders plain towards the Channel ports and the supply complex in the rear of Ypres. Bitter fighting ensued drawing in many of the weak British formations which had been through the March battles and made up to strength from raw troops, many mere boys.

Among reserves hurried to the scene were the 33rd (New Army) Division, moved from the Arras area by rail. In their vanguard was the machine-gun battalion commanded by

[1] Liddell Hart, *Foch: Man of Orleans.*

142

Lieutenant-Colonel Graham Seton Hutchison, a Regular soldier of the Argyll and Sutherland Highlanders. At the head of cyclist patrol he pedalled up the valley of the little River Lys on the morning of 12 April and was appalled by what he saw. Men of the 41st, 31st and 49th Divisions were streaming back exhausted after days of non-stop fighting. Jumping into a motor ambulance Hutchison returned to his men and ordered them forward. Stunning an obstructive transport officer with his revolver, he loaded eight Vickers guns into a lorry and sped to the danger point. Under the muzzles of these weapons three companies of stragglers were rallied and 'persuaded' to take up supporting positions.

On the morning of 13 April the Germans, attacking under cover of the mist, overran some of Hutchison's forward guns but the others riddled masses of cavalry and infantry as the fog lifted. During the day various improvised units arrived to help plug the gap between the towns of Strazeele and Bailleul—sanitary men, cooks, batmen and orderlies from corps headquarters took their place in the line, and it was reported that there was even a platoon of Town Majors under an Area Commandant. But when the Germans came on afresh the following day the situation deteriorated. In the face of an apparently relentless advance one of the improvised units gave way. A cluster of khaki figures stood up in the shallow trenches they had been defending. Rifles were thrown down and hands went up. What happened next Hutchison has described himself:

'Such an action as this will in a short time spread like dry rot through an army and it is one of those dire military necessities which calls for immediate and prompt action. If there does not exist on the spot a leader of sufficient courage and initiative to check it by a word, it must be necessary to check it by shooting. This was done. Of a party of forty men who held up their hands, thirty-eight were shot down with the result that this never occurred again.

'It is necessary to state this in order that those who were not present can properly appreciate the danger in which our line, the Channel ports and the British Isles themselves were threatened in this way. It was not a time when either sympathy or sentiment could in any way be permitted to weigh as a consideration for any in the battle. Neither the wounded, the exhausted nor the afraid could be permitted either consideration or help; for each man as long as he lived had to use his weapon. Nothing else mattered.'[2]

Colonel Hutchison was an unusual man. From what he wrote after the war, one gains the impression that he genuinely enjoyed combat. A keen amateur artist, his publications are vividly illustrated with scenes reflecting what he must have felt was the glory of battle. His fertile imagination may well have been excited by Haig's famous message of 11 April, in which he declared: 'There is no other course open to us but to fight it out. Every position must be held to the last man; there must be no retirement. With our backs to the wall and believing in the justice of our cause each of us must fight on to the end.' But whatever the reasons that influenced him, and however grave the crisis which confronted him—and there can be no question that a break-through at this point would have been serious—one is prompted to ask: If it was felt necessary to shoot British troops as an example to others, why did so many have to die?

Hutchison himself knew the men had come from soft jobs at headquarters and were under officers with little fighting experience. It is hard to believe that they would have been much use in any case, but had he shot two and inspired thirty-eight, there would have been greater logic in his action. To shoot thirty-eight to inspire two does not make sense. A much more widespread panic at Sapignies in March was stopped by a sergeant in the South Lancashire Regiment who shot two men out of hand.[3]

Of course, it could have been that the gunner who was ordered to open fire loosed a longer burst than Hutchison intended. Or that Hutchison himself was in a slightly hysterical state after seeing so many British troops retreating in disorder during the previous days and was just as much a victim of the ruthless demands of total war as the thirty-eight men he condemned to death.

In the spring of 1918 few people were as confused as the ordinary soldier. All around him he saw the carefully built-up structure of the rear areas dissolving. A young Irishman who had a bird's eye view of the chaos was Private Martin Power of the 2/7th Manchester Regiment in the 66th (Territorial) Division. He was in the cells awaiting court martial

[2] Seton Hutchinson, *History and Memoir of the 33rd Battalion, Machine Gun Corps.* See also *The 33rd Division in France and Flanders 1915–19.*

[3] Smith and Kincaid, *The 25th Division in France and Flanders.*

at the time. On 9 March his battalion marched twenty miles to take up its position in the Fifth Army's line. Power, only eighteen years old, was on sentry duty that night. Worn out by the long trek, carrying more than sixty pounds of equipment, he fell asleep. In the middle of the night he felt someone shaking him roughly. He opened his tired eyes and found himself staring into the muzzle of a revolver held by an infuriated captain.

'The officer had been all for shooting me while I was asleep,' Power recalls, 'but the sergeant said that as I was a Roman Catholic I ought to be woken up so that I could say my prayers first. When I came to, the captain didn't have the nerve to kill me in cold blood and I was sent back to the reserve line to await a court martial.'

Power was still under arrest when the German offensive involved his division in desperate fighting. Time and again he volunteered to go back to his battalion but each time he was refused permission. Gradually, however, all the rear personnel were called forward, including the regimental policeman guarding Power. The Irish boy waited obediently in a village behind the lines, looking after the regimental band instruments, until the Germans were too close for comfort. Then he joined a gang of stragglers and found himself a rifle. When the retreat was over he learned that most of his comrades had become casualties and that the battalion's records, including his own court martial papers, had been destroyed. Posted to the 2nd East Lancashire Regiment, he was careful not to fall asleep on duty again. The next time he might not be so lucky.[4]

The problem of preventing men from sleeping on duty was never really solved during the war. In 1918, with so many young soldiers pushed to the front, it was particularly difficult.

A medical officer in a Scottish regiment noted that 'in many cases you were dealing with boys, some of whom were not properly grown; and it was always an anxiety to these boys to have to march ten to fifteen miles carrying a matter of 80 to 100 lbs and a good bulk of that pressing on the chest. These boys used to dread the march and I know one or two who undoubtedly developed neuroses.'

He, himself, used to make it a point to march with the batta-

---

[4] Personal recollections of Martin Power Esq.

lion in order to encourage the youngsters and see they got help.[5]

Officially, only two men were shot for sleeping 'on post' during the whole war.[6] But the problem had been causing major concern from the very beginning. Childs records the fact that Field-Marshal Sir John French wanted to avoid inflicting the death sentence for this offence at all costs.[7]

'But things got very bad in this regard and one day Lord French caused a paragraph to be inserted in General Orders drawing attention to the prevalence of this offence and stating that if it continued he would be under the painful necessity of ordering the death penalty to be carried out.'

Both the recorded cases were certainly after French had left France to take over command of the Home Forces, being carried out during the period 1916/1917. But gaol sentences for this offence were not uncommon.

Private Sam Horsfall, of the 21st London Regiment, relates that at Christmas 1915, his battalion, which had been through the battles of Festubert and Loos, was called hurriedly into the trenches. Anticipating a ten-day spell in rest they had been celebrating well rather than wisely.

'The weather was awful and as we entered the communication trenches they were full of water, although they were shallower where bodies had slithered in off the parapet. In the front line the water was up to the firing step and although we bailed it was no use. The water just flowed back. We were worn out.'

Horsfall was found standing asleep after the time when he should have been relieved as sentry.

'The company commander making his rounds told me that owing to finding others in a similar position he had to make an example of me.'

While awaiting trial, Horsfall was deprived of the privilege of receiving or sending letters and thus could not have revealed his plight to his family even if he had wished to—which he didn't. Paraded before the battalion a few days after his court martial he heard for the first time his sentence—two years' imprisonment, suspended.

Whether it was due to his 'crime' or not, Horsfall found him-

[5] Evidence before the 'Shell Shock' Inquiry, 1922.
[6] *Statistics of the Military Effort of the British Empire.*
[7] *Episodes and Reflections.*

self given many exceedingly unpleasant duties during the year that followed. On the Somme he was ordered to take a message across no-man's-land to battalion headquarters after his company looked like being cut off. Somehow he made it. The following day when he paraded with his company which had been relieved 'the captain cast his eyes along the thin line until they met mine. Then he approached me with outstretched hand and said "I won't let this pass unnoticed". I did not take this seriously at the time, but not long afterwards, when we had been made up to strength, the adjutant rode into the centre of the company on his horse and read a paper saying that Sir Douglas Haig had remitted my two year sentence for outstanding conduct on such and such a date.'[8]

At Cambrai, Captain Ernest Thurtle, whose subsequent efforts to abolish the death penalty for cowardice have already been mentioned, had struggled all night to place dummy tanks in position before the opening of the attack on 20 November. There had been trouble with overhead cables and barbed wire, and almost everything that could go wrong did go wrong. When finally the job was completed he led his men back to the spot where four men under a corporal had been placed to cover them against possible attack by an enemy patrol. Every man, including the corporal, lay asleep. It was as grave an example of dereliction of duty that might be found, but Thurtle, aware of the peril in which the men might find themselves, did nothing. Like most soldiers serving in France he was not sure just how frequently the death sentence was actually applied, or in what circumstances, and did not wish to find out at the expense of the lives of his own men.[9]

Sometimes, it was impossible to stay awake. During the March Retreat, men of the Royal Naval Division nodded off in the firing line during lulls in the fighting. Tough Regular Royal Marine sergeants stayed on their feet and roused the slumbering riflemen when the next German attack began. Towards the end of the Fifth Army's retirement a number of men were taken prisoner lying fast asleep over weapons pointed in the direction of the enemy. Supporting troops coming up behind the front could not appreciate the ordeal the embattled divisions had suffered and officers like Lieutenant-Colonel Hutchison were apt to be critical of their morale. In fact, for

[8] Personal recollections of Sam Horsfall Esq.
[9] Thurtle, *Time's Winged Chariot* and statements recorded in *Hansard*.

the first time in the war, the British were inflicting more casualties on the enemy than they were suffering.

Both on the Somme and in Flanders the hammer blows aimed at destroying the British Army fell almost entirely on men from the United Kingdom. It was they who had to endure the initial bombardments so carefully designed to smash the defences. It was they who had to conduct the fighting withdrawal. As they fell back, one of the most welcome sights that met their eyes were deploying Australian divisions, still maintained at their old strength of four brigades. The Aussies enjoyed a high reputation as fighting men—Ludendorff, the dominant figure on the German General Staff, classified them as among the elite formations opposing him. Sir Douglas Haig took a more ambivalent view. There is no doubt that he would have liked the Aussies better if he could have had some of them shot. But the Australians would have none of it.

13

Australian Exception

The difference in the attitude to discipline of the British and Australian soldiers is perhaps best illustrated by an incident which took place at Cassel, in Flanders, where Haig opened his advance headquarters before the Third Battle of Ypres. A British Military Police sergeant was standing surveying the passing throng of soldiers with an eagle eye when he was approached by a rangy Australian.

'I say, mate,' said the Australian confidentially, 'what've they done with all the Sheilas in this place? Where's the nearest knocking shop?'

And when the sergeant just stood there speechless the Aussie added by way of explanation, 'You know. The red light street . . . the nearest brothel?'

When the Redcap had recovered he put the Australian under arrest immediately as being drunk, explaining later that he thought he must have been to come to an M.P. with such a question. The soldier had no desire to be arrested, however, and to make matters even more difficult, his comrades regarded the sergeant's action as an unwarranted reflection upon their social life. A massive brawl ensued in which every Australian soldier within coo-ee range joined. It took a persuasive, good-humoured and formidable Australian Assistant Provost-Marshal to break it up and get his compatriots to disperse. Henceforth Cassel was placed out of bounds to them.[1]

In truth the Australians were not amenable to formal discipline. They did not salute as frequently as the soldiers of other armies and they did not give their respect freely. It had to be won. But it is hard to see why anyone should have expected them to be any different. Australia, as far as population was concerned, was a small country, full of little com-

[1] See Bean, *Australian Official History*.

149

munities where nearly everyone knew everyone else. This parochial outlook was natural to the battalions of volunteers raised in the various States. Furthermore, Australia was historically 'agin' official authority, and her geography encouraged the cult of the self-reliant individual. It was still a pioneering country and had not then been conditioned to the petty tyrannies of urbanization.

Whatever they may have lacked in smartness, the Australians made up for with their enthusiasm. Their dash at Gallipoli, alongside the New Zealanders, had won them the admiration of the British soldiers fighting in the same area. But as with all other soldiers, they were only human. Under the Australian Defence Act the position of soldiers who deserted or refused to take part in a battle was clear.

'No member of the Defence Force shall be sentenced to death by any court martial except for mutiny, desertion to the enemy or traitorously delivering up to the enemy any garrison, fortress, post guard or ship, vessel, or boat, or traitorous correspondence with the enemy; and no sentence of death passed by any court martial shall be carried into effect until confirmed by the Governor-General.'

This plainly ruled out capital punishment for men who avoided service in the front-line trenches. Therefore, in cases where they felt it was necessary to make an example of a man, he was sent home in disgrace. And, for a time, this threat to the pride of the troops was thought to be deterrent enough. When the Australians moved to France and the arena of the great artillery battles, other factors were brought to play.

On 15 July, 1916, as a diversionary effort to draw German reserves from the Somme, the 5th Australian Division was committed to a barren and costly assault at Fromelles, suffering 5,000 casualties. A few days later the 1st Australian Division attacked at Pozières, up the road from Albert to Bapaume. The village was a vital observation point and the Germans were not disposed to give up lightly. Its houses and windmill became the target of an ever-growing concentration of guns, which effectively flattened them. As the 2nd Australian Division took over from the 1st, the barrage thundered on unabated.

'Casualties in consequence were very severe,' wrote General Sir Hubert Gough, who was responsible for the attack, 'and so was the work entailed. Communications and trenches, dumps of ammunition and stores which had been collected were many times blown to pieces; consolidation, moving down the wounded, bringing up fresh stores, ammunition and reinforcements, and a hundred and one other necessary tasks were only carried on in circumstances of great danger and arduous effort.'[2]

The *Australian Official History* described the effect of this torrent of high explosives more graphically:

'The shelling at Pozières did not merely probe character and nerve; it laid them stark naked as no other experience in the A.I.F. ever did. In a single tour of this battle, divisions were subjected to greater stress than in the whole Gallipoli campaign. The shell fire was infinitely worse than that experienced in the Third Battle of Ypres.'

Just as thousands of British troops became 'shell shock' casualties under this strain, Australian soldiers broke down too. No longer was it sufficient to threaten to send home men who failed. Even prison sentences were looked upon as a merciful release from the appalling conditions. As the winter set in, the morale of the Australians, unaccustomed to the mud and the rain, suffered still more. In December, 1916, Sir Douglas Haig had written to the War Office expressing his alarm at the number of Australians deserting while en route from England to the front line. He urged that the Dominion government should amend the law and allow the death penalty to be inflicted as a matter 'of grave urgency'. In this he was supported by the Army Council in London who had sent a telegram to the authorities in Australia expressing their view that the subject was one 'of the utmost gravity for the discipline of the whole army'. The move to introduce capital punishment had begun in the spring of 1916 when Sir William Birdwood, who had commanded the Australian and New Zealand Army Corps at Gallipoli and then brought them to France, recommended that a sergeant in the 1st Pioneer Battalion should be executed.[3]

Fully cognisant of the fact that this was not permissible in law, Birdwood asked that the whole subject should be taken up. With the connivance of Haig, the British put to the Commonwealth government the proposition that Australian troops should be made subject to the Army Act. There was no response. In the light of the campaign being fought to introduce conscription it was hardly a propitious moment to make the suggestion.

[2] Gough, *The Fifth Army.*
[3] Bean, *Australian Official History.*

In December, when the number of Australians convicted of absenteeism reached 130 out of the Fourth Army total of 182, General Rawlinson wrote to Haig saying that he could not be held responsible for the discipline of the Australian forces under his command unless the death penalty was introduced immediately. The execution of three deserters was recommended by the brigadiers and divisional generals involved. But despite all representations the Dominion government refused to alter the law.

Bad staff work and a misplaced faith in the capabilities of tanks cost four Australian divisions 10,000 casualties at Bullecourt, a fortified village included in the outer defences of the Hindenburg line. As a result, when the IInd Anzac Corps was sent north to take part in the Messines attack, desertion and absenteeism increased, noticeably in the 4th Division. Knowing full well that any death sentence passed upon them (courts martial still went through the formalities) would be suspended automatically, some men openly refused to go into the trenches when an attack was pending. Major-General Holmes and Brigadier Glasgow both requested that the law be altered to allow the death penalty, but without success.[4]

Haig even promised that if the Australian government sanctioned the death penalty he would use it 'very sparingly'. But by this time Sir William Birdwood had come round to the politicians' view that such a move would prejudice efforts to introduce conscription.

By the time the Third Battle of Ypres had opened, General Monash of the 3rd Division had joined in the campaign for capital punishment. While temporarily acting as commander of the IInd Anzac Corps he had confirmed four death sentences in the 4th Division and commuted them to ten years' gaol. In a letter to his wife he wrote:

'I had a long talk with the Army commander [Sir Herbert Plumer] about it, and I am writing to . . . urge strongly that in some clear case of cowardly desertion the law should take its course.'[5]

After achieving a notable success at Broodseinde at the beginning of October the Australians remained in the line as the weather broke. Then with the coming of the rains the incidence of desertion increased again. Men began to disappear

[4] Bean, *Australian Official History.*
[5] Cutlack, *War Letters of General Monash.*

when battalions were sent up to take their place in what passed for trenches. They reported again when the unit came out of the line and told whatever story they thought would serve them best. Out of fairness to the great majority of men who stuck to their posts, the Australian commanders saw to it that many dodgers actually did serve punishment sentences at field prisons, instead of receiving suspended sentences. This had the effect of drawing Haig's attention to the fact that nine Australians in every 1,000 were in gaol, compared with only one per 1,000 in the British Army and two in the Canadian Forces.[6]

The Commander-in-Chief was genuinely dismayed and talked of the lack of discipline in the Australian forces having serious consequences. In private he blamed Birdwood, who, he stated, had taken the easy way out in order to maintain his own popularity. According to Haig the Australians were neither as clean nor as smart as the Canadians, were so unruly and full of revolutionary ideas that their wounded had to be sent to separate camps to convalesce. This state of affairs he laid squarely on the refusal of the Australian government to allow capital punishment.

The attack on Birdwood was most unfair, and not a little influenced by the fact that Birdwood had originally been a nominee of Kitchener and had remained a firm favourite of the Dominion authorities ever since. In his way, Birdwood, although a British Regular and a cavalryman (12th Lancers) was adapting to the Australian mode of discipline rather than forcing them to bend to an alien code. He went so far as to have the names of men sentenced to death and then to gaol for disciplinary offences published in their home towns and made it clear that when the war ended there would be no amnesty for men serving gaol sentences. Otherwise he applied himself to looking after the interests of his men. He saw to it that a limited number of men were sent home on leave (up to then the Australians took their leave in England) under the guise of guarding troopships against submarine attack.

With Birdwood's approval, his Chief of Staff, Brudenell White, entered into a correspondence with G.H.Q. in which he pointed out: 'These fellows are not used to a tough winter, and a winter in conditions such as we had on the Somme last year would hit us very hard, and might raise casualties to a degree beyond our power of replacement.' The sequel to this was the

[6] See Blake (Ed.), *The Private Papers of Douglas Haig*.

153

withdrawal from the line of Australian divisions for varying periods for training, the absorption of reinforcements and rest.

Inevitably, General Childs had his own view of the Australians. In his considered opinion they were fine fighting troops 'but they had with them a percentage of the dregs who were a nuisance and a danger not only to the armies in France, but to the civil population.' A number of men, he stated, not only deserted but made themselves a 'menace and terror' to the countryside. Knowing they could not be shot they even robbed British transport at pistol point on its way up the line. The description applied to these brigands, who did not stop short of rape and murder, fitted exactly the British soldiers who, just over a century earlier, had earned a similar reputation by terrifying the district around Belem Hospital for convalescent soldiers near Lisbon. In their case they were known as the Belem Rangers. Boulogne Bushrangers might have been a suitable title for the Australians.

By contrast, as Haig noted, the conduct of the Canadian, New Zealand and South African contingents was excellent. As the death penalty could be applied in all three forces he drew the obvious conclusions.

Like the Australians, the Canadians benefited from having a Parliament which watched their interests closely. But their discipline was akin to the British and strictly enforced. When out of the line they were drilled constantly as this was shown to be beneficial for morale. A special hospital with a permanent court martial in attendance was set up to deal with cases of self-inflicted wounds (729 Canadian other ranks and seven officers sought this way out during the war) and it was not unknown for a man who had sustained a genuine injury, say tearing his hand on the barbed wire, to conceal his wound until it had either healed or was so bad he had to report it.[7]

Formed into a corps of two divisions in September, 1915, the Canadian forces in France had expanded to four divisions by the beginning of 1917. On the Somme, at Vimy and at Passchendaele they played an important part. Mainly thanks to their commander, Sir Arthur Currie, one of the few men not afraid to argue with Haig,[8] they had not been split up and used to patch the front in 1918. Instead they remained intact until the Allies

[7] MacPhail, *Official History of the Canadian Forces.*
[8] Currie implied after the war that Haig had once accused him of 'insubordination' because of his attitude.

turned to the offensive in August of that year. Throughout the war the Canadians were fortunate in being protected by their leaders to a degree not vouchsafed most of the other British formations. All the same, twenty-five of their number were shot by sentence of court martial.[9] It might be argued, at a stretch, that fear of the death penalty helped to make them a powerful striking force. But on 8 August, called by Lundendorff 'The Black Day' of the German Army, five Australian divisions, which had never been subjected to the death penalty, attacked alongside them and achieved equal success.

[9] The Secretary of State for War (Sir Laming Worthington-Evans) stated in answer to a question on 31 March, 1925, that twenty-five Canadian and five New Zealand soldiers were shot during the war for disciplinary offences.

14

America's Answer

On 15 July, 1918, the Army Headquarters in Washington received an acid cable from General John Pershing, commanding the United States Expeditionary Force in France.

'Prevalence of mental disorders in replacement troops recently received suggests urgent importance of intensive efforts in eliminating mentally unfit from organizations new draft prior to departure from United States. Psychiatric forces and accommodations here inadequate to handle greater proportion of cases than heretofore arriving, and if less time is taken to organize and train new divisions, elimination should be speeded.'

As the Americans required a mental age of only eight from recruits in the early days of the war, Pershing's complaint is not surprising.[1]

Despite this initial handicap, and even allowing for the experience of the other Allies, the Americans responded very efficiently to the special requirements of a war in which the heavy artillery was the dominating factor. The relationship of psycho-neurosis cases to the intensity of the fighting was watched carefully. In the 26th Infantry Division, eighteen were reported during a long spell on the, for once, quiet Chemin des Dames early in 1918. Moved to the Toul sector, where the enemy broke into their trenches, the same division reported fifty-two psycho-neurosis cases in three days in April. A sharp attack supported by heavy artillery fire produced forty-three cases in a single night. Later at Château Thierry, 191 men were evacuated with nervous disorders in five days of fighting to clear the woods.

American doctors also noted what had been commented on in

[1] See Miller, *The Neuroses in War* and *The Medical Department of the U.S. Army in the World War*, Vol. 10.

British hospitals where patients with a variety of complaints were housed. During air raids, the psycho-neurosis cases would frequently hide, perhaps under a table, at the sound of a bomb being dropped. Some might even 'take cover' when a door slammed or during a thunderstorm. In contrast, men with severe shrapnel or gunshot wounds would behave with complete indifference and even joke about their situation.

United States observers also said that in Canada returned soldiers who had suffered head wounds, perhaps with the loss of a portion of the skull, almost never showed symptoms of 'trench neuroses' which was something that usually afflicted unwounded men.

It was concluded that a wound solved the mental problem for many men who had been seeking a compromise between doing their duty and the basic instinct of self-preservation. Others, who were sufficiently adaptable, managed to adjust themselves to the circumstances.

'The neurosis provided a means of escape so convenient,' states the official American medical historian, 'that the real cause for wonder is not that it should play such an important part in military life but that so many men should find satisfactory adjustment without intervention.'

Leaving nothing to chance, the Americans set up a system which gave every division their own psychiatrist and staff by the time the war ended. Not all the senior medical officers agreed with this. One divisional surgeon, outranking the psychiatrist, put his staff on the task of dressing the lightly wounded during a fierce battle. As a result 'several hundred cases of slight war neuroses were evacuated who would never have left their division if they had been examined by a trained psychiatrist'.

With the American forces, as with the other armies in the field, the problem of maintaining discipline inevitably had to be faced. Unlike the British they could draw on extensive experience in their own country, for conditions during certain periods of the Civil War closely resembled those which arose in France. The numbers and the organization of the units involved was not dissimilar. Even the War of Independence had features from which lessons might be learned.

George Washington had shown a great deal of sympathy and understanding where deserters were concerned.

'Men just dragged from the tender scenes of domestic life

and unaccustomed to the din of arms, totally unacquainted with every kind of military skill, are timid and ready to fly from their own shadows' he said after the panic flight from the Brooklyn Heights. 'Besides, the sudden change in their manner of living brings on an unconquerable desire to return to their homes.'

Notwithstanding these sentiments, Washington had not hesitated to introduce the cat o'nine tails to instil discipline into his army, handing out 'thirty or forty lashes according to the crime'. Nor did he hesitate to hang publicly anyone he considered to be a traitor.

During the Civil War the 'unconquerable desire' of men to return to their homes was observed on a massive scale. At first the crime of desertion was looked upon lightly. In the north, Lincoln, notoriously kindhearted, resisted requests that he should indulge his right as Commander-in-Chief to exercise the death penalty.

Besides, there seemed to be no shortage of volunteers. States vied with each other to raise regiments of patriotic volunteers in colourful uniforms. This fervour sustained the Union Army after the disillusion of the First Battle of Bull Run but as the marching and manoeuvring and the bloody clashes before Richmond failed to provide victory and the troops settled down to the monotony and discomfort of a long war, men began to drift away. After regiments had been slaughtered in hopeless frontal attacks at Fredericksburg in the winter of 1862 and the Army of the Potomac had undergone a soul-destroying and futile march through chill, knee-deep mud the following month morale plummeted. The appointment of a new commander, Hooker, briefly revived past enthusiasm and hope. But, like Nivelle fifty-four years later, the General became a victim of his own propaganda and after his army had been mangled at Chancellorsville in May, 1863, many men felt they'd had enough. Of the 17,000 Union casualties, 6,000 were reported as 'missing'.[2] Allowing for undiscovered corpses and prisoners, a considerable number of these were undoubtedly deserters. Significantly they came in similar proportions from a corps which had been surprised and routed, from a crack corps which had fought well and from one which had not been engaged. The runaways went to swell the ranks of more than 80,000 troops whose absence from the Army of the Potomac

[2] Catton, *History of the American Civil War* and *Glory Road*.

could not be accounted for. Just before Chancellorsville, in exactly the way in which the French President was persuaded in 1917 to forgo his right to review all death sentences, Lincoln accepted the arguments of his generals that examples must be made.

After offering an amnesty which gave deserters a last chance to rejoin their regiments, the first ritual shooting began. Bands played the condemned men to the execution grounds in the slow time of a funeral march. Firing squads followed the band; next came the coffins, each carried by four men, and behind each coffin came a deserter under escort. In the case of one parade in the Vth Corps, five coffins followed by five men were paraded in single file to five open graves. With their eyes covered with black blindfolds, they heard a few words of prayer from chaplains, then sat on the edge of the coffins as the order to fire was shouted to the waiting squads. There were twelve men in each firing party. One of their weapons contained a blank charge. As the echoes of the fatal volleys died away, the bands struck up merrily and the watching troops were marched off.[3]

Desertions continued, despite such ceremonies, and by the end of the war the Provost Marshal General estimated that the total number in the Union armies during the war totalled 201,000. Of these only 76,000 were caught.[4]

Desertion among soldiers of the Confederate States became a grave problem early in the war, mainly because a shortage of equipment, and shoes in particular, positively encouraged straggling, which is only one step removed from defection for good. The streets of Richmond were full of stray soldiers after the battles in the Peninsula and before the Second Battle of Bull Run a handful of men were executed as a warning to others of what they might expect.[5] All the same, as the Army of Northern Virginia invaded Maryland in the late summer of 1862, 'Stonewall' Jackson had to issue an order that men who left the ranks without orders were to be shot forthwith. A Provost Marshal was appointed by the Commanding General, Robert E. Lee, but achieved little. The civil authorities counselled leniency.

During the winter, six men of the Stonewall Brigade, which

[3] Catton, op. cit.
[4] Boatner, *The Civil War Dictionary*.
[5] Freeman, *Lee's Lieutenants*.

Jackson had commanded at the First Battle of Bull Run, were court martialled for desertion. One man was given six months' hard labour, two were to be flogged and three to die. Lee endorsed the death penalties, but Jefferson Davis, the Confederacy's President, commuted the sentences to flogging, after a plea from Paxton, the commander of the Stonewall Brigade. In October, 1862, the Confederate Congress passed an Act authorizing courts martial consisting of three officers similar to those of the British Army in the 1914–18 war.

The first signs of a major drop in morale occurred soon after Gettysburg (1–3 July, 1863). As the Confederates retreated 5,000 unwounded men deserted. Lee was shaken to learn that twenty-two of the runaways belonged to the renowned 22nd North Carolina Infantry. Towards the end of July he issued an appeal for absentees to return to their regiments. In it he stated:

'To remain at home in this, the hour of your country's need, is unworthy the manhood of a Southern soldier . . . let it not be said that you deserted your comrades in a contest in which everything you hold dear is at stake. . .'

Jefferson Davis followed this by offering a general amnesty and releasing all men on trial or imprisoned, with the exception of those who had been convicted twice for desertion. He also introduced a system for giving more leave (shades of Pétain in 1917).

The response to these measures was disappointing. Lee thereupon tightened his grip on cross-roads, bridges and fords where stragglers could be seized. More than 1,000 were caught in two weeks, but not all surrendered willingly. One party fought back and some of the Provost Marshal's men were killed. Ten of the ringleaders of this band were sentenced to death by court martial and this time Davis did not spare them. They were tied to stakes and shot in a hollow square formed by men of their own division who marched past the bloody corpses.[6]

What had been a drain on the army through desertion in the early years of the war became a stream with the development of trench warfare and siege conditions in the summer of 1864. The fact that in battles such as Cold Harbor the Confederates repelled Union attacks with heavy losses did nothing to maintain morale. As the frosts of winter settled on the mud and

[6] Freeman, *Lee's Lieutenants.*

sandbag ramparts guarding Richmond, the shivering grey regiments dwindled visibly.

Conscripts could no longer be trusted to wait without officers in the streets of the capital, lest they abscond. General James Longstreet, veteran Commander of the 1st Corps offered commissions (in the Negro regiments then being formed) to soldiers who apprehended or obstructed deserters, but the few men who took advantage of this inducement had little effect on the general situation.

The politicians counselled leniency and offered amnesties, the generals demanded executions, and the stream of Southern soldiers who crossed to the Union lines continued unchecked. The total number of deserters will never be known but two months before the end of the war in April, 1865, it was believed that there were about 100,000.[7] Many thousands more vanished from the army in the remaining weeks before Lee's surrender. As in the retreat to Corunna and the siege of Burgos nearly sixty years before, as in Flanders sixty years later, mud and misery had conquered where the fear of death had failed.

With the comprehensive example of the Civil War courts martial procedure to guide them – and Civil War generals were still on the active list as late as 1898 – the United States Army had a wealth of experience on which to draw, plus that of her Allies. Considering that the American army in France expanded from 200,000 men to more than two million during the last year of the war, the administration of law and the maintenance of discipline was highly efficient. Certain snags arose, however, notably the regulation which required serious offences to be tried by a general court martial, a cumbersome process compared with, say, the British field general court martial. In the war of movement that developed during the last four months of the war, these courts proved to be impractical and had the fighting continued there is little doubt that the Americans would have implemented a plan to set up permanent courts martial composed of convalescent combat officers. These courts would have been attached to each corps and possibly each division. In the event, only one such body was formed which 'was sent where most needed in the summer and fall of 1918'.[8]

[7] Boatner, *The Civil War Dictionary*.
[8] Final Report of the Judge Advocate, General Headquarters A.E.F., August, 1919.

In order to avoid wasting time, the American forces were instructed to deal with all minor offences at regimental level. In this respect the law favoured officers who had to be tried by general court martial for all offences, a requirement which could not be fulfilled under the circumstances prevailing. As a result many officers who might have been guilty of minor offences escaped punishment, whereas a soldier was dealt with by his commanding officer, or by a special court martial authorized to deal with lesser charges.

Taking the same line as their Allies, the United States Army adopted a policy of giving suspended sentences to prevent troops in combat formations escaping from the front line through their crimes.

Where self-inflicted wounds or malingering were suspected medical officers in fighting units were ordered to retain patients in the combat area until they had been examined by the divisional psychiatrist. If a man was accused of a crime for which he might be shot, the divisional psychiatrist was expected to obtain the additional opinion of a consultant. Considering the size of the force involved, death sentences were rare in the American Expeditionary Force, a total of forty-four being passed, of which eleven were carried out.[9]

Under the 48th Article of War, the commanding general of the army was empowered in the time of war to confirm and order the execution of soldiers convicted of murder, rape, mutiny, desertion or espionage. Sentences of death in other cases had to be approved by the President, who was also the only authority who could commute a death sentence, whatever the charge.

This situation was varied during the period the American Expeditionary Force was in France so that General Pershing could remit the extreme penalty but in July, 1919, all powers of life and death reverted to the President as in peacetime. Four men who were then under sentence of death had their punishment confirmed by the President. According to the Final Report of the Judge Advocate, at A.E.F. Headquarters in August, 1919, 'Murder and rape were the only offences for which the offender suffered death in the American Expeditionary Force.'

Apart from the first-hand evidence of their own active service units the Americans also had the benefit of the ex-

9 ibid.

perience of scores of doctors of the United States Army Medical Corps who served with British Infantry battalions, particularly in the final year of the war. In view of the statement that only murderers and men guilty of rape were executed in the American Army, it may be assumed that it was from information based on British (and to some extent French) practices that the U.S. Army Medical Department concluded:

' . . . before the clinical character and remarkable prevalence of war neurosis among soldiers had become familiar facts, not a few soldiers suffering from these disorders have been executed by firing squads as malingerers.'

The history makes a further comment of interest:

'Instances are also known where hysterics have committed suicide after having been falsely accused of malingering. Mistakes of this kind are especially liable to occur when the patients have not been actually exposed to shell fire on account of the idea so firmly fixed in the minds of most line officers and some medical men that the war neuroses are due to some mechanical shock.'

Notwithstanding the medical advances made during the war, the firing squads of the British Army continued to carry out their duties throughout hostilities and for a period afterwards.

*　*　*

In the last nine months of the war, when the ravaged British infantry was reinforced with thousands of teenagers, observers noted a relaxation of discipline in some battalions. Offences which might have led to gaol sentences, field punishment, or worse earlier in the war, were sometimes treated leniently. A boy in the 13th Royal Fusiliers who had been docked two days' pay for eating his iron rations, ran away and was found twenty miles behind the line. His offence was plainly desertion in the face of the enemy but 'the sentence was trifling' when he was court martialled. An officer in another regiment recalled that a sergeant who had been executed in 1915 would not have had to pay for his life in 1918, 'but the old Regular Army had a much fiercer way of looking on anything approaching cowardice.'[10]

If some units made allowances for boys who fell asleep, or who were unable to keep up on the march because their equipment was too heavy for their immature bodies, others

[10] Chapman, *A Passionate Prodigality.*

maintained strict discipline. Ninety-five executions were carried out in France and Belgium in the twelve months ending 30 September, 1918. Ten of these were for murder, but the majority were for desertion in the face of the enemy. Two were for cowardice. The figure of ninety-five was only one less than for the previous twelve-month period.[11]

A soldier in the 2nd South Wales Borderers 'B' Company recorded the fate of one of his comrades.

'He deserted two or three times, but he was not a coward, as a braver man never went on active service. He told me that the reason for his conduct in that way was that he was the sole support of a widowed mother, and that the Government only gave her an allowance of 5s. 6d. ($27\frac{1}{2}$p) a week. He said he would never soldier until they paid her more. The last time he deserted was in July, 1918. He was arrested at St Omer early in August, court martialled and sentenced to death, the sentence being confirmed by Sir Douglas Haig. The execution was carried out at dawn on 10 August, 1918, between the town of Hazebrouck and the village of Bore, by men from his own Company, and he was buried in Bore cemetery.'[12]

Private Fred Bestwick who joined a Lewis gun section of the 7th Durham Light Infantry in the early summer of 1918, was present on two occasions when his battalion paraded with other units of the 8th Division to see death sentences pronounced. One of the men was 18, the other 21. Both were shot at dawn.

'The whole idea of this disgusting spectacle was to frighten others from deserting, but that was not so easy.

'Young soldiers, new to the front line, standing in trenches, shells falling all around, friends being killed, trenches and bodies blown to pieces, with no sleep for nights on end . . . suddenly went mad. I've seen them.

'Their nerves gave way. Their discipline gone, their one thought was to get out of this hell. The first thing they did was to throw down their rifle and run – anywhere, not knowing where they were going but terrified.

'They kept running until exhausted. If an N.C.O. was near he would hit out either with his fist or the butt of his rifle and stop any panic among the remainder. Eventually, if a man got away, he would be caught by the Redcaps when asked to show

[11] *Statistics of the Military Efforts of the British Empire.*
[12] Letter to Ernest Thurtle, M.P.

his pass.

'The troops often debated deserting among themselves after death sentences had been announced. But the general opinion was, "How are you going to get any grub when you're on your own?" This, and the difficulty of getting transport away from the line, seemed an unsurmountable problem.'[13]

Unquestionably the youth of many of the British troops was a factor which had to be coped with. Yet experienced officers who saw them in France considered that the 'A-4' boys, as they were called after their medical and enlistment category, were among the best trained drafts sent to France. Some were almost too well trained, having had so many dire warnings about various kinds of gas that they were panicky at the first suspicion of an attack. By and large, however, the boy soldiers proved more than equal to their formidable tasks. Haig commented on the tremendous resistance put up by the 50th Northumbrian and 51st Highland divisions in Flanders in April, 1918, only a fortnight after their battalions, sadly reduced in the March offensive, had been filled up with A-4 boys. It is often forgotten that these striplings were well to the fore in the three months which saw some of the heaviest casualty lists of the war—August (122,272), September (114,831) and October (121,046).

Why it was thought necessary to carry on executing soldiers right through the war is not clear. Research into the literature of the period reveals nothing to indicate that G.H.Q. ever made a study to find out the actual effects of their policy. The conduct of British troops from 1914 onwards would appear to prove that all categories were able to adapt themselves to the hitherto undreamed of pressures of twentieth century warfare. The Regulars and Territorials at Ypres, the Kitchener battalions of the Somme and at Arras, the conscripts at Passchendaele and the boy soldiers of 1918 showed a degree of obedience that was unparalleled by any other army. And they remained so, despite the fact that from the spring of 1915 to the end of 1917 they were involved in a continuous series of attacks to break through the German defences. During these years, neither French nor Haig expressed doubts at any time that the troops would carry out their orders or considered that an offensive would have to be postponed because of poor morale. The Russian, Italian and French armies, each of whom applied the

13 Personal recollections of Fred Bestwick Esq.

death penalty liberally, all reached a stage where their commanders could not guarantee their obedience. Even the redoubtable German army gave cause for grave concern after the terrible fighting at Verdun in 1916 and at Ypres in 1917. Troops chalked 'Cattle for Wilhelm and Son—butchers' on the trucks taking them to the front. Ernst Junger, a lieutenant in the 73rd Hanoverian Fusilier Regiment, records that, while searching for his unit in a village just behind the Passchendaele sector, an N.C.O. just shrugged his shoulders and ignored him when he asked the way. He had to extract the information at revolver point. It was the first time he had come across such defiance.[14]

It was symptomatic of a development that had been causing General Ludendorff concern for some time. In September, 1917, he required that special attention should be paid to the morale of troops manning the lines of communication and 'patriotic instruction must be specially fostered among them'. What he called 'work of enlightenment among the troops' was begun.[15]

Unlike the British generals, German military leaders did not have absolute powers over their men.

'The administration of discipline by the English is very rigid,' Crown Prince Rupprecht, commanding the army group facing the British in Flanders, wrote in his diary on 21 September, 1917. 'Whilst on our side there is known to me only a single case in which a soldier on account of aggravated refusal of duty in the face of the enemy was shot, I gather from a compilation of British orders which have been found, that at least 67 English soldiers have been shot under martial law in the period between 27 October, 1916 and 30 August, 1917.'[16]

Ludendorff envied Haig this savage method of dealing with the problem of desertion which grew as the war dragged on.

'The loss by desertion was uncommonly high' he wrote in his *Memoirs*. 'The number that got into neutral countries—e.g. Holland—ran into tens of thousands, and a far greater number lived happily at home, tacitly tolerated by their fellow citizens.

'They and the skrimshankers at the front, of whom there were thousands, reduced the battle strength of the fighting troops,

[14] Junger, *Storm of Steel*.
[15] Ludendorff, *My War Memoirs*.
[16] Quoted in *Official History of Australia in the War*.

especially of the infantry, to which most of them belonged, to a vital degree.'

Ludendorff complained bitterly that instead of making the regulations more stringent, the German government eased them:

'During the first half of the war the Reichstag had made the penal laws more lenient. The commanders responsible for maintaining discipline were deprived of their most effective punishment, in that a sentence of "close arrest" no longer involved being tied to a fixed object. No doubt this punishment was extraordinarily severe, but to abolish it altogether was fatal.'

Frequent amnesties also had a bad influence, he declared, adding:

'The judges had come to regard military offences with a leniency which was often incomprehensible. A contributory cause of this was that the cases which had occurred at the front were not dealt with immediately by the unit, but further in the rear in quite different circumstances, and after a certain time had elapsed.'

In June, 1918, Ludendorff was calling for 'the most severe measures' against shirkers and deserters. Before the Allied offensive of 8 August he expressed concern about morale and a week after it he talked of the 'element of uncertainty which the insubordination of some of the troops had introduced into our calculations.'

Never, even in the darkest days of March and April, 1918, do we find Haig expressing such doubts. Unwilling to concede, as the Duke of Wellington had done, that British soldiers were quite capable of running away in the stress of battle, he had a blind faith in their willingness to fight. Otherwise he could hardly have used them as ruthlessly as he did, the United Kingdom troops in particular. After Passchendaele the Canadian Corps, under the watchful eye of Currie and the Dominion government, did not take part in any major battle until the following August. A complaint by the Australians resulted in their 1st, 2nd and 5th Divisions spending four months in quiet sectors after the second Battle of Bullecourt, and it has already been noted how the Australians' plea earned them special consideration during the winter of 1917–18. By contrast the United Kingdom divisions were used as military workhorses. If the Canadians and Australians were in the van of the attack of

8 August, it was mainly because the troops from the home country had born the brunt of the three great German offensives at Cambrai, on the Somme and in Flanders.

Assuming, therefore, that British troops were at least as reliable as their opponents, and probably showed greater stamina, one is entitled to ask if the threat of the death penalty for personal failure in action was an important factor in sustaining their high standard of discipline. For the answer to be in the affirmative it would have to be proved that the law was not only rigorously applied but that it was obviously and openly applied. This was not the case. Even in the case of the execution superintended by Crozier, it is noticeable that the battalion was drawn up on the other side of the wall so that the end of the unfortunate drink-sodden Crocker could not be seen. A former corporal in the Hood Battalion serving in the same brigade as Dyett states that 'the rumour of the execution flew round the division in no time'. But it was only after the war when he spoke to a Military Policeman who had been present, that he actually confirmed the incident. Some victims like the boy in the 11th Middlesex, probably shot in a disused colliery yard, and the 18th Manchester soldier executed in a quarry, were put to death almost in secret. Even where troops were paraded, the behaviour of the authorities was strangely contradictory as this eye-witness account reveals.

'I was a transport driver of the 10th Durham Light Infantry, 43rd Brigade, 14th Division. In the early part of 1916 we were on the Arras front. While the battalion was in the line the Brigade transport camp was at a village called Warlus. On the evening of 20 May, 1916, we were informed that reveille would be at 2 am the next morning and we were to parade in full equipment, with ammunition. At three o'clock the next morning we were marched to the outskirts of the village where we found the rest of the brigade transports. At 3.30 am we were called to attention and to our surprise a prisoner with escort was marched down in front of us. Then came the Assistant Provost Marshal with some papers in his hand.

'The prisoner's cap was taken off and he was told to take one pace forward. Then the A.P.M. commenced to read the papers which were to the effect that Private —— of the 7th King's Royal Rifle Corps, 41st Brigade, 14th Division, was found missing from his battalion on the night they went into the line. He was arrested and charged with desertion. The man pleaded that he was drunk and missed his way. He was tried by court martial, found guilty and sentenced to death, the death sentence being confirmed by Sir Douglas Haig.

'The man was then told to take a pace back again, which he did without a quiver—a braver man at that moment wasn't to be found in France. He was then marched away to the place where he was to be shot. We were then ordered to about turn and the Brigade Transport Officer threatened that any man who turned round would be put on a crime [charge]. So we stood in silence for what seemed hours, although only minutes. Then the shots rang out and one of the Yorkshire fainted, the strain was that great. Still we stood in silence until we heard another shot, which I afterwards heard was the doctor's shot to make sure he was dead.'[17]

It was as if the authorities deliberately fostered an air of mystery on such occasions. Certainly, despite pronouncements and promulgations, doubts remained in the minds of many soldiers as to the frequency of executions and the details of the last grim rites. George Coppard, writing in 1969 from his contemporary diaries,[18] was under the impression that in 1917 the policy was changed and instead of being shot men were sent out on dangerous patrols or raids. The number of men shot at dawn, in fact, reached a peak during this period, and he may have been misled by the number of men given suspended sentences. A lieutenant who spent four years with a Regular battalion in the 6th Division states:

'There was only one occasion that suggested a party of men had had to carry out such an appalling sentence, but even then it was only a whisper.'

And a retired public school teacher, who served in the 34th Division, could recall only one rumour of a death sentence being carried out, that of a case in August, 1918.[19] Although, therefore, plenty of announcements were read out, the broadcasting of such information on parades and in orders does not appear always to have achieved its object. As the carrying out of death sentences in public was an unusual event, the essential exemplary aspect of the punishment seems to have been abandoned.[20]

[17] Letter to Ernest Thurtle, M.P.   [18] *With a Machine Gun to Cambrai.*
[19] In a letter to the author.
[20] In fairness, in the 1920 debate on the Army Act an M.P. stated that he had been told by a general that he had paraded his whole division to see one sentence carried out.

On soldiers who were closely involved, the effect of executions seems to have been just the opposite of what was intended.

A Royal Engineer 'on rest' was sitting in a cafe enjoying a beer alone when a military policeman walked in. Like most ordinary soldiers he did not have a high regard for Redcaps and when the newcomer asked him to have a drink he refused. White-faced, the M.P. said, 'For Christ's sake have a beer with me.' He was in such distress that the sapper agreed. Sitting at the table the policeman put his hands in his pockets and pulled out a packet containing a few cigarettes, a box of matches and a handful of coins. Then with tears streaming down his face he explained, 'He gave me these.' The M.P. had been on duty all night guarding a young soldier awaiting execution for running away from the trenches under shell fire. Just before he was taken to his death, the boy had given his escort his last possessions saying calmly, 'I shan't need these. You'd better have them.'[21]

A sergeant in the 1st West Yorkshire Regiment, in the 18th Brigade of the 6th Division, was in charge of the guard on a lance-corporal awaiting execution for desertion.

'On the evening of the 10th I handed him over to the new guard and proceeded with my platoon to the trenches. Next day I was ordered to pick the two worst characters in my platoon to form part of the execution party. Lance-Corporal ——— was a clean, smart, brave soldier, respected by all his comrades.

'The two men I selected for the firing party went with the adjutant. When they came back, tough characters though they were supposed to be, they were sick, they screamed in their sleep, they vomited immediately after eating. All they could say was, "the sight was horrible".'

'Lance-Corporal ——— had been very lucky in gambling with his comrades and had won a fair amount of money while the battalion was back at rest. This had been his downfall, as he had gone on a drinking bout only a few hundred yards from his battalion. This execution took place at the Asylum, Armentières.'

The same West Yorkshire sergeant had another experience only a week later.

'A private in my regiment was charged with desertion. He had been absent about 18 days. He was tried and convicted at Houplines, near Armentières.

[21] From a letter to the author.

'I was sergeant in charge of the Guard. I had thirty-two prisoners, mostly twenty-eight-day men. Amongst these men were all those who had formed the firing party for Lance-Corporal ——. At 8 pm I received an envelope marked, "Open this when you are alone". The instructions contained in this were: "You must warn a party of twelve men from the prisoners you have (those who shot Lance-Corporal —— must not be included)." At 4 am next morning I entered the guard room with an escort. I gave strict instructions that no man was to move until his name was called out, and he must then get up and go outside. Of course, they knew that Private —— was to be shot that morning.

'It was then I witnessed a scene I shall never forget. Men I had known for years as clean, self-respecting soldiers, whose only offence was an occasional military "drunk", screamed out, begging not to be made into murderers. They offered me all they had if I would not take them for the job, and finally, when twelve of them found themselves outside, selected for the dreaded firing party, they called me all the names they could lay their tongues on. I remained with the guard for three days and I leave you to guess what I had to put up with. I would not go through three more such nights for £1,000. This execution also took place at the Asylum, Armentières.'

Another sergeant who had been in charge of a firing party of the 13th Middlesex Regiment knew the prisoner well, which made it all the worse for him. He recorded the boy's last words, 'What will my mother say?'[22]

Parliamentary interest in the death penalty subsided during the last nine months of the war. The tremendous battle of the period absorbed everyone's attention. And, besides, the War Cabinet's decision to classify executed soldiers as 'died on active service' could be relied on to avoid many awkward questions from the parents of the thousands of teenagers now in the fighting line. The truth was to be jealously guarded for some time to come.

[22] Letter to Ernest Thurtle, M.P.

PART III

1918-39

'It is clear to us that during 1916 and 1917 the
nervous system of the recruit did not receive
adequate consideration.'

REPORT OF THE 'SHELL SHOCK' ENQUIRY

15

Probe by a Judge

In 1919 a committee was set up under the chairmanship of Mr Justice Darling to enquire into the 'laws and rules of procedure regulating courts martial'. Mr Horatio Bottomley, who had published the details of the Dyett case in *John Bull*, was among the members (having become an M.P.) and so was Major-General Sir Wyndham Childs, the Deputy Adjutant General. For twenty-two days the committee studied statements and took evidence from a variety of witnesses including Field-Marshals French and Haig, but when they had finished their deliberations the wall of secrecy remained unbroken. It was recommended that the transcript of evidence should not be made public.

Though the tone of the report[1] of the committee was moderate and tended to support the conduct of courts martial during the war, some disturbing facts were disclosed.

'Evidence had been given before us to the effect that in some instances superior authorities have actively discouraged officers from appearing on behalf of accused persons,' stated paragraph 54. It revived memories of the allegation made in 1917 that of more than twenty soldiers shot by sentence of court martial in 'part of the month of October' only one had been defended.

Deprecating this practice, the committee declared that any officer should feel himself free to defend a man of his unit if asked to do so, although it was regarded as undesirable that officers should try to make a reputation for themselves as 'prisoner's friend'.

In April, 1918, the Under-Secretary of State for War, Mr Macpherson, had personally moved an amendment to the

---

[1] *The Report of the Committee constituted by the Army Council to inquire into the Law and Rules of Procedure regulating Military Courts Martial* was published at a price of 2d.

Army Act which varied the court martial oath so that, although secrecy had to be observed, an exception could be made 'so far as it may be permitted by instructions from the Army Council for the purpose of communicating the sentence to the accused.'

Obviously the Army Council did not feel like going as far as giving permission, because the Darling committee stated clearly:

'Under the existing system, unless the accused is acquitted of all charges against him, he does not know until promulgation whether he has been convicted of all such charges . . . nor does he know until promulgation what his sentence is. In our opinion it is unfair and unnecessary to prolong his suspense.'

In other words the ghastly procedure of announcing death sentences to soldiers eight or nine hours before they were due to be executed had been carried on throughout the war. As will be seen, it was continued even after the signing of the Armistice.

The committee recommended that the sentence of a court should be given in writing at once to the prisoner. In addition they did not consider it necessary for sentences to be read out on parade except in special circumstances where it was felt to be necessary.

An explanation of the absence of contemporary newspaper reports of courts martial was also given. There appeared to be an impression in 'certain quarters', stated the committee, that a court martial was a secret tribunal. This was a complete mistake. Even on active service a court martial was open to the public, although the court could sit in camera if any danger to witnesses was likely to arise from their being identified. (This stipulation which applied to civil courts may well have been mentioned because of the situation existing in Ireland in 1919.)

A glimpse of the part played by certain commanders was also permitted. The Committee recommended that views on sentences should be restricted to general notices in orders and in no case should an officer in a position of 'superior authority' comment upon an acquittal, except in formal and innocuous terms laid down in King's Regulations. The committee was satisfied that during the war some senior officers had gone so far as to issue circulars on the subject of sentences which were couched 'in terms which cannot be justified'. It was suggested that the Army Council should 'deal severely with any attempted interference with the judicial discretion of the Courts'.

The need to encourage officers to specialize in military law, the re-writing of the Army Act in plain language and the adoption of the French practice of restricting the membership of courts martial to officers over 25 years of age, were among other recommendations made by the committee.

There was another important suggestion. The committee stated: 'It appears that under Section 124 of the Army Act the person convicted is the only person entitled to obtain a copy of the proceedings of a court martial.'

This had been clearly stated during the war when Dyett's father had tried to obtain details of the evidence against his son. Macpherson, then the Under-Secretary of State for War, had set his face against this on the technical ground that as the prisoner was dead no power on earth could force the Adjutant-General to hand over the papers. The Darling Committee thought otherwise.

'Where such a person is dead, we think that the right (of access) might well be extended to his legal representatives or (if there be none) to his next of kin.'

Having in mind possible cases of espionage or trials involving civil disorders of the kind then current in Ireland, the committee added the proviso that this should not apply when a trial had been heard in camera.

The state of the ignorance of soldiers as to their rights was also revealed. All men had the right to present a petition 'upon receipt of which the proceedings are again considered'. It was 'possible that all soldiers are not aware that any petition against the legality of conviction or the severity of sentence will be considered. We think a definite statement to this effect should be included in King's Regulations and in the case of death sentences . . . added to Army Form 3996.'

The last paragraph was a virtual confession that scores of men had been executed without being given the chance to make a last desperate effort to save themselves.

As if to soften this grave admission the committee revealed that eighty-nine per cent of the death sentences passed had been commuted to a lesser penalty. They doubted very much 'whether any court, necessarily not possessing the information which he (the Commander-in-Chief) possessed as to the discipline and morale of the Army would have ventured to exercise clemency to any such extent.'

In their conclusion, the committee made it quite clear that the application of military law during the First World War was based on attitudes formed more than a hundred years earlier. They declared that the principles on which punishments for offences were inflicted remained the same as when the Duke of Wellington wrote in respect of a death sentence he confirmed despite a commendation to mercy:

'I consider all punishments to be for the sake of example, and the punishment of military men in particular is expedient only in cases where the prevalence of any crime, or the evils resulting from it, are likely to be injurious to the public interests. I beg the court to consider their recommendation in this light, and to apply it to the existing circumstances and situation of the Army, and to what is notorious in regard to this crime.

'I beg to inform the Court Martial that a very common and most alarming crime is that of striking and otherwise resisting, sometimes even by firing at, N.C.O.s and even officers, in the execution of their duty. It will not be disputed that there is no crime so fatal to the very existence of an Army, and no crime which officers, sworn as members of a General Court Martial, should feel so anxious to punish, as that of which this soldier has been guilty.

'It is very unpleasant to me to be obliged to resist the inclination of the General Court Martial to save the life of this soldier, but I would wish the court to observe that if the impunity with which this offence, clearly proved, shall have been committed, should, as is possible, occasion resistance to authority in other instances, the supposed mercy will turn out to be extreme cruelty and will occasion the loss of some valuable men to the service.'

With this in mind, the committee declared that in their opinion 'a Commander-in-Chief who is entrusted with the safety of his Army must not be fettered in his decision as to a point which so affects the discipline of that army.'

The doctrine of the 'iron hand', formulated to control an army containing a high proportion of illiterates addicted to looting, plunder and rape, in the moment of victory as at Vittoria or in the hour of despair as at Burgos, had triumphed. It had been applied in all its severity to an army whose behaviour in a foreign country was irreproachable, whose rank and file were the best educated soldiers ever to leave Britain's shores and whose courage had been proved for all to see. There had been coercion and malpractices. There had been injustice.

178

But the full extent of this was concealed in the suppression of the transcript of evidence given at the Enquiry from the penetrating gaze of disinterested parties.

One person who was particularly concerned with the administration of military justice at the time was 200909 Lance-Corporal Percy John Smith of the 10th Royal West Surrey Regiment. Lance-Corporal Smith had enjoyed an interesting career since he contrived to join the army in September, 1914, at the age of sixteen. Because of his youth he had been retained in England until early in 1918 when he paraded with the band to play him off as a one-man draft for the battalion in France.

Having survived the hard fighting of the last year of the war, when he was twice buried by shells, Lance-Corporal Smith marched into Germany with the Forces ready to fight if the Germans declined the Armistice terms. The period was an exacting one. Divisions had to be prepared for all eventualities. As late as April, 1919, British officers were instructed to carry their pistols with them at all times as there were rumours of a plot to murder them en masse. Minor mutinies broke out. General Heneker, commanding a division, wrote in his diary on 20 May:

'Trouble in 15th Hampshires. Two companies refused to parade. Went in morning and talked strongly to them. Officers are bad. Looked sulky but don't expect more trouble—captured a ringleader.' The following day he was discussing the possibility of advancing: 'VII Corps goes thro' in buses, we follow marching and must be prepared to fight.'

With many men being demobilized the strengths of battalions rose and fell while the tasks seemed to multiply. Lance-Corporal Smith found himself in a battalion so short of men that he was on guard for twenty-four hours and was still required to do certain duties on his twenty-four hours off. He was enjoying the pleasure of a highly irregular sleep, having taken off his equipment and boots, when he was roused from his blankets in the guardroom. In fact, there was no guard. A weary sentry had come in and shaken the man who should have relieved him. On receiving a reassuring grunt he had gone to bed without seeing that the new sentry had taken over. And he had not bothered to wake Smith, the guard commander, to report.

It was a bad breach of discipline, not made any better by Smith's reply to the officer who caught him out. This youngster had arrived the previous day straight from Sandhurst and when he started to lecture Smith, the fed-up little man exploded.

Banging his chest he exclaimed:

'1914 not 1919, you bastard.'

Needless to say, from being in charge of the guard Smith immediately became one of the guarded. He was accused of failing to post a sentry, being asleep without wearing his equipment, insubordination and swearing at an officer, etc., etc. On the recommendation of his Commanding Officer, Smith was court martialled and remanded to await sentence. For fourteen days he was held prisoner in a cellar under the chemist's shop in the village. Then the Regimental Sergeant Major arrived to say that he was coming up for sentence. With Smith's assistance, he removed the corporal's stripes, tacking them on so that they could be ripped off on parade without any trouble. Then Smith was marched forth into the centre of the customary hollow square.

The thing that stuck out in his mind afterwards was the face of one of his cronies in the front rank. Smith could hardly contain himself at the expression of his friend who obviously thought the proceedings highly amusing. A staff officer then rode into the centre of the parade ground and read out the sentence: 'to suffer death by being shot'.

It was the first intimation that Smith had received that his life had been in peril, but like a flash he bellowed, 'I wish to appeal,' being completely unaware that there was no appeal in such cases.

The whole thing came as such a surprise to him that he was still grinning when he shouted and the R.S.M. snapped at him, 'Take that smile off your face'.

It disappeared quickly enough as the promulgating officer carried on to announce that Smith's penalty had been reduced to twenty-one years' gaol. As various other amendments eventually reduced the term considerably his spirits rose again and he was still trying to work out how long he would have to serve when the band struck up a gay march and the officers rode away with the battalion. The R.S.M. put his mind at rest.

'You're all right, Smith. You'll be out in two years.'

While Smith returned to his cellar to ponder his fate that

night, the jovial comrade who had watched from the front rank of the parade wrote home to report the exciting events of the day. By the time the news reached Smith's parents the details had become somewhat garbled with the result that Smith Senior, who had a business in Croydon, ran up the street in his shirtsleeves, caught the first London train and went to the War Office, where he threatened to carry out some executions of his own if his boy was shot.

Smith, however, had already extricated himself from the scrape by remarking to the officer who had defended him that he shouldn't really have been in the army at all as he had enlisted for only four years, which had expired the previous September. Within a couple of days he was delighted to find himself on a boat heading for home, reappointed corporal and, as he had been a sniper, posted with other crackshots around the vessel to watch for drifting mines.[2]

Smith's case demonstrates that military law was still firmly applied immediately after the war. Official records show that between 1 October, 1918 and 30 September, 1919, six men were shot for desertion and eight for murder. Figures were not readily available, however. The War Office was still extremely reluctant to tell the public what it was entitled to know. It was not until 28 April, 1920, that the administration plucked up enough courage. A government spokesman stated in answer to a Parliamentary question that 3,076 sentences of death had been passed and, of these, 343 had been carried out. Within a short time this announcement provoked an extraordinary sequence of events.

A prominent socialist called H.V. Clarke, who had been employed at G.H.Q. during the war, wrote to several leading newspapers saying that to his knowledge no fewer than 37,900 soldiers had been put to death for disciplinary offences. He declared that in his own time he had copied the records of the executions from General Routine Orders. According to his count they were as follows:

1914	528
1915	10,488
1916	12,689
1917	13,165
1918	1,035

For fairly obvious reasons no newspaper would publish these

[2] Personal recollections of P. J. Smith Esq.

figures. For not so obvious reasons, they did not take the trouble to ask to see Clarke's sources. Miss Sylvia Pankhurst was more enthusiastic but unfortunately published the figures before seeing the evidence, mainly because her left-wing publication *Dreadnought* was about to go to press and this was a tit-bit too good to leave out.

Certainly it did not escape the sharp eyes of the Special Branch. The day the *Dreadnought* appeared detectives called at Clarke's home while he was out. Hearing of this on his return, Clarke destroyed all but one sheet of the copies he had made of the Routine Order announcements of death sentences. Racing to the office of the *Dreadnought* in Fleet Street, he could not find Sylvia Pankhurst, who was out at the time. When she returned she went immediately to call on him but in the meantime, shaken to hear that detectives had called again at his home, he had destroyed the last sheet of his 'evidence'.

In her autobiography Miss Pankhurst states that Scotland Yard men called on her on 7 June and asked her to publish an apology or a withdrawal prepared by the Director of Public Prosecutions. This eventually appeared although in Miss Pankhurst's view Clarke, who said he had spent five months copying out the record of executions, was a sincere man and passionately in earnest.

'If his figures were incorrect, then he was suffering from delusions,' she declared.[3]

What Mr. Clarke's 'evidence' was we shall never know, but it is highly unlikely that any army would have sacrificed the equivalent of two divisions to encourage the others when its disciplinary policy was based on the principle that 'any penalty inflicted on the troops must be one that will not cause a shortage of men'.

The affair was followed apparently in silence by one man who knew all the answers, Major-General Childs, but he had other problems to absorb his interest. To him went the job of clearing up some of the more unpleasant features of victory. His advice was in demand everywhere. Great pressure was mounted by M.P.s to secure the release of soldiers serving gaol sentences. Childs successfully opposed this on the grounds that it would be unfair to those men who had done their duty properly—but as a sop he agreed to have all cases reviewed regularly to see if there were any mitigating factors. The

[3] Pankhurst, *The Home Front.*

government consulted him with regard to the pension entitlement of nearly 4,000 men suffering from self-inflicted wounds. It was decided against granting them. But the biggest task of all was dealing with the thousands of returning prisoners. Childs arranged for a standing tribunal to be set up, with a V.C. holder and two other distinguished active service officers as members. Every soldier and officer was required to render a report of the manner in which he was captured, the tribunal—'in effect a court of honour'—being able to require the attendance of men if necessary. The result was satisfactory as far as Childs was concerned even if lacking in credibility.

'No courts martial were necessary,' he wrote, 'and I am proud to reflect that the report of the Standing Court of Inquiry overwhelmingly satisfied me that there was no established case of cowardice in the face of the enemy—a monumental record, in fact, of the courage of the British Army.'[4]

The idea that under the Army Act currently in force not one of the prisoners could have been charged is ludicrous. No doubt if the men whom Hutchison mowed down with his machine-gun in Flanders had succeeded in surrendering they would have been included in the mass exoneration.

Even the Casement Brigade, formed in Germany from Irish prisoners of war, were completely cleared after stating that to a man they had joined only to escape from the bad conditions of the camps in which they were held.

The haste with which these and other slates were wiped clean was almost indecent.

It would have been much more honest if it had been stated that as the Allies had won the war no action would be taken against returning prisoners because it was against the national interest. It would be unfair to blame Childs for the line adopted. He was merely a convenient tool of the government. Childs, whom successive chiefs had called 'Fido', was transferred eventually to a job to which his special qualities were particularly suited—head of the Criminal Investigation Department of New Scotland Yard.

4 *Episodes and Reflections.*

16

The 'Shell Shock' Enquiry

The first annual debate on the Army Act after the war saw a determined attempt on the part of some M.P.s to get rid of Field Punishment No. 1 known to the troops as 'crucifixion'. According to the rules laid down, a soldier under sentence (up to twenty-eight days if given by his commanding officer and up to three months by court martial) might be kept in fetters or handcuffs and 'secured' to prevent his escape.

'When in irons he may be attached for a period or periods not exceeding two hours in any one day to a fixed object,' said the Manual of Military Law. He was not to be treated like this more than three days out of four and not more than twenty-one days in all.

In peace time offenders had been tied up to gun wheels, but during the war British soldiers were frequently 'attached' to the railings of buildings. At Calais a case had been reported of men being strapped (the rules said that straps or ropes could be used in lieu of irons) to a wooden frame in the main road regardless of the weather and Sylvia Pankhurst claimed that one of the conscientious objectors taken to France had been 'crucified' at a cross roads within range of shells.[1]

Although the Regular soldiers had accepted Field Punishment No. 1 as one of the hardships of their calling before 1914, it became universally loathed during hostilities because it exposed the offender to the stares and jeers of French civilians. One M.P. pointed out that he had seen men tied up even to signposts in the middle of a village. Despite the general agreement that the penalty was humiliating there were still people who urged its retention. One was Sir George Courthope, Member for Rye. Referring to his own role as president of a field general court martial in Flanders, he said, 'I had to try

[1] *The Home Front.*

twelve men in one noted regiment, men of undoubted gallantry, for an offence which, in spite of extenuating circumstances, and but for the existence of the penalty (Field Punishment No. 1) there would have been no other course open to the court martial but to condemn the men to death.'[2]

Drunkenness in action was a serious offence which had to be visited with severe penalties on the spot. He firmly believed that but for the existence of field punishment many men guilty of the crime would have been put to death.

The Secretary of State for War, Mr. Winston Churchill, agreed with this point but declared that personally he was against degrading men in this way and said that he would gather opinions from ex-officers and N.C.O.s.

Mr Churchill's inquiries bore little fruit for Field Punishment No. 1 was still a feature of the Army Act the following year. On the occasion of the annual debate, however, the knotty problem of the death penalty was raised again. An ex-officer tried to secure for condemned men the right to appeal. Although he failed, the first of some interesting facts came to light.

'I was told by one General a few days ago,' said an M.P. opposing the call for an appeal procedure, 'of one case where it was his painful duty to carry out a sentence of death. He paraded the whole division in order to see the sentence carried into effect. The result was that there was not a single other case in his division in the course of the whole war.'

In 1921, even more interesting facts emerged. Captain J. H. Thorpe, the Member for Rusholme, who had had a great deal of experience in France, stated that he could remember innumerable cases where a soldier came before a court martial and said that he had no-one to defend him. It had been his duty as a court martial officer—he was a barrister—to look after his interests.

'While British officers have an extraordinarily high sense of justice and honour, they are painfully uninstructed in the first principles of evidence and law,' he declared, adding:

'My own custom was—and I dare say I shall be told it was wrong—that after the trial of a man in a case where the sentence may possibly be the sentence of death, I invariably, for my own conscience's sake, asked the man whether he thought he'd had a fair deal.' Captain Thorpe wanted a qualified court martial officer to act as judge-advocate at every field

[2] *Hansard.*

185

general court martial where a man might be condemned to death, imprisonment or loss of rank.

Another Member, Major M. M. Wood, painted a most revealing picture of what went on in the minds of some of the officers who sat in judgement on soldiers.

There was the court martial president who told him that he always imposed the maximum sentence laid down in the Army Act because he knew there was a confirming officer who would reduce the sentence if he saw fit.

At the same time he knew a confirming officer who never commuted a sentence because, in his opinion, the members of a court, having seen the prisoner, were in a better position to judge what was the proper sentence to inflict.

'I remember an officer telling me that on one occasion he was sent down by headquarters at the front specially to do court martial duty. He was quite satisfied with the guilt of the prisoner. But it took him a whole hour, he said, to persuade the other members of the court that the man was guilty. It was a question of desertion and the death sentence and the man was eventually shot.'

This officer had given as his explanation for this highly improper action:

'What would they have said to me at headquarters if I had gone back and told them that this man was acquitted when the evidence was so clear?'

The cold statistics resulting from such actions appeared in March, 1922. A large book was published by the War Office price 10s 6d. Written in gilt letters on the oatmeal coloured cover were the words 'The Statistics of the Military Effort of the British Empire during the Great War'. In Part XXIII 'Discipline', facts about courts martial were printed. It revealed that 346 members of the British Imperial forces, including Native labourers and Chinese coolies subject to the Army Act had been executed for a variety of offences. The breakdown as far as theatres of war were concerned was as follows:

France	322	Salonica	3
East Africa	5	Egypt	2
Mesopotamia	4	Italy	1
Constantinople	4	Palestine	1
Gallipoli	3	Serbia	1

Only three of the men shot by firing squads were officers. Two had been condemned for desertion and one for murder. In the case of the other ranks, ninety-one were stated to have been under suspended sentence at the time they were sentenced to die. Forty had previously been condemned to death—in thirty-eight cases for desertion.

Desertion was officially the offence for which the greatest number of men paid the supreme penalty. Excluding one man reported as shot for desertion in the first two months of the war, the figures for other ranks were compiled for yearly periods starting 1 October to 30 September of the following years:

Offence	1915	1916	1917	1918	1919	1919
Desertion	40	62	78	77	6	
Murder	1	6	3	10	8	8
Cowardice	5	6	5	2		
Quitting post	2	2	2	1		
Striking a superior		1	2	3		
Disobeying an order		4		1		
Mutiny			2	1		
Sleeping on duty			2			
Casting away arms			2			
Totals	48	81	96	95	14	8

Of the officers and men who died, 291 were Imperial troops, five belonged to colonial units and thirty-one were serving in what were classified as 'Overseas Contingents'. Ten Chinese, five 'camp followers' and four coloured labourers were included also in the total of 346.

Figures of the number of trials for cowardice rose as the size of the army overseas increased—126 up to 30 September, 1915, 136 for the next twelve months and reaching a peak of 161 in the period ending 30 September, 1917. A striking fall in the number of trials for this offence occurred in the twelve months ending 30 September, 1918, when only ninety were recorded. But in this period there was a corresponding jump in the number of men tried for desertion and absence without leave, the figures reaching 2,596 and 10,977 respectively.

In all ten officers and 531 men were tried for cowardice, and 21 officers and 7,361 men for desertion while on active service. The total number of cases of self-inflicted wounds was 3,894 of which twelve were officers.

The figures caused little stir, perhaps because by 1922 most people were desperately trying to forget the war. But they make an interesting study when read in conjunction with the report of the War Office Enquiry into 'Shell Shock' which appeared the same year. Some witnesses were sympathetic, some not. General Lord Horne, former commander of the First Army and a recognized artillery expert, said he 'looked down' on a unit which had a high number of cases of 'shell shock', putting it in the same category as one in which there were many little fingers missing from the left hands of the men—i.e. poor morale. A former inspector of infantry training thought that a battalion of countrymen with less intelligence would stick out a situation which townsmen, with greater intelligence, would not. And a Ministry of Pensions neurologist was against giving a wound stripe to a man who 'had simply broken down mentally' whereas he thought a man who had been blown up or buried was entitled to one.

A great deal of time was devoted to discussions on the relationship of 'shell shock' to cowardice and the definition of the latter.

Professor Roussy, consultant neurologist to the French Army, told the committee: 'Cowardice, I consider, is lack of self-control of the individual in the presence of a situation in which there is an element of danger and in which there is an element likely to cause fear. The man who flees the battlefield as a result of not exercising sufficient control is a coward.'

Most of the front-line officers and doctors showed considerable understanding of the effect of active service conditions on ordinary soldiers.

Major-General Sir H. S. Jeudwine, whose 55th Division had been through some of the hardest fighting of the Third Battle of Ypres and Cambrai and then distinguished themselves in April, 1918, thought the highest incidence of break-downs were caused during the static period of the war when men had to sit still in the trenches seeing their comrades killed all round them and not knowing when it would be their turn.

Lieutenant-Colonel G. Scott-Jackson, of the Royal Northumberland Fusiliers, said that the most cases he had experienced in his own battalion was when they were the targets of a heavy mortar at Kemmel.

'If bombarded by heavy artillery you are practically stupid and your mind is almost a blank. You lie down and pray for it to finish. But you have to watch trench mortars and if you are cunning enough you dodge them; it is the concentrated attention which is the important factor.'

Viscount Gort told of a case of a Guards officer who was buried during the First Battle of Ypres and evacuated home. When he returned in 1915 he had been a failure but after rejoining the battalion in 1918 he had done well.

An interesting comparison with an earlier war was made by the veteran Major-General Sir Alfred Bayly, who had held the title of Inspector of Temporary Non-effectives.

'I saw the men who retreated from Maiwand (1880). They had been through a fifty-mile march and, to look at, most of these men were exactly the same as the men who are now known as "shell shocked". It was pretty much emotional upset when they threw away rifles and everything else as surplus weight.'

In his view 'emotional shell shock' was not completely curable 'if the patient had any possible chance of being returned to the fighting line.'

Like some other witnesses he believed recruits of all ages had been 'pushed' too much.

Regimental officers painted some interesting little cameos of front-line conditions.

'I have seen three or four men at very brief intervals fall out in a condition of acute shock. They were all fresh in the field and no shell had burst within twenty yards of them. We'd had no rest all night and had been under heavy dispersed fire all the morning, a constant stream of wounded had passed through us, we were moving parallel and close to a barrage. Our own guns were on the other side about a hundred yards off; there was a lot of noise and noise alone jangles one's nerves.'

'I have encountered a minor stampede started by an officer of low morale calling 'gas' when there is no gas. He had already denounced the 'butchery' of his platoon during the action.'

'I saw a lot of . . . troops in an absolutely terrified condition during that retirement (March, 1918).'

'I met Medical Officers in France whose duties were interpreted simply by the seeing of the sick and the issuing of one or two tablets for half an hour every morning . . . they undoubtedly failed in the best interests of their profession and their country.'

There was the case of the Gordon Highlander who was sentenced to death after being found in a dug-out on the Somme, when his battalion had attacked. Although he swore he had been blown there by a shell he was court martialled and condemned to death. The sentence was commuted and the very next time the Gordons went into action he won the D.C.M.

There was the story of three 'rather noted' boxers who gave exhibitions to the troops but who 'cracked' in the trenches. And there was a pathetic description of men who, after heavy shelling, lay in a torpor and allowed themselves to be carried away as if unconscious but were able to say, later, exactly what had happened.

Colonel Fuller, one of the leading exponents of tank warfare, equated panic with 'crowd shell shock'. Normally this was only a temporary condition and 'once stopped a little rest will soon set the men up again'.

A medical officer who had experience of conditions on the ground and in the air took the view that the greatest single cause of what was known as shell shock was 'loss of sleep and inadequate rest'. He declared:

'The credit balance of nervous energy varies in individuals just as bank balances do. Some become bankrupt and succumb . . . Most real men take a lot of depressing . . . and so they draw on an overdraft and manage to carry on.'

Another doctor frankly refused to make a distinction between shell shock and cowardice, saying:

'Cowardice I take to mean action under the influence of fear and the ordinary type of shell shock was, to my mind, persistent and chronic fear.'

In their summary of the findings the committee said that shell shock had been 'a costly misnomer'. No such thing existed. The war had produced no neuroses that were not already known in civilian life but the stresses and special conditions of modern warfare had led to some complaints appearing in an exaggerated form and in large numbers.

Patients could be divided into three categories—concussion cases (relatively few); emotional shock, due to prolonged strain probably including some terrifying experience sometimes triggered off by a trivial event; and mental exhaustion cases resulting from great strain and hardship over a period.

As far as cowardice was concerned, the witnesses had been agreed that it was a military crime which should be punished by death on occasions and the committee accepted this. However, it stated that cowardice might be beyond an individual's control and that specialist medical opinion was essential to decide doubtful cases of war neuroses. Men who had already proved their courage should receive special consideration in the case of a subsequent lapse.

Sweeping criticism was made of the recruiting system during the war. There had been no check on a man's nervous and mental stability during the first eighteen months and with conscription the medical problems became worse in many cases . . . 'it is clear to us that during 1916 and 1917 the nervous system of the recruit did not receive adequate consideration. During the final year of the war . . . the administration was placed on a much sounder basis.'

The report of the Enquiry ended by stating that no soldier should be allowed to think that loss of nervous or mental control provided an honourable avenue of escape from the battlefield. All efforts should be concentrated on preventing slight cases [of 'shell shock'] leaving the active service area where 'treatment should be confined to rest and comfort for those in need of it and to heartening them for return to the line.'

As far as disciplinary measures were relevant, the committee stated that it was 'extremely difficult to distinguish cowardice from neurosis since in both fear is the chief causal factor.' The committee recommended that the best possible expert advice should be obtained when any question or doubt arose at any stage in the court martial process.

The year 1922 saw yet one more vain attempt to ameliorate the severity of Field Punishment No. 1 so that it would be 'of the character of personal restraint or of hard labour, but shall not be of a nature to cause injury to life or limb'. In fairness to the Army Act, this proviso was implied. But the assertion that some commanding officers awarded field punishment for trivial offences stung the Under-Secretary of State for War, Sir Robert Sanders, to spring to their defence. He quoted Field-Marshals Sir Douglas Haig and Sir William Robertson as having spoken in favour of it the previous year. General Macready, the Adjutant-General, had solemnly warned that without the power to tie soldiers to a gun wheel for two hours a day calls for the death penalty would be more frequent. Abolition would have 'a disastrous and far-reaching effect'.

Always there were people who warned that to do away with the traditional penalties would rock the Army to its very foundations. Field Punishment No. 1 was eventually discarded the following year and the sky did not fall nor the troops mutiny. With the advent of the first Labour Government in January, 1924, under Ramsay MacDonald, genuine prospects of getting rid of the death penalty also appeared. Now they were in office, however, the new leaders of the country had to contend with the wily and experienced heads of the armed forces. The military authorities influenced the Secretary of State for War, Mr Stephen Walsh, to persuade reformers to drop amendments so that the Army Council and Service representatives could go into the whole question. Only Jimmy Maxton, the veteran Glasgow Socialist, refused to toe the line. But his amendment motion that any soldier, sailor or airman condemned to death should have the right of appeal to the Court of Criminal appeal was defeated by 193 votes to 120.

Captain the Viscount Ednam, who had warned that 'No one wants the death penalty but it has got to be, and without it a great deal of harm will be done to the Army' was delighted.

Ernest Thurtle got his opportunity to make his contribution to the campaign to abolish the death penalty for cowardice and desertion after his election to Parliament in 1923, when he stood as the Labour candidate for Shoreditch. He had been badly wounded in the fighting at Cambrai but had recovered enough to fight two elections before eventually succeeding. He was hardly a slick politician; much more the old-fashioned idea of a socialist, with strong patriotic sentiments. Perhaps for the very reason that he had been born in America, at Port Jervis, New York State, his desire to show his patriotism was all the stronger. In fact, young Ernest was a bit of a mixture when it came to antecedents. His father, a Norfolk man who was an expert in training gun dogs, returned from America when Ernest was two years old and the family moved to Alfrick, Worcestershire. Four years later when Thurtle senior died of tuberculosis, Ernest and his mother moved to Griffithstown, near Pontypool, Monmouthshire, where he was educated and spent his youth. He was already married and had revisited America with his bride, a daughter of George Lansbury, the

Socialist radical journalist, when war broke out.

Thurtle's fight to prevent soldiers being shot at dawn was based on his view of military law. He defined this as 'the power which enabled non-fighting people, the majority, to send fighting men, the minority, to be killed or maimed in any cause the majority may decide proper. And the fighting man may not refuse on pain of death or, at least, penal servitude.'

In his first major contribution to the campaign, Thurtle gave a vivid account of an incident in which the higher command decided to instil some life into a tired battalion then holding the line at Arras after nearly eighteen months of heavy fighting.

'There had been numerous raids by the enemy and they had been somewhat successful. Brigade headquarters and divisional headquarters became annoyed and a message was sent up to the battalion that if another raid happened somebody was going to be "for it". A few days later, in darkness and drizzle, another raid did take place and one or two prisoners were obtained by the enemy. An inquiry was ordered, arrests were made, a court martial took place and a sergeant and two corporals were executed as a result.

'That particular sergeant came from the North of England. He was married and had a family. He had left a well-paid job but, in spite of that, was put up before a firing squad of his own comrades and shot in cold blood.'[3]

The experience of Lieutenant-Colonel Hugh Mowbray Meyler, Member for Blackpool and a solicitor in civilian life, was even more disquieting. Colonel Meyler had been appointed president of a court martial to try a nineteen-year-old soldier on a charge of failing to join his company when it went up the line early in 1915. The boy had been found in a dug-out when they returned from the trenches.

'I was called to brigade headquarters before I ever sat on that court martial,' said Colonel Meyler, 'and I was told that General Headquarters expected that the court martial, if it found the man guilty, would sentence him to death and leave it to them to decide if it was carried out.'

The only legal help the young soldier had was an officer totally inexperienced in legal matters. There was no direct evidence that the man had been warned that his company was to go into the trenches but there was strong circumstantial

[3] *Hansard.*

evidence which led to him being found guilty and remanded to await confirmation of sentence. The findings were sent off on their passage to General Headquarters.

'It was a slow process,' said Colonel Meyler.

When the man's company went back into the line they took him with them, under escort, because there was nowhere else for him to go. For three days he served in the line within a hundred yards of the Germans, then marched back with the battalion when they were relieved.

'They had a long way to go and arrived (at their billets) about midnight. Just a little before they arrived there were delays. We wondered why, but we found out. The adjutant rode up to the commanding officer and told him that the death sentence had been confirmed. I was ordered to detail the firing party. And I did . . . that firing party came from 'A' Company of a battalion and shot this man the next morning who came from 'B' Company of the same battalion. You may say that regulations do not allow this to be done. I have seen it done myself.

'The prisoner had no idea he was in any danger of being shot. It was only on his arrival back at his battalion rest area that he was told.

'In the morning at 6.30 three battalions from the brigade were marched out and when the sentence of the court martial was read out, one of his comrades dropped in a dead faint. As the battalion stood on parade to march off, we heard the rattle of the volley that killed him.'

There was bitterness in Colonel Meyler's words.

'I was president of the court martial as well as the officer who had charge of him in the line and had to detail the firing party. Do you think it did my morale any good? It is a good many years now: it is more than nine years ago and I have not forgotten any detail of it.'

An incredulous voice interrupted the silence of the House.

'Were you president of the court martial?'

'I was president of the field general court martial. I was the officer who had charge of the man in the line and the man who detailed the firing party.'

'Absolutely irregular' chorused a number of Members.

'*Was* that a regular proceeding?' asked one of them.

'I was fighting in the line . . . I had no copy of the Manual of Military Law with me,' replied Colonel Meyler, who served in the Middlesex and Border Regiments before going to a balloon spotting squadron.

He agreed with Mr Thurtle that many ex-soldiers were opposed to the death sentence. 'I am referring not to senior officers, because I know that they have the idea . . . that they are affecting the psychology of the soldiers. It was those who lived cheek by jowl with the soldiers who knew the real psychology.

'You train your soldiers not to be impressed by fear, to despise fear, and then you go and bring out . . . this death sentence which is supposed to improve their discipline by means of fear. The whole thing is illogical.'

Colonel Meyler's frankness encouraged yet another Member to unburden his conscience.[4] He had sat on a court martial in the winter of 1914, he said, which sentenced five men to death. He did not know what had happened to them but 'I had an uncomfortable feeling that even with my limited knowledge of the law I could have got off each one of these men on a technicality if I had been in a position to act as a friend. What does an ordinary Territorial captain know about court martial? Nothing . . . less than nothing. I was sitting on this court martial for this reason . . . that the brigade had been . . . practically annihilated.'

The great majority of the M.P.s present refused to be moved, however. Some just could not bring themselves to believe that injustice could have occurred in a system so hedged about with regulations.

There were a number of Members who expressed misgivings but found it hard to believe that mistakes could occur under the system. Young Captain Anthony Eden asked if it were not a fact that no man could be tried by court martial (for sleeping on duty one supposes) if it could be proved that he had been on duty more than a certain number of hours. But others were less sympathetic. 'More sob stuff', was a typical remark from the back benches during speeches by abolitionists.

Thurtle gave a moving account of a man who was sentenced to death because he had gone absent to solve a marital problem. He had talked to the padre who was present who had reported that at the execution the prisoner 'squared his shoulders and filled his lungs and faced the volley as any V.C. might face a volley.'

4 Mr. W. H. Ayles, Labour M.P. for N. Bristol.

'How are we to know this is not a sentimental story patched up?' asked Lieutenant-Colonel Spender-Clay.

When Thurtle pointed out that there was no evidence that any senior officer or commander had been shot since the execution of Admiral Byng, Colonel Sir Charles Yate, the seventy-six year old Member for Melton, who had enlisted in the 44th Foot (1st Essex) and was a veteran of the Afghan War of 1881, rumbled, 'They do not run away.'

'They never get near the fighting line,' flashed back Mr Thurtle.

But the majority of Members were still against reform. One of them, Captain Robert Gee, who held the Victoria Cross and M.C. and had spent twenty-two years in the Royal Fusiliers, stated in one debate that he had deliberately visited sergeants' messes, corporals' rooms and soldiers' canteens and discussed the matter. In every case—and he had called on twenty-seven regiments—the men did not want the Army Act to be changed; they 'preferred to be tried and dealt with by their own officers.'

Captain Gee had won his V.C. during the German counter-offensive at Cambrai when he recaptured the village of Les Rues Vertes single-handed. A tough, good looking man, he was among the more formidable opponents of Thurtle's reform. Victory was not going to be easy with men like the Member for Bosworth to contend with.

17

Inquests and Authors

The tenacity with which successive governments clung to the grisly secrets of wartime justice was equalled during the 1920s only by the lack of curiosity of the British public. It was almost as if they deliberately sought relief in the opiate of ignorance. The French, by contrast, seemed set upon the path of painful revelation, but they had a judicial procedure which afforded the means of redress to those who sought it.

In 1920, the father of a Private Santerre received a medal awarded to his dead son whom he knew had been shot for a disciplinary offence. He wrote back to say that he did not want it. He could not accept that his son had died gloriously for France. He demanded justice. At Douai, a tribunal, with the power of annulment—'rehabilitated' Private Santerre as a soldier.[1]

The following year, Monsieur Jadé, the Deputy for Finistère, raised the spectres of four corporals. In March, 1915, M. Jadé had been a company commander in the 336th Reserve Infantry Regiment. He watched from the trenches as two other officers led their companies in a forlorn attack on the Moulin de Souay, a heap of bricks some thirty miles north of Rheims. Machine-guns drove back the French as they tried to hack their way through unbroken barbed wire. One of the companies had lost too many men to make another assault but the other, the 21st, was ordered forward again. At zero hour (L'Heure H) they refused to follow their commander over the parapet.

The next day a party led by four corporals was ordered into no-man's-land in broad daylight to make a further attempt on the wire. A storm of bullets drove them to take cover in shell holes where they remained until nightfall when they crept back

[1] See Wilkins, *Mysteries of the Great War*, also reference in Army Act Debate, Hansard for 29 March, 1927.

to their own trenches.

Thirty-two privates were court martialled on charges of displaying cowardice in the face of the enemy. They were acquitted on the evidence of a sergeant major who said they could not have heard the order to advance on the day of the first attack. The corporals were all found guilty of cowardice on the second day and were executed in front of the whole regiment.

M. Jadé asked the French Government to hold an inquiry into the incident but this was refused. In 1926, however, under pressure from various pacifist organizations with growing political influence and from veterans' associations, a Court of Cassation, with power to annul sentences, was set up in the Cherche-Midi, the court-cum-gaol in the Boulevard Raspail, Paris. Others sat in other provincial centres. At Metz, the attack on the Moulin de Souay was brought up. There it was revealed that General Reveilhac, the divisional commander, had at one stage ordered his own guns to open fire on the infantry who refused to leave the trenches but that the artillery commander had refused without a written order. The suicide mission led by the corporals had also been his idea.

Tragically an order reprieving the doomed men had arrived just after they had been shot and two, who had only been wounded, were given the coup de grâce by an officer.[2]

The four corporals were 'rehabilitated' by the Court of Cassation and a monument to their memory was erected at Sartilly, in the Departement of the Manche. Sixty years later a film 'Paths of Glory' was made which closely resembled the incident. It was highly successful.

The 'Case of the Bloodstained Trousers' concerned Private Lucien Bersot, a middle-aged peasant serving in the 60th Infantry Regiment. The garments were offered to him by a corporal when he complained that his own were only cotton and not thick enough to keep him warm in the cold winter of 1915–16. As they had just been removed from a corpse at a field hospital Private Bersot did not consider them suitable. He refused to put them on. When a passing lieutenant repeated the order he replied jokingly:

'But they are soaked in blood and guts. Put them on yourself and see how you like it. A French citizen does not need to walk round in a dead man's shit.'

[2] Wilkins, *Mysteries of the Great War*.

Bersot got eight days' extra duties on the spot but he kept his thin cotton trousers. However, when the colonel of the regiment saw the report he decided that this was not enough. And when two of Bersot's comrades tried to persuade the lieutenant to intercede he declared that this was mutiny. All three were tried in a château at Mardoncons on the Aisne, one being acquitted, one sentenced to hard labour for life and Bersot condemned to death. At the inquiry into the trial it was revealed that Colonel Auroux of the 60th Regiment who had ordered the trial had also sat on the court martial as president. The sentence was annulled but an attempt by Bersot's widow to press charges against Auroux failed.[3]

Near St Mihiel in August, 1915, when a company refused to attack after digging trenches for forty-eight hours in drenching rain which turned every man 'into a ball of mud with a rifle sticking out' the corps commander was alleged to have ordered the entire unit to be machine-gunned. Being talked out of this, he lowered his demands gradually from seventy-five victims to twenty. Later six, chosen by lot, were court martialled and shot. In July, 1929, they were cleared of the charges at a Court of Cassation. They too were commemorated by a monument.

As the trials went on it became obvious that not only had justice been badly administered but that unusual severity had often applied, particularly in 1914. Private Francois Laurent, shot in October of that year for inflicting a wound on himself, was proved to have sustained a genuine injury to his hand. His widow was awarded a pension. So were the dependents of six soldiers of the 298th Infantry Regiment selected by lot from twenty-four men court martialled in November, 1914. The last letters of two of the men were read at the trial. One of them, Private Henri Floch, wrote to his wife:

'On 27 November, about 5 pm after a violent bombardment lasting two hours we were in a front line trench finishing our dinners when the enemy came over and made me and two others prisoner. In a moment of confusion I managed to make my escape. I followed my comrades and later I was accused of having abandoned my post in front of the enemy. Twenty-four of us were brought before a court martial yesterday. Six were condemned to death of whom I was one. I am no more guilty than the others, but an example must be made. My pocket wallet will be sent to you and its contents.'

[3] Van Paassen, *Days of Our Years.*

Another of the six condemned men, Private Quinault, wrote in a similar vein, almost suggesting that he and Floch had composed their last letters together. 'I am no more guilty than the rest of my comrades, but our lives are sacrificed for others . . . ah, there is something!'

Undoubtedly the case that caused the greatest outcry was the inquiry into the execution of Lieutenant Herduin and Ensign Millaud of the 347th Infantry Regiment, which had been the target of a heavy bombardment and constant attacks at Verdun in June, 1916. When the regiment had been reduced to 350 men, their commanding officer killed and all the senior officers put out of action, the French artillery sent a rain of shells into the position. Herduin and Millaud, with a detachment of forty-two men, decided to fall back under cover of darkness and their conduct was held to be responsible for the general collapse of their own regiment and another alongside them. Nivelle, commanding the Second Army, made some stern inquiries of the divisional commander. He in his turn ordered the immediate execution of the two young officers for cowardice. Herduin, who held a decoration for bravery already, demanded a court martial in vain.

According to the official account of their deaths, Herduin's last words were:

'Soldiers, you are going to shoot me. I am not a coward, nor is my comrade, but we did abandon our post. We should have stayed there to the end, to the death. If you find yourselves in the same situation, do not retreat . . . remain to the end . . . and now, aim well, right at the heart! Proceed! Fire!'[4]

This was somewhat different from the account of his last words given at the trial of Cassation at Colmar in 1926. Apparently when the firing squad, formed from men of his own regiment, hesitated, Herduin called to them:

'We are charged with not having done our duty. It seems we did not hold out long enough. But I assure you we did our full duty. We did not deserve death. This will later be acknowledged. And now, you too, do your duty. Don't make us suffer. Aim straight at the heart. To my wife and my boy, goodbye.'[5]

Earlier he had written to his wife, Fernande:

'Insist that you get my pension. You have a right to it. My conscience is clear . . . those higher up always look for victims

[4] Horne, *The Price of Glory.*
[5] Van Paassen, *Days of Our Years.*

to get themselves out of a scrape.'

Madame Herduin obeyed her husband's last wishes. After she threatened to sue the divisional commander for murder and won a libel case against a newspaper which defended him, the French government was happy to settle for a large sum and admitted that Herduin had died because of 'erroneous application of the regulations'.

As late as December, 1933, the *Daily Telegraph* reported from Paris:

'War tragedies of an especially painful nature are now being reviewed by the French military courts. On several occasions men were executed as traitors or deserters who were really innocent. Efforts are now being made to rehabilitate their memories.'

The trials, as has been stated, had, in fact, been going on for years. But no-one in Britain considered them to be particularly newsworthy, and a correspondent who sent a report to an American chain of thirty newspapers did not get a line into one of them.[6]

From a military point of view, the blatant exposure of the nastier side of disciplinary enforcement is undesirable if it also exposes unfairness and injustice. And the revelations of the Courts of Cassation may have had a more profound effect than is realized on the morale of the French troops and the nation when committed to battle in 1940. The role of the State in these trials, which it did little to discourage although few newspapers carried reports, is interesting. Could it have been that having seen the generals reap the glory of the victories of 1918, the politicians were happy to see them shown up in a poor light during the years that followed?

Deprived of official legal outlets, the truth gradually filtered out to the British public via books. Most of the major literary works made some reference to courts martial. Edmund Blunden's *Undertones of War* describes how he and another junior officer, having sat in judgement on a tough old cook who had been drunk in the trenches, blithely said 'death' when asked by the elderly president of the court martial what the sentence should be. And when this worthy looked horrified they argued hotly that it was what was prescribed in regulations. Nevertheless the cook escaped with some minor punishment. The execution of two men of the Royal Welch Fusiliers who shot

[6] Van Paassen.

another N.C.O. in mistake for their hated platoon sergeant came out in *Goodbye To All That* by Robert Graves. He described also his own relief at finding a more hard-boiled captain to take his place on a court martial due to try an Irish sergeant who had thrown down his rifle during heavy shelling and bolted with the rest of his platoon. As the charge was cowardice and death was the only penalty allowed if a man was found guilty, Graves felt he could not bring himself to condemn a man for something he might possibly have done also in similar circumstances.

There were other books and other references. But the air of mystery remained. The literary style, the emphasis on other aspects of the war, plus the restrained, sometimes classic English did not make the crude impact of the dramas played out in the Courts of Cassation. In 1929, the fourth edition of a small book by A. P. Herbert was published. Winston Churchill wrote an introduction in which he summed up the British attitude:

'This story of a valiant heart tested to destruction took rank when it was first published a few months after the Armistice, as one of the most moving novels produced by the war. It was at that time a little swept aside by the revulsion of the public mind from anything to do with the awful period just ended.'[7]

The story was that of a young officer, given the name Harry Penrose, who served in the Royal Naval Division at Gallipoli and later in France, where he broke down, was court martialled and shot.

It was carefully explained that though the incidents were factual, they were a collection from a number of cases and drew on a variety of sources. The truth was that Penrose, the central figure of *The Secret Battle*, was based on Edwin Dyett, the tragic young officer shot in January, 1917. There was every reason for A. P. Herbert to know the facts. He was serving in the Royal Naval Division at the time.

The details of the case, as far as they were drawn from the Dyett trial, were deliberately disguised to avoid any possibility of libelling the officers involved, but in two important respects they tallied with the allegations made in *John Bull* and in Parliament later. The vital testimony that led to the prisoner being found guilty was attributed to a witness who had a personal grudge against him—and the summary of evidence was handed to the prisoner's friend only the day before the trial.

[7] Foreword to *The Secret Battle*.

A. P. Herbert concluded the book by saying that it was not an attack on the death penalty—he thought he might even believe in capital punishment. What he did not believe was that his friend should have been shot for cowardice. In his view, Harry Penrose—alias Edwin Dyett—was 'one of the bravest men I ever knew'.

Strangely, although *The Secret Battle* was widely read, it did not make a great impact on the public. To obtain a real response one had to mention—drink! Different people had different views on this subject. One of the medical officers who testified before the 1922 Shell Shock Committee had stated categorically 'had it not been for the rum ration I do not think we should have won the war'. He said that in his battalion of the Black Watch they had always tried to give the men a good meal and a double ration of rum in coffee before they went 'over the top'. But General Pinney, who commanded the 33rd Division for a period, forbade the issue of the morning tot thus inflicting his own teetotal convictions upon his men. Foremost among the opponents of the demon drink was Brigadier Crozier.

At one stage he had urged strongly that spirits should not be available to the troops in France—although he had not hesitated to avail himself of the anaesthetic qualities of whisky and rum in connection with the execution of the unfortunate Crocker. Writing after the war he stated:

'In 1917 a class of young men were being granted commissions who, until then, had no idea of rising to the heights of social beverages—whisky, gin, cocktails and the like. Half the cases of indiscipline on the part of officers which came through my hands (and there were a good many) were directly or indirectly attributable to drinking having been made easy.'

He concluded, 'The record of beer and the Bible in the war leaves me stone cold. Both sides suffered from alcoholic debauchery, while both used the Bible as propaganda for peace.'[8]

The opening of *Journey's End* in 1930 led to a spate of letters to *The Times*.

Brigadier C. D. Baker-Carr, who had been commandant of the machine-gun school in France for two years, wrote:

'I have no hesitation in saying the average officer was remarkably temperate. In actual fact I am unable to call to

[8] Crozier, *A Brass Hat in No-Man's-Land.*

203

mind a single case of drunkenness on the part of an officer while he was at the school. On the last night of each course there was usually a merry, somewhat boisterous party. Undoubtedly a few officers may have exceeded the limit of strict sobriety, but they were few and far between.

'There were officers who were sentimentalists, shirkers, drunkards or cowards; there were officers who were level-headed, conscientious, temperate and brave, but the number of the former is so infinitesimally small that it is altogether negligible.'

General Sir Ivor Maxse hastened to his support:

'I took a distinguished young French officer to see *Journey's End* and afterwards, in the Strand, turned to him and asked him what he thought of it. He replied: 'If British officers had really behaved like those we have just seen in the play we would have lost the war.' With that remark I entirely agree.'

Colonel Seton Hutchison wrote to say that never at any time, either in attack or defence, had he witnessed an officer 'originating from whatever class' who was intoxicated.

A member of the Ladies' Army and Navy Club stated that she was sure that nearly every woman who had had relatives or friends at the front would be grateful to Hutchison and Maxse.

Not everyone was prepared to give unreserved approval of their views, however. Referring to attacks on war literature as a whole, Captain Churchill-Longman, who had been twice wounded during four years' active service, asked:

'Why should not the drunkard in *Journey's End* be the central figure of the play? Does the man who wrote *All Quiet on the Western Front* know more about war than the writer of *Hints on Training* issued by XVIIIth Corps [commanded by Maxse] in May, 1918. After all, one is no more credible than the other.'

Perhaps the most touching letters came from a former officer who signed himself 'M.C. and Bar'.

'In an attack in 1916 a company of a service battalion of the K.O.Y.L.I. was "standing to" in a jumping-off trench preparatory to an attack. As it was early afternoon and the position was very exposed, it was absolutely physically impossible for the customary ration of rum to be taken round personally by an officer. The company commander (a barrister) who was subsequently killed in the attack, therefore attached a note to the rum jar apologizing for not being able to get round with it himself, wishing the men luck and adding some words such as

"Think of the other fellow and pass it on". The men did so with the result that when it reached the last man in the company the jar was only half-empty.'

It was in the same month of 1930 that the furore over drink in the trenches arose—Prohibition was big news at the time—that Thurtle launched his most determined assault on the Army Act. In the same month the cathedral of St Martin was opened again, rebuilt on its ancient site behind the famous Cloth Hall in war-shattered Ypres. Times were changing. Or so people thought.

18

Brass Hats at Bay

Pleading a case against the stringent measures of the Army Act was not exactly a popular occupation. It smacked too much of Bolshevism in one camp and not enough of it in the other. Nor did the public feel it was an urgent issue. There wasn't much of an army left—unless you counted the mounting army of unemployed. There were plenty of heroes from the Somme and Ypres to be found on street corners. How many 'shell shock' cases emerged only when their spirits were eroded by the struggle for existence we shall never know. There were also technical reasons which made the debates unpopular. They generally took place late at night, and they dragged on. The chamber was full of Members who were only too happy to recount their personal experiences. For men who had not been on active service the speeches became a bore. Debates often ended in the early morning by which time the daily papers had gone to bed. By the time the evening editions were on the streets the events of another day claimed attention. So good 'human stories' were missed—such as the fight of one M.P. to obtain a pension for a widow in West Ham who had been refused a pension because her husband was shot for desertion and had been forced to seek Poor Law Relief for herself and her children.

No-one bothered to report that it was well-known during the war that orders were given to the Machine Gun Corps that if any men were found deserting from their posts they were to be shot down, '. . . that is to say the death penalty was to be executed not by courts martial but by those responsible for discipline in the field'. One M.P., Captain Gunston, actually claimed that when volunteers were required for 'shooting parties' they were 'never lacking'. He thought it was because 'on the whole the men were keener on the death penalty than the officers.' And Lieutenant-Colonel Reginald Applin, who had won the D.S.O. in 1902, announced that he had served in the 1914–18 war 'with a very gallant corps which had no death penalty. When a man—or an officer—was considered to have let those people down, a court martial was held by the men around the camp fire at night. Sentence was passed and the man was executed on the next occasion by his judges.'

Colonel Applin, who had commanded the 14th Hussars, had also served in the Machine Gun Corps and was the author of a book on machine-gun tactics.

Different methods used by firing squads were discussed. Incidents were described of condemned men being covered by a white sheet with an aiming point on it (this tallied with another report from Salonika where a yellow shroud had been used[1]).

Miss Ellen Wilkinson, the Member for Jarrow, recalled visiting the home of a widow who had just heard that her son had been shot. It was towards the end of the war and although the Army had not notified her, she had learned the facts from men returning from France. When General Knox described his experiences during the Kerensky offensive and the consequences of not applying the death penalty 'Red Ellen' rounded on him.

'If the deserters from Kerensky's army had been shot—and I am quoting from Kerensky's own book—they would have to shoot something like one fifth of the entire army.' she said. 'You cannot get away from the fact that what the Bolsheviks did in order to restore the morale of the army—apart from the reintroduction of the death penalty—was to institute a terrific propaganda in the ranks to make the soldiers believe what they were fighting for. It had been destroyed by propaganda and this was used to restore it.'

The Labour Party had declared its full support for Thurtle's campaign in 1925. That year he stated that thirty of the soldiers executed during the war had been 'lads under twenty-one years of age, too young to be regarded as citizens of this country, but young enough to be shot in cold blood because their nerves failed them.'[2]

He praised the attitude of Sir Ian Hamilton during the Dardanelles campaign and cited the case of the five Worcestershire soldiers who were reprieved.

'I am bound to say,' declared Thurtle, 'in reading through

---

[1] Wilkins, in *Mysteries of the Great War*, describes the sheet as a 'yellow San Benito'.
[2] *Hansard*.

the routine orders in connection with France and Flanders, that I never detected anything like the same humanitarian spirit which I found in the orders issued under Sir Ian Hamilton.'

Pointing out that the Australians did not execute soldiers he asked: 'Is the Minister going to rise in his place to-day and say that Australian troops may be trusted to fight with courage and determination without the dread death penalty hanging over them, but that British troops are not to be trusted?'

This brought a colourful if irrelevant reminiscence from Lieutenant-Colonel Dalrymple White, who stated that among the Australians were many confirmed deserters who hid in the woods.

'They were big, burly fellows, fond of gambling at Crown and Anchor,' he declared. 'They were armed with revolvers. In two cases at least we had Australians who were murdered by these desperadoes. They used to boast openly that gambling and making money was a better game than being killed in the line. They were very stout men, always breaking away from their escorts on the way to Rouen and in more than one case they managed to break out of Rouen Prison.'

George Lansbury, too, joined in the debate, with the disquieting revelation that two men in the South Lancashire Regiment, who had gone absent as their unit was entraining at Waterloo, were captured in England and taken to France and shot there. Subsequently this was confirmed by Thurtle who discovered that the men had been caught at Woolwich two months after deserting.

Occasionally an element of humour crept into the debates, such as the tale of a British Sergeant and four men who, after being pinned down in a shell hole among their dead comrades for two days and two nights, decided to crawl forward and give themselves up to the first Germans they encountered. As they crept round the corner of a trench they met a German N.C.O. and six men. Both parties immediately put up their hands and a furious argument ensued as to who was surrendering to whom. In the end it was decided that it would be safer for the Germans to go back to the British lines and the sergeant was later decorated for making the capture.

Colonel Applin introduced a flavour of bygone days to the House by citing an old Zulu custom in defence of the death penalty for sleeping on duty. 'A man who has been found sleeping is brought before his chief; and the chief turns to his induna (sub-chief) and says: What is the penalty? and the reply is "death". A man steps forward and puts his spear through him then and there.'

Less entertaining but more pertinent was a speech by Mr Gerald Hurst, the distinguished lawyer and Member for Manchester's Moss Side, who said that he had defended soldiers in 'the East' on charges of falling asleep at their post. After he had secured their acquittal 'all field officers in my division were called together and told by the General Officer Commanding that they were not to defend soldiers any more at courts martial.'

Mr Hurst, who had been commissioned into the 7th Manchester Regiment, was not only a highly experienced barrister —later he was knighted and became a K.C.—but a much-travelled soldier who had seen service in the Sudan, Gallipoli, Sinai and Flanders. He was not the sort of man who could be ignored. If he said something it could be taken as correct. His intervention was typical of the part played in the debates by the lawyers on both sides of the House. Almost without exception, in the post-war years, those who had seen courts martial on active service expressed concern and dismay.

The question of soldiers who fell asleep on duty was a familiar one to the House. Once when driving it home, Thurtle had made an impassioned plea:

'If this House could be kept up for ninety-six hours without any sleep at all, I will guarantee that, willy-nilly, seventy-five or eighty per cent of the Members would be falling into deep slumber,' he thundered.

From the other side of the House came a sepulchral voice:

'Not if there was a death penalty attached.'

*   *   *

The first major breakthrough by Thurtle and his supporters came in 1928, three months after the death of Sir Douglas Haig at the age of 67. They were surprised to discover that the Government had included eight amendments to the Army Act, which removed the death penalty for:

Leaving a commanding officer to go in search of plunder.
Forcing a safeguard.
Striking a sentinel.
Breaking into a house in search of plunder.

209

Sleeping or being drunk on sentry duty.

Striking or offering violence to a superior officer.

Disobeying an order in such a manner as to show defiance.

Altering or interfering with air signals without authority.

Mr Morrison pointed out acidly that 'we have been told in past debates that the abolition of the death penalty in such cases would have been prejudicial to discipline, that it would injure the fighting morale, and that these (penalties) had to be retained as a deterrent.'

Clement Attlee, speaking in support of the amendments, was assailed for not having altered the Army Act when Labour was in power. (He had actually voted against a move to abolish the death penalty soon after the war in which he had served as an artillery major.)

He confessed frankly that the Labour Party had been faced with the annual Army Act debate soon after taking office and had, like the Liberals and Tories before them, taken the advice of a committee which had been able to consult the leading military experts of the day. Now views were changing, and he invited the Government to do away completely with the death penalty for disciplinary offences.

Mr Duff Cooper, speaking for the Government, revealed why, although unwilling to go as far as Attlee had suggested, they were prepared to abolish capital punishment for the crimes listed. As Attlee had said, the military members of the Army Council and the civil members as well, no longer felt that this would endanger discipline. But there was another point to be considered, and there seems little doubt that it was what had prompted the reforms. The great number of offences for which a soldier could be shot had been a gift to propaganda experts. 'I am not referring to any Members opposite,' said Duff Cooper, 'but to an entirely different type of agitation from the Communist Party.'

The year 1928 was also notable for the embarrassment caused to both sides in the argument by the intervention of Brigadier Crozier. In an article in the *Daily Express* he boldly expressed the view that inflicting the death sentence was most unpleasant and that the sooner nations got together and stopped making war the better. However, if executions were going to be carried out in future conflicts, then 'I suggest that a paragraph be inserted in the Army Act to the effect that, whenever possible, executions be carried out by machine-gun fire. It is not fair for men to have to be put to such a terrible strain as is entailed by the execution of a comrade in any case, but, in these days, to neglect to rely on the scientific accuracy of machinery is short-sighted and inhuman.'

At least Crozier was consistent in his views. He saw no reason why, if ordinary soldiers were to be shot for cowardice, generals should not suffer a like fate for a similar offence.

'If cowardice is a triumph of matter over mind, then I know of one general who should undoubtedly have been tried for cowardice, instead of which he was promoted.'

It had to be admitted that the argument about the accountability of generals had its points.

In the following year, 1929, when an attempt to remove the death penalty for cowardice failed, Viscount Sandon, Under-Secretary for Air, speaking in support of the Government, pointed out that it was easy to put all the blame for disasters at the front on the generals at the top but 'occasionally it was the fault of the enemy!'

He recalled his own experience during the Third Battle of Ypres when a battery was badly hit by German shells.

'It was that area between the St Julien Road and Military Bridge and I remember being summoned up to take over because every officer there, and a good many men as well, had been killed only two or three hours before. It was a unit I was with only a short time and was one of the finest . . . but honourable Members can imagine what the state of the morale would be in any collection of human beings in circumstances of that character. When I arrived, the first thing that happened was that the sergeant came and said, "I am not feeling well, can I go to the wagon lines?" I let the man go although there was only one other non-commissioned officer left. Shortly afterwards he came up, with some other men and they also said they were not feeling very well and that they wanted to go back to the lines. Then, of course, I realized what was going on. I am making no reflection on these men . . . conditions in that sector at that moment were worse than could be borne by any human being, unless there was some authority, of which they were aware, acting on their minds to keep them at their post.'

After this moderate attempt to rationalize the retention of the death penalty, the words of Duff Cooper, then Financial Secretary of the Treasury, struck a harsh note out of keeping with his tone the previous year.

'There is such a thing as cowardice,' he stated, bleakly, 'and it ought to be punished severely.'

In 1930, however, with a Labour Government in power, the mood of the House was changing. Twelve years had passed since the signing of the Armistice and the British Army had been reduced to a fraction of the mighty instrument it had been in 1918. Even so, Ernest Thurtle did not have it all his own way. The new Secretary of State for War, Mr Tom Shaw, found his loyalties divided. He was unable to persuade the Army Council to agree with the move to drop the death penalty entirely and suggested putting off a decision for a year. Thurtle would not be appeased. He circulated a vivid pamphlet entitled *Shootings at Dawn*. In it he quoted the experience of a soldier who attended the execution of a sergeant and two corporals of a Kitchener battalion of the Durham Light Infantry, probably those mentioned in the 1921 debate as having been shot because of the determination of divisional headquarters to make an example of someone. It took place in bitter weather at Rollecourt, near St Pol. According to a witness the men arrive in manacles which were removed so that they could take off their tunics before being tied to stakes. Three firing parties of twelve inflicted the penalty, aiming at envelopes pinned over the hearts of the condemned men. The witness had the unpleasant job of burning straw which had been heaped near each post to sop up bloodstains.

Also included in the pamphlet was the statement of a former private in the 1st Battalion, the Buffs, who formed part of the firing squad when one of his friends was shot in a double execution:

'We were told that the only humane thing to do was to shoot straight. The two men were led out blindfolded, tied to posts driven into the ground, and then we received our orders by sign from our officer, so that the condemned men should not hear us getting ready. Our officer felt it very much, as he, like me, knew the fellow years before. The other fellow I never knew but his case was every bit as sad as he was only a boy.'

The pamphlet helped to swing faint hearts behind new legislation aimed at abolishing the death penalty for cowardice which was the subject of a motion on 3 April. A counter-proposal aimed at rejecting the changes in the Army Act was proposed by Lieutenant-Colonel Sir Lambert Ward but this amendment was rejected by 288 votes to 165. Thurtle had won the first round. It was then proposed to drop the death penalty for the offences of leaving a guard or picket without orders, intentionally giving a false alarm, and leaving a post without being properly relieved. But the Old Brigade had not given up yet. Lieutenant-Colonel Sir George Courthope moved an amendment with the object of retaining the ultimate sanction for these offences. Drama followed. In the first case the House had voted on a motion that 'Those words be inserted'.

The 288 Noes had won the day. Now, in the noise and confusion of the chamber, no one seemed to have grasped that the form of the question being 'put' had changed and the chairman construed the 288 Noes as carrying Courthope's amendment. The House dissolved into uproar until Mr Emanuel Shinwell, a future Minister of War, managed to make himself heard.

'My point of order, with great respect,' he said 'is that the assumption was that the question was being put in precisely the same form as the previous question had been put.'

He pressed on calmly despite loud interruptions.

'I say it was a perfectly well-founded assumption, and it was obvious that the honourable and right honourable Gentlemen on the other side were as much victims of that assumption as the honourable Members on this side.'

Nevertheless the vote was allowed to stand and Members began to drift from the Chamber. Thurtle then proposed that the death sentence should be dropped for desertion also, as it was almost indistinguishable from cowardice—a man who left the trenches during an attack and reappeared the next day could face either charge. This time both sides were careful to note the wording of the motion and the abolitionists won by 219 votes to 135. No-one could deny, however, that the result of a vital part of the debate was the opposite of what was intended, and on 7 April the amendment that had foxed the House was brought up again.

This time Sir George Courthope was not so fortunate. He made a desperate attempt to persuade the Commons to retain the death penalty for soldiers who left their post before being properly relieved. Without it, he said, men who were lying out in no-man's-land might be tempted to quit vital listening posts, adding a graphic description:

'The man on duty of this kind found himself lying soaked to the skin and chilled to the bone, straining every nerve of eye and ear for sight or sound which might indicate danger threatening his comrades in the trenches behind him. Every sound may seem to be the movement of an enemy advancing upon him. Later in the season when the plant growth took place, it was remarkable to notice the wind among the poppies. It sounded like hosts of men creeping on.'

By removing the threat of the death penalty from an individual in this position the House were 'taking from him one of the things that helps him stick to his job.'

Lieutenant-Colonel Sir Godfrey Dalrymple-White, who had joined the Grenadier Guards in 1885, was very concerned about the effect of any relaxation of the Army Act on the North-West Frontier 'where we fight against very cunning and crafty foes, whether Waziris or Afridis; men who can creep in on the sleeping troops'. If the amendment to the law were carried through there was nothing to prevent a whole outpost, including the officer who commanded it, leaving the scene and opening the way for 'the wild tribes'.

Neither Sir George nor Sir Godfrey made any impression and the death penalty for the three offences—leaving a guard, intentionally giving a false alarm and leaving a post without proper relief—was dropped and replaced by imprisonment.

Even then the struggle was not over. In the Lords on 16 April, Viscount FitzAlan moved to leave out the amendments to the Army Act which had been approved by the Commons. If men had only gaol in front of them, he said, the temptation to acts of cowardice would be, in many cases, almost irresistible. Two trump cards were then played. A little old man with a rosy pink face and silver moustache arose—Field-Marshal Viscount Plumer, who as Herbert Charles Onslow Plumer had joined the 65th Foot (York and Lancaster Regiment) after leaving Eton in 1876. 'Old Plum' as he was known behind his back had won a considerable reputation during the First World War as a man who took care of his troops. This was due, in part, to the fact that after he took over command of the Second Army in May, 1915, his men remained on the defensive at Ypres, having their hands full enough with the guardianship of the Salient. After this passive role in 1916, and when it seemed the rear areas had become almost permanent, Plumer had sprung the mines at Messines. Later he took over the responsibility of the major effort in the Third Battle of Ypres that autumn. His earlier reputation stood him in good stead when scapegoats were being sought for the shambles which culminated in the terrible struggle on the approaches to Passchendaele. Gough, who had been responsible only for the opening phase of the attack, bore the brunt of the criticism. Plumer was happily removed to Italy just as things reached their worst. In producing him to speak for the Army, the opponents of reform knew well that they had a protagonist whose laurels were unsullied by ugly accusations of ruthlessness.

At 73 the old warrior's voice was thin but the message was clear enough. 'Old Plum' regarded the power to inflict the death penalty as essential to a Commander-in-Chief. Most emphatically, he declared, the punishment of imprisonment was not severe enough. It gave an offender a path to safety. In his eyes, the only deterrent for a man who might wilfully endanger the lives of his comrades was the knowledge that whereas they might 'incur' a glorious and honourable death at the hands of the enemy, he, if convicted by court martial, would die a dishonourable and shameful death.[3]

He was confident that if the law, as amended by the Commons, remained unchanged the effect in the future would be to prejudice morale and lower the high standard which had hitherto been the proud tradition of the British Army, however distant that future might be.

The Field-Marshal, who had seen his first action against the Egyptians at Tel-el Kebir in 1882, resumed his seat to applause. Attention now turned to a more substantial figure whom the Lords had no difficulty in hearing—Field-Marshal Viscount Allenby, the conqueror of Palestine, known as 'The Bull'. Allenby argued that the death penalty indicated the enormity of an offence and created a moral atmosphere which caused a soldier to abhor such crimes and, indeed, anything that might affect his honour as a soldier. That moral influence would be undermined if there was no death penalty. He stressed that the offences for which he wished to retain capital punishment could endanger the lives of a great number of men, cause the failure of military operations and possibly bring about a national disaster. Any action that reduced the abhorrence with which offences had traditionally been regarded, would have a serious effect on discipline. He sat down amid much nodding of heads and appreciative murmuring. Lord Thomson, the Secretary of State for Air, who spoke for the Government, seems to have been

[3] *The Times* report of the House of Lords debate of 16 April, 1930.

215

put out by the illustrious opposition, although he argued that the laws had been designed originally for troops bordering on the criminal classes and that many aircraftsmen were better educated than the officers at Waterloo. He rambled into an irrelevant dissertation in which he likened a deserter to a man who played cards with his friends all night, won a great deal of their money and cleared off in order to enjoy it. It was not an inspiring performance. The Government was defeated by forty-five votes to twelve.

The triumph of the noble Lords and the Field-Marshals did not last long. The Commons were outraged. One Member described the action of the Upper House as 'a piece of arrogance, impertinence and outstanding audacity'.

On 19 April, their Lordships were required to reconsider their position. The Marquess of Salisbury indignantly defended the country's two most distinguished living soldiers from the remarks made in the Commons. Lord Parmoor, Lord President of the Council, regretted that the noble Marquess had thought fit to refer to a speech made by an individual in 'another place'. And Lord Thomson, somewhat apologetically, said that in view of the great authority of the Field-Marshals their remarks would be considered by the competent authorities between then and the next debate of the Army Act . . . the upshot of it all being that the Lords agreed to drop their opposition to the reform.

Thurtle had won. Although certain rare circumstances, such as being proved to be a traitor or spy, could cost an offender his life, a soldier who cracked under the strain of modern war was no longer liable to be led out at dawn to face the rifles of his comrades.

T. E. Lawrence had supported Thurtle earlier with a letter in which he had written: 'I have run too far and too often (but never fast enough to please me at the time) under fire to throw a stone at the fearfullest creature.'[4]

Now, snubbing Allenby who had been his titular superior during Lawrence's operations in the Middle East, he wrote of the reforms:

'I feel it is a blessed victory. The old state of the law hurt me. It was such a damnable judgement upon our own flesh and blood.'

[4] Thurtle, *Time's Winged Chariot*.

19

The Lost Statistic

Throughout all the debates on the Army death penalty, the things that weren't said were often the most significant. Only by constant questioning and probing were the facts eventually brought to light. All except one. In none of the debates did anyone mention 'The Missing Statistic'. According to the 1922 details of the war effort of the British Empire, only three men were shot for mutiny, two in the period ending 30 September, 1917, and one during the following twelve months. The figures were forty-seven men short of the truth. All of them were Indians.

Early in 1915, the 5th Light Infantry were the only Regular battalion in the Singapore garrison. The British troops had sailed for Europe and the remaining units were volunteers and police, plus a few artillerymen. No-one in authority was particularly concerned. The only other major power in the Far East, Japan, was an ally of Britain and the main task facing the Indian soldiers was guarding interned German civilians. These individuals gave little trouble in their quarters in Tanglin Barracks. They had been very popular with the European community before 1914 and their hospitality was renowned.

The 15 February dawned apparently just another fine day in the colony, enlivened in the afternoon by the sound of fire-crackers as the inhabitants of Chinatown celebrated a public holiday. Only a few men with sharp ears detected the heavier reports of rifle shots. Gradually the news spread—the 5th Light Infantry had mutinied. They had tried to free the German prisoners. Two officers and a warder had been killed at the gaol. A civilian and his wife had been shot, and the doctor from the General Hospital had been ambushed while driving in one of the island's few cars and murdered in front of his wife.

In fairness to the Germans, only a handful took advantage of the opportunity to escape, even though it was later learned that they had already begun tunnelling their way out. The mutineers dispersed after failing to seize their colonel who barricaded himself in his bungalow with his second-in-command and the latter's wife. The crew of H.M.S. *Cadmus*, a sloop in the harbour, rescued them the following day, assisted by various detachments. With the aid of a highly disciplined body of Japanese civilians, order was restored. About half of the 5th Light Infantry were discovered to have remained loyal but they had been without arms when the rebels struck. They helped to round up the dissident members of their battalion. Six hundred men were recaptured, many of them in mosques where they had taken refuge. Not all of them were held to be fully responsible for their actions but in the courts martial which followed two hundred men were given severe sentences. Of these, forty-seven were condemned to death. The punishment, it was announced, would be carried out in public. Furthermore, Mansoor, an Indian who kept a coffee shop in the Pasir Panjong where the mutineers had met regularly, would be hanged in public first.

For some reason, when the gallows had been half built, the authorities had second thoughts. Mansoor was executed in the gaol after all. But the soldiers, all Rajput Mussulmans, were destined to meet their fate in a most theatrical fashion. The stage was the space outside the perimeter wall on the Outram Road side of the Criminal Prison on Pearls Hill. Opposite, on a site which was levelled in the 1920s for a new general hospital, was a gentle slope providing a natural terrace for spectators. On the afternoon of 21 April, thousands of Europeans, Eurasians, Chinese, Malays and Indians gathered there. The crowd contained quite a few white women. All eyes were concentrated on a long row of heavy posts which had been driven into the ground a few feet from the prison wall.

The 'privilege' of shooting the mutineers—for as such it was described—was given to the units who had suffered casualties in the fighting. Ten men of the Royal Artillery were the first to march into the middle of a square formed by police and other troops on the 'floor' of the amphitheatre. Soon afterwards the only officers condemned to death were marched out between an escort of gigantic Sikh policemen with fixed bayonets. Neither Subedar Dunde Khan nor Jemadar Chisti

Khan showed any sign of fear. Although in plain clothes, they marched onto their last parade as smartly as if they had been in dress uniform. The police tied their wrists and ankles behind two central posts and the prisoners stood to attention while the sentences were read out in Malay, Chinese and Urdu. Previous honourable service to the Raj by the men's family was proclaimed. As no blindfolds were used the men had no option but to watch the firing squad obey their orders. According to an eyewitness the arms drill of the artillerymen was impeccable.

'On the command "Fire!" one man pitched forward; the other seemed to lean almost nonchalantly against the post to which he was tied. Then slowly he slid to the ground.'[1]

As the echoes of the volley died away, a shrill, melancholy wail arose from the prison where the other mutineers were held.

As the bodies were removed by gaoled comrades of the dead officers most of the crowd on the hill, who had watched in silence, dispersed. Others remained and sought better positions. They did not wish to miss the rest of the performance which went on throughout the afternoon. Before each execution the spectators reappeared and a huge gathering was waiting when the finale was enacted. A long file of men of the Malay Volunteer Force, which had suffered heavy casualties in the capture of the rebels, marched in column onto the execution ground and turned to face the posts which were eight paces away. Then into the arena came the condemned men, shabby and insignificant between the files of bearded and turbaned Sikhs. There were twenty-one prisoners in all. The firing squad totalled 105 men, five rifles to each of the mutineers.

It was too much to expect that such a large number of doomed individuals would stand quietly while the verdict on each one of them was read out three times. One distraught wretch gave a low wail and in a few moments all twenty-one of them were swaying at their bonds, praying and weeping, drowning the words of the sentences. In dismay the officer in charge of the firing party took it upon himself to get the business over with. But his commands could not be heard above the uproar. Some rifles came up hesitantly to the 'Present' and a ragged volley rang out. A few of the prisoners fell and lay still, some dropped writhing and many stood staring at their execu-

---

[1] This account is based primarily on papers, documents and photographs placed with the Imperial War Museum by A. H. Dickinson, C.M.G., O.B.E., an officer in the Straits Settlement Police at the time.

tioners, shouting and cursing. Scattered shots put paid to them as the firing squad carried on, some even stepped a pace or two from the ranks to deliver a second shot at closer range.

The last act of the scene was carried out to the prolonged farewell wails from the gaol as warders walked up and down the line of posts, mercifully shooting any man still alive. From the onlookers there came not a murmur of protest in any language.

An inquiry into the reasons for the mutiny revealed that the British officers had been at loggerheads and some had formed a clique against their Colonel, a man of weak personality.[2] The two Indian officers had exploited the situation and so had the other ranks. Dissidents passing through Singapore to and from India had done the rest and the ringleaders had persuaded half the battalion to follow them on their disastrous course. What was left of the battalion was re-formed and the 5th Light Infantry, which had a long and distinguished history, including campaigns in the Arakan in 1824, in the Sikh Wars and in Afghanistan, sailed for service in the Cameroons.

Somehow the compiler of statistics overlooked the forty-seven mutineers when he came to fill in the figures of men executed for disciplinary offences during the First World War.

And no-one else missed them.

[2] The Dickinson papers contain a copy of the original report.

PART IV

1939-45

'It is very wrong to disturb large numbers of healthy normal men and women by asking the questions in which psychiatrists specialize.'

WINSTON CHURCHILL

20

The Generals try again

When World War II began there were still 120,000 veterans of the 1914–18 conflict in receipt of pensions for primary psychiatric disability or who had received final settlements for illness of that nature. Many of these victims had shown symptoms long after the Armistice. There were men like the cab driver who had served in the artillery for four years without showing signs of strain. A slight collision brought about his complete collapse and it was discovered that he was suffering from total amnesia as far as his war service was concerned.[1] And a case is on record of a former infantryman with four years' active service in Gallipoli and France who did not crack until forty years afterwards when he spent three days crouched behind a settee which he identified with a trench. With scores of examples to draw on, the British medical profession was infinitely better informed as to what to expect in 1939 than it had been in 1914. Many doctors with front line experience had shown considerable courage in refusing to hide the abuses of the stringent disciplinary methods enforced in the trenches, a leading expert stating that men who were shot at dawn 'were in many cases suffering from an acute neurosis'.[2] As far as the Army was concerned, nearly all the generals and senior officers had experience of trench warfare and most were concerned to see that the heavy losses caused by futile attacks in Flanders and on the Somme were not repeated. The soldiers too, thanks to the cinema, had a much better idea of what to expect. Unvarnished eye-witness stories of World War I and the work of a number of pacifist organizations had added a healthy element of intelligent suspicion to their reasoning.

[1] Miller, *The Neuroses in War.*

[2] Dr J. R. Rees, quoted by Ahrenfeldt, *Psychiatry in the British Army in the Second World War.*

A much more careful system of screening men for different arms of the service was applied and, with the introduction of National Service before the outbreak of hostilities, there was none of the chaos associated with the rush of Kitchener volunteers in 1914. As the British retreated before the German Blitzkrieg in 1940, both Regular and Territorial troops put up a sterling performance against a better equipped foe, despite a gruelling introduction to tactical bombing. The Dunkirk perimeter was held without the need of the death penalty. Although stories still persist of panics and even of two summary executions on the beaches, any evidence of the indiscipline of a few is completely outweighed by the conduct of the great majority.[3] Although it was not known at the time, one of the most significant failures in morale was in élite German troops hit by a handful of British tanks and infantry at Arras on 21 May. Exaggerated reports of the strength of the forces attacking the 7th Panzer and SS Death's Head Division induced a state of ultra-caution which had far-reaching effects on the campaign and possibly on the war.[4]

The British Army recovered remarkably quickly from its unhappy experiences in France (and in Norway earlier) but after welcome victories in the Middle East a severe crisis arose following Axis successes in the desert.

The Churchillian view of enforcing discipline was traditional. He believed that a soldier who failed in his duty should be shot. When Sir Charles Wilson, later Lord Moran, showed him the manuscript of his book *The Anatomy of Courage*, in which he described his experiences as a medical officer in an infantry battalion in the trenches, the Prime Minister condemned it. He said it might discourage young soldiers. The book was turned down by Macmillan's at the time and did not appear until the war was almost over.[5]

In 1942, Churchill was faced with the duty of putting his avowed ruthlessness to the test. At the end of May, the German Afrika Korps and their Italian allies, struck against the Gazala line in Cyrenaica. Within a month, Tobruk, which had been regarded as impregnable, had fallen, and the Eighth Army had been harried back across the Western Desert. The incidence of absenteeism, particularly in the rear areas, reached a dis-

[3] See Sargent and Slater, 'Acute War Neuroses which occurred at Dunkirk', *Lancet* (2) 1940.
[4] See Liddell Hart (Ed.), *The Rommel Papers* and Guderian, *Panzer Leader*.
[5] Moran, *Churchill : The Struggle for Survival*.

quieting level. General Sir Claude Auchinleck, Commander-in-Chief, Middle East, requested that the death penalty should be restored for desertion in the face of the enemy and cowardice. He believed that if it were known that he possessed the power to order executions it would provide a 'salutary deterrent to those men to whom the alternative of prison to the hardships of battle conveyed neither fear nor stigma.' General Sir Harold Alexander, who replaced 'The Auk' in August, declared himself also in favour of shooting deserters.[6]

It was a difficult decision to have to make when the existence of Britain was at stake. Memories must have gone back to the late night debates of the Twenties. But in the end, no doubt after consulting the Prime Minister, the executive committee of the Army Council turned down the suggestion unanimously. Whereas they did not doubt the military desirability of this severe measure it was impossible to restore it—for political reasons.

Unable to turn to instant solutions to improve morale—the most effective of which would have been an outright victory—the authorities had to resort to other measures to stop the drain in manpower. By the middle of the year the proportion of psychiatric cases among battle casualties had risen to ten per cent. Most of these were simple exhaustion cases and with the setting up of an Army Rest Centre run by the 200th Field Ambulance it was able to restore six out of ten men to the front line between July and November, 1942. The effectiveness of similar treatment had been noted earlier during the siege of Tobruk when some psychiatric cases were treated on the open beach and others in a deep concrete bunker, in a hill which had a heavy anti-aircraft gun on its summit. About half of the Tobruk patients were sent back to the line but it was admitted that not all of them were fully stable.[7] Apart from medical aid and the arrival of better equipment, a new commander for the Eighth Army, General Sir Bernard Montgomery, applied his own therapy. It has become fashionable to sneer at what have been called Montgomery's 'gimmicks'. Yet it is doubtful if those who look down on his elementary psychology would rather have seen the death penalty in its place. The priority which 'Monty' gave to restoring the morale of the Eighth

[6] Ahrenfeldt, op. cit.
[7] Ahrenfeldt.

Army was the first step which took him along the road to the ranks of the truly Great Captains.

Montgomery, who was as hard on his subordinate commanders as he was sensitive to the requirements of his troops, had not forgotten his own experiences when on the receiving end of enemy attacks, both at Le Cateau in 1914,[8] and as G.S.O.1 to a formation which was involved in one of the debâcles in 1918. It would have been interesting to see how he might have tackled the serious deterioration in morale which was observed in Malta during the same year.

Lieutenant-General Sir William Dobbie, the Governor of Malta, was looked upon by Churchill as a latter-day Ironside, filled with a religious zeal which led the Prime Minister to liken him to General Gordon.[9] With these virtues of antiquity went some old-fashioned drawbacks. During the terrible bombing attacks which went on with variations in intensity for more than eighteen months, the nerves of the garrison of the island were fully tested. In such a restricted area there were few places where a psychiatrist could be of greater help. Yet no specialist psychiatrist was requested and there was 'intense hostility towards psychiatry on the part of the medical and non-medical authorities'.[10] It may be summed up in the wording of an instruction posted in all battery positions when the bombing was at its height in March, 1942. Anxiety neurosis, said the notice, was the term employed by the medical profession to 'commercialize' fear, and that if a soldier was a man he would not permit his self-respect to admit an anxiety neurosis or to show fear. In this month, when Malta was being bombed four times a day by forces of one hundred bombers, an observant medical officer suggested that rest camps for gunners should be set up. This advice was declined and the same officer noted that one in four men of the garrison showed a pathological degree of response to air attack which got worse in April.

The attitude of the authorities was not helped by the knowledge that Churchill himself had little time for psychiatrists and had stated in 1942:

'I am sure it would be sensible to restrict as much as possible the work of these gentlemen, who are capable of doing an immense amount of harm with what may very easily degene-

8 Montgomery, *Memoirs*.
9 Churchill, *The Second World War*.
10 Ahrenfeldt.

rate into charlatanry . . . it is very wrong to disturb large numbers of healthy normal men and women by asking the questions in which psychiatrists specialize.'[11]

Sadly, the one man who might have made the best use of a psychiatrist's advice was General Dobbie himself. During April the fearful strain became too much for him and he cracked. Field-Marshal Lord Gort was sent to replace him. Even so, it was more than a year before a psychiatric specialist was brought into the island. By then, July, 1943, medical and surgical specialists were reporting that nearly all officers in Malta were suffering from 'ineffectiveness and loss of grip, great sleepiness and jumpiness' and that many of them were drinking heavily. The conditions proved once more the vulnerability of the 'Iron Man' approach to modern war.

Yet another example was Major-General Orde Charles Wingate. Like many martial mystics, Wingate believed that if a man was tough physically and strong morally, he would be immune from illness. He preached this doctrine to the men who took part in the first Chindit raid behind the Japanese lines early in 1943. As a result a number of his officers failed to enforce necessary preventive measures and disastrous losses were suffered from disease—malaria and dysentery in particular. When the survivors of the 1943 expedition were interviewed by medical experts afterwards many 'other ranks' were in a highly nervous condition and blamed the organizers of the operation, 'each man attributing his own survival entirely to his own efforts plus an element of luck.' Wingate's doctrine of the 'Iron Man' was exploded when he caught typhoid.[12]

The nature of the country, as well as the periods of intense fighting and the unhappy start to the war, made fighting in Burma particularly arduous. After the first campaign in the Arakan, one medical expert classified the whole of the 14th Indian Division, as a psychiatric casualty.[13] It was fortunate, therefore, that in General Sir William Slim, the Fourteenth Army had a commander who was perhaps unique among senior officers in admitting his own human weaknesses, a factor which seems to have helped him make allowances for others. Slim, a natural psychologist, did in his quiet way what Mont-

[11] Ahrenfeldt.
[12] Ahrenfeldt. See also Mosley, *Gideon Goes to War*.
[13] Lieutenant-Colonel A. A. White, Psychiatrist to Eastern Command.

gomery did more obviously. His nickname of 'Uncle Bill' reflects the success of his methods. No efforts were spared to reassure the troops that if they were wounded they could rely on prompt treatment and evacuation—a vital factor in both world wars—and to treat men whose nerves broke; psychiatrists, with drugs carried by mule pannier, tended men actually in the front line on occasions. Seven out of ten of the British psychiatric cases and six out of ten of the Indian casualties of this nature were thus returned to active service with their units throughout the Burma campaign.

In any theatre where preparations to deal with psychiatric patients were neglected, circumstances eventually made their introduction inevitable. According to the type of warfare—desert, jungle, mountainous or European, armoured or infantry—specialist treatment had to be made available in order to stop wastage of manpower.

The absence of a psychiatric adviser and trained orderlies when the British First Army took part in the invasion of North Africa in November, 1942, was recognized as a mistake at the outset and two qualified doctors were sent out within a month. In January one of their tasks was to report on the condition of a brigade which panicked—as it turned out this was put down to a mass reaction by troops who contained a high proportion of dull, backward and neurotic men—after three days of mortar bombardment, heavy casualties and insufficient food and sleep.[14] From 1943 onward much greater care was taken in the Mediterranean theatre, corps exhaustion centres being established. While at Salerno, in Italy, where some of the fiercest fighting of the war occurred, forward psychiatric centres were set up to 'avoid secondary deterioration and wastage of manpower'.

The British forces which took part in the invasion of Europe in 1944 were well equipped to deal with troops who fell victims to nervous illness during the intense fighting. An advanced section of a psychiatric hospital had started to function at the beginning of July and by the middle of the month divisional and corps exhaustion centres had been established. In the Second Army, which was engaged in an unrelenting battle to draw the German armour on to its front and free the

---

[14] Ahrenfeldt; see also *The Official History of World War II, Mediterranean and Middle East*, Vol. 4.

Americans for the thrust from the south, the proportion of psychiatric cases (mostly exhaustion) among battle casualties reached 20 per cent during the period July to September. But two out of three men were returned to their fighting units. Deserters were numerous and, with the normal sentence being three years' penal servitude, field punishment camps were filled to overflowing in the early part of the campaign. About a quarter of these men, it was noted, had already seen considerable active service.

It is useful at this point to show comparative desertion figures for the two wars. In each case the period is for the twelve months up to 30 September of the year indicated unless otherwise stated.

Year	Event	Desertions per 1,000 men under arms	Year	Event	Desertions per 1,000 men under arms
1915 (from Aug 4 1914)	First and Second Ypres; Loos; Gallipoli	20.7	1940	Norway; Dunkirk	4.48
			1941	Fall of Greece; Crete	10.05
1916	Somme	9.19			
1917	Late Somme; Arras; Messines; Start of Third Ypres	7.41	1942	Gazala; fall of Tobruk; Burma defeats	8.49
1918	Passchendaele; Cambrai; March 21– August 8	7.41	1943	Alamein; Tunis; Sicily	5.90
1919	Victory offensive; Army of Occupation	7.99	1944	D-Day; Kohima; Falaise	6.19
			1945	Battle for Germany; Defeat of Japan	6.24

From this it would appear that the harsher measures of World War I had even less effect than the disciplinary regulations of World War II. If one takes into account the fact that the documentation of the civil and military population was much more comprehensive in the war against Hitler—explaining the high figure for 1915 which was probably a phenomenon ensuing from the Kitchener volunteers rush—there may be said to be little difference.

Undoubtedly the increased care given to the selection of

personnel for fighting units was a policy which paid off. Where formations were strung together haphazardly their performance was unreliable as was seen in North Africa on occasions. An experiment in 1944 gives some indication of the high standard insisted on. In order to ease the desperate shortage of infantry, two thousand men were posted from the Pioneer Corps to an infantry division for training and aptitude tests. Many of these men had orginally been transferred from other arms to the Corps on the recommendation of psychiatrists. Despite the crying need for men, only three per cent of the Pioneers were considered to be suitable as infantrymen at the end of the ten weeks of training.[15] Perhaps the greatest testimony to the efficiency of the British system came from a study made by American researchers who studied troops in the Mediterranean theatre of war. They estimated that an American infantryman became ineffective after between two hundred and two hundred and forty combat days. A British foot soldier could be expected to last four hundred fighting days. The Americans, however, had special problems not entirely related to selection.[16]

If the United States had gone through four years of war instead of the few months in which they saw serious combat in World War I, their leaders might have taken a different attitude to the men under their command. Despite the heavy casualties they had suffered in 1917–18, the theory persisted that all American soldiers were brave by nature. In the Mediterranean, the Far East and in Europe, there were instances of their generals falling back on the Sikh War and Crimean tactics of using the courage of the soldiers as a bludgeon. Hence the neglect of the use of specialized armour on the D-Day beaches and the slaughter at Tarawa.

In view of the reputation of Americans, it is surprising to note that at the start of World War II, the United States Army had no plan for the psychiatric treatment of fighting troops, no unit to provide treatment, not even a medical specialist in this field at headquarters. Hospital treatment for nervous breakdown was virtually forbidden and morale and discipline were

[15] Ahrenfeldt.
[16] Report of investigations by Lieutenant-Colonel J. W. Appel and Captain G. W. Beebe, U.S. Army.

solely the concern of field and regimental officers.[17] Among the nasty shocks which this occasioned, few were as unpleasant as the attack at El Guettar in North Africa at the end of March, 1943.

The task of the American assault was to cross a plain and seize a range of rugged hills, seamed with gullies and ravines. In command of the IInd Corps, which was given the task, was Lieutenant-General George S. Patton, a veteran of World War I. After inadequate reconnaisance and with imperfect maps, the assault troops, many of them belonging to the raw 9th U.S. Infantry Division, were committed at night. The result was disastrous. One battalion was lost for thirty-six hours, all its senior officers becoming casualties. A column directed by Major-General Manton S. Eddy was shot up on the Gabes road and came to a halt under heavy fire 'badly demoralized and severely hurt'. Survivors were still straggling back two days later. Another group which went astray and lost contact eventually sorted itself out as a provisional battalion fighting an isolated battle all on its own which did little for the confidence of the troops.[18]

For days at a time, according to official American reports, the proportion of battlefield casualties evacuated bearing 'neuro-psychiatric' labels was as high as one in three.

The effect of this reverse upon Patton, as Corps commander, may have been responsible for his much publicized conduct later. Patton had expressed his own feelings towards neuroses cases quite clearly:

'Any man who says he has battle fatigue is avoiding danger and forcing on those who have more hardihood than himself the obligation of meeting it. If soldiers would make fun of those who begin to show battle fatigue, they would prevent its spread, and also save the man who allows himself to malinger by this means from humiliation and regret.'

Applying this theory, Patton struck, with his gloves at a clearing-station a patient who had been labelled 'psychoneurosis anxiety state'. He explained his action by saying that he believed if he could make men angry enough with him they would redeem themselves. At the 93rd Evacuation Hospital,

[17] See Kardiner and Spiegel, *War Stress and Neurotic illness;* see also *The U.S. Army in World War II—The Medical Department: Medical Services in the Mediterranean and Minor Theaters.*
[18] U.S. Official History.

San Stefano, Sicily, on 10 August, 1943, when he was involved in a scene with another patient who said that he was not wounded but 'only scared', the incident had more serious repercussions. Ironically Patton himself, in the words of the United States official medical historian, 'was probably suffering from the accumulated tensions of the preceding weeks of intense combat. He was on his way back to the front where every available man was needed.' In other words, Patton was as much a neuropsychiatric case as the soldier he struck.[19]

In Tunisia, the number of American casualties from battle fatigue, nervous breakdown and exhaustion who eventually returned to the fighting line fell to the sorry figure of two in a hundred. In Sicily the recovery and return rate started off at fifteen per hundred neuro-psychiatric cases but improved to more than a third.

By the end of October, 1943, every American division had its psychiatrist—a stage which had been accepted as necessary in 1918. But they had to contend with a malpractice which also dated from World War I, that of keeping infantry divisions in an unpleasant and dangerous area for a long period without relief. The debilitating consequences of this had been clearly seen at Ypres by the British and the need to avoid unbroken service in such an area was a feature of the 1922 Enquiry into Shell Shock. After the hard winter conditions of 1943 an experimental centre was set up by the U.S. 88th Division. By the end of the year many other special training and rehabilitation units had been opened and nine out of ten battle fatigue casualties were being returned to the front line as recovered.[20]

One of the problems diagnosed by the American medical services actually lay in the battle indoctrination given to soldiers. During this it had been stated that 'every man has his breaking point'. As a result some soldiers assumed the moment they experienced fear and anxiety that they were approaching that point. As it was less of a disgrace (having been recognized officially) to show symptoms of distress, it was not unusual for individuals so afflicted to give full vent to their feelings instead of repressing them. A study of the rifle battalions of the Fifth Army in Italy showed that all soldiers who were not otherwise

[19] *U.S. Medical Service in the Mediterranean and Minor Theatres.*
[20] op. cit.

disabled ultimately became psychiatric cases.[21]

Some idea of the strain ground combat troops could endure before reaching breaking point is evident in certain case histories. A thirty-year-old artillery sergeant who landed at Lingayen Gulf in January, 1945, had already seen intense fighting elsewhere. Shortly after going into action his unit was overrun by five Japanese tanks. These were disposed of by the gunners after the infantry had withdrawn but he became disgusted with the conduct of the runaways and the staff responsible.[22] Not long afterwards his unit was trapped in a pass and suffered severe casualties. When the survivors were sent to a 'rest area' they were blasted by Japanese guns before they could even dig slit trenches. Moved once more, this time to a casualty clearing station, the weary gunners were roused from their first night's sleep by a Japanese 'Banzai!' attack which they had to help to repel. Only after this did the sergeant break down, recovering six months later after treatment with drugs and by hypnosis.

A younger man, a tank gunner who had fought in North Africa, Sicily and St Lô in the Cherbourg Peninsula, suddenly abandoned his turret when attacked by German fighter bombers. He was brought back and seemed normal. But a week later he froze and was unable to fire when enemy tanks appeared. Still he was retained in the tank crew. It was only when he once again froze after his Sherman had been hit outside Aachen and the crew had to push him out that someone had the sense to realize that he had been pushed beyond the limit.

Where desertion was concerned, the United States Army had a unique problem in containing within its ranks many soldiers with immigrant connections in Italy, France, Sicily, and eventually Austria and Germany. The numbers were relatively high and after the Runstedt Offensive, in the winter of 1944, desertion increased considerably. It was at this period that the only death sentence for cowardice was carried out. It has been said since that the shooting of Private Ernie Slovak, who his goaler described as 'a nice little guy', occurred because he had no friends. A simpler explanation is that the American commanders were reacting in the classical way to a state of frustration created by their own failure to anticipate the German thrust. They had to take it out on someone.

[21] op. cit.
[22] Kardiner and Spiegel—case histories.

233

Had the situation in North Africa become worse, pressure for the use of the death penalty might have grown there too. A slap from a disappointed general in certain circumstances is merely a substitute for a firing squad. The rage of Hitler against his own troops when the tide turned is perhaps the finest example of the backlash of the losing commander. In the autumn of 1943 the German troops of Army Group Centre were driven back in disorder in Russia. Among them, fighting against encirclement and under constant pressure from the air and marauding T-34 tanks, were the haggard remnants of the crack Gross-Deutschland Infantry Division. Their object was to escape across the Dnieper near Kiev. Thousands of German soldiers were killed and captured on the banks of the river which is about eight hundred yards wide at this spot. Those who did cross regarded their deliverance as little short of miraculous. They were met by military police and herded at machine-gun point into camps hemmed in with barbed wire. After being kept waiting for hours in mud and rain, they were marched into huts where interrogation teams cross-examined them.

A soldier who produced nine unused cartridges was screamed at and rated for not having fired them at the enemy. In his exhausted state, the treatment reduced him to tears. A lieutenant who had lost his map case and his binoculars in the retreat was posted on the spot to a group of tattered scarecrows about to be formed into a penal company.[23]

Penal companies had been a feature of the German army in World War I. In World War II the experiment was tried of forming a penal division of criminals serving gaol sentences of up to nine years led by high grade officers and N.C.O.s. As many of the men had been convicted of offences against the régime and were politically opposed to the Nazis, the results were not encouraging. It was planned to send the formation, designated the 999th Division, to Russia. But a trial posting of one battalion to the Eastern Front ended in wholesale desertions. A spell in Belgium as occupation troops was also un-satisfactory. The unit, renamed 'African Division 999', was sent to Tunisia where one regiment was destroyed by the Americans, many of its men surrendering. The other regiment, although it fought with some success when split into small

[23] Sajer, *The Forgotten Soldier.*

detachments, was rounded up when North Africa fell.[24] Hitler, it seems, had much less success than the Duke of Wellington in making gaolbirds into soldiers. In the long run he relied on the fear of death to control his troops.

Firing squads, which had been a rarity during World War I, were the certain end of soldiers of any rank who failed to carry out the Fuhrer's impossible orders. As the Wehrmacht retreated into Poland flying squads of Feldgendarmes patrolled the straggling columns. They had licence to hang on the spot any soldier caught helping himself to official food supplies. Round the necks of the corpses they hung notices saying 'I am a thief and a traitor to my country'. In Berlin, as the Russians drew nearer, SS squads hanged soldiers from lamp-posts almost at will. Some of them were mere boys returning to anti-aircraft batteries after showing off their newly acquired uniforms to their families. On their chests placards proclaimed 'I hang here because I left my unit without permission'.[25] As the Reich crumbled and defeat loomed ever larger, the death penalty was used indiscriminately almost as a charm to ward off doom itself.

The Russians, too, supplemented their commissars, propaganda and special unit cheer leaders, with execution squads. N.K.V.D. 'Rear Security Detachments' of machine-gunners used their weapons to stem any 'unauthorized withdrawals'.[26] Nor were the Security Police immune. N.K.V.D. men who gave way during the German drive on Stalingrad were also executed. Generals met the same fate. General Pavlov, commanding what was known as the Western Front, his chief of staff, Major-General Klimovski, his signals chief, Major-General Grigoriev, were all court martialled and shot in the summer of 1941. Major General Korobkov, commanding the Fourth Army, and Lieutenant General Rychagov of the Red Air Force were also tried on charges of cowardice and faced firing squads.[27]

The principle was exactly the same as that applied in the case of Admiral Byng. But the philosophy was less of an encouragement to other Red generals than the appearance of the large and well-equipped tank armies which they later led to victory. As far as the ordinary Russian soldier was concerned

[24] Burdick, *Army Quarterly*, Vol. 102, No. 1.
[25] Ryan, *The Lost Battle*.
[26] Clark, *Barbarossa* and Seth, *Operation Barbarossa*.
[27] See Clark and Seth.

it is more likely that the knowledge of the appalling treatment he could expect at the hands of the Germans if he became a prisoner greatly outweighed his fear of the disciplinary code of his own side.

21

Who ever heard of L.M.F.?

A unique morale problem which faced the British and Americans during World War II concerned the men who flew the huge bomber fleets. In 1922 Air Vice-Marshal Sir John Salmond, who had commanded the Royal Flying Corps and the Royal Air Force during the last year of the 1914–18 conflict, had told the War Office Committee of Enquiry into Shell Shock that all combat pilots would inevitably break down in time if not relieved, although the length of their flying efficiency would differ according to the temperament of the individual.

Dr W. H. R. Rivers, consultant in psychological medicine to the Royal Air Force, told the same committee that he had studied three groups of personnel: pilots, observers and balloon spotters. His conclusions:

'The pilots frequently had severe concussions and were much more knocked about than either of the other two groups; but such psycho-neurosis as they had was very slight indeed, almost trivial compared with the cases seen in the army. All they needed was to talk to get rid of the repression and then go off for a holiday.

'The observers (who also manned a machine-gun) had definitely more severe symptoms on the whole, and those in the balloon section were the most severe cases of psycho-neurosis I have seen anywhere.'

He put down this disparity in reactions to the same situation to the lack of occupation in the second two categories, the observer having to sit tight, leaving critical decisions to the pilot, while the balloon spotter frequently hung as a sitting target immediately over a disputed part of the battlefield. (Balloon crews were eventually the only Allied personnel to be issued with parachutes during the war.)

Despite the better endurance record of pilots, the morale

problem was still considerable in fighter squadrons. A young American who had been trained by the Royal Flying Corps and joined a British unit in France wrote in his diary for 11 July, 1918:

'One of our dashing young airmen, who, according to his own story had done innumerable deeds of valor but had never been caught in that act, changed his tune yesterday. He landed after he had been out alone and his plane had about fifty holes in it. The altimeter and Aldis sight were both hit. He was as limp as a rag and had to be assisted to his quarters. There he remained as sick as a dog for two days. When questioned about what happened to him he would get hysterical and sick at his stomach again. The Wing doctor came over to see him and sent him to hospital, tho' there's nothing wrong with him except he's badly frightened. That's the last of his illustrious career. He'll go home and write a book on the war now. I always did think he was yellow. What I believe happened to him is this. He's been telling so many lies about what he's been doing that he believed some of them himself and decided he'd go out and really have a look at the Hun. The first ones he saw shot him up and his constitution couldn't stand the fright. One thing about this game out here: those that are good are awfully good, and those that are bad are awfully sour. Thank God the Huns have the same trouble.'

And on 27 August he wrote:

'One of our noblest he-men, a regular fire-eater to hear him tell it, has turned yellow at the front. He was quite an athlete and always admitted he was very hot stuff. He was ordered up on a bomb raid and refused to go. The British sent him back to American headquarters with the recommendation that he be court martialled for cowardice. He would have been, too, if his brother hadn't been high up on the A.E.F. staff. He pulled some bluff about the machines being unsafe and they finally sent him home as an instructor and promoted him. He may strut around back home but I'll bet he can never look a real man in the eye again.'[1]

Fighter pilots were a special case. Once contact had been made with the enemy they were too busy looking after themselves to be concerned about the behaviour of others. The combat area could cover a vast distance and mechanical defects and failures added to the hazards. Pilots were on their

[1] *Diary of an Unknown Aviator.*

own and had to be judged by their combat reports. The need to minister to their morale was therefore paramount, regular rest being essential. In World War II the Germans did this by withdrawing squadrons and sending the flying personnel to ski and other resorts where all recreational facilities were provided—including feminine company.[2] British squadrons were posted to quiet areas at the beginning of the war and later used resorts in liberated areas. A great responsibility descended, however, on the junior leaders who had to be able to detect combat fatigue—'twitch'—or simple exhaustion and nervous strain. Wing-Commander 'Johnnie' Johnson, who finished the war with thirty-eight victories to his credit, relates how when he reported sick with an old shoulder injury early in his career he was suspected of trying to avoid flying duties and was offered a job training pilots on Tiger Moths.[3] Another high-scoring Hurrican pilot flew when suffering from the first depressing symptoms of jaundice rather than raise doubts about his courage. Where genuine cases of loss of nerve were suspected, such as the sergeant-pilot of 54 Squadron who began to dive *through* the enemy formations and break away after the first attack, action had to be taken discreetly. To prove the man guilty of any serious offence was almost impossible, particularly if he had taken part earlier in a number of strenuous engagements. In this case the offender was sent on leave pending posting and unpleasantness was thus avoided.[4]

With bomber crews disciplinary action was not so easy. A four-engined plane which abandoned a mission without good reason involved six, seven or eight men. In the case of Royal Air Force operations most of them took place at night which helped to conceal anyone who decided to avoid a heavily defended target area. A burst from the plane's own guns on the wing tips to simulate night fighter attacks, bombs jettisoned in the North Sea and alterations to the navigator's log were offences which, if detected, would amount to mutiny.[5] As a deterrent to any such acts the authorities resorted to a humiliating form of punishment in which a man was stripped of his flying brevet for 'lack of moral fibre' (L.M.F.) or 'forfeiting the commanding officer's confidence'.

[2] Johnson, *Wing Leader*.
[3] ibid.
[4] Deere, *Nine Lives*.
[5] Actual incidents recalled by R.A.F. veterans.

Undoubtedly as a means of inflicting a sense of shame upon an individual it was successful. Whether it was fair is a far different matter. For, just as many of the men who were shot for failing to do their duty in World War I might be suffering from a variety of psychiatric conditions, so veteran airmen were also afflicted. On a great number of them fell the strain which Dr Rivers had noted in observers and balloon spotters during the previous war due to long hours of sitting and waiting and watching with their lives in the hands of the pilot. Selected from volunteers and highly trained to a man, they were still only human.

On occasions, flying personnel were stripped of their 'wings' at formal parades in the classic tradition, the brevet being torn from its housing after the stitches had been unpicked. On other occasions the punishment was carried out almost privately. Take the case of a flight sergeant wireless operator/air gunner of 76 Squadron (motto: Resolute). He had taken part in raids on Essen, Hamburg, Düsseldorf, Berlin and other heavily defended German cities. On four occasions his plane had been hit by flak.

On one raid a propellor had been shot off. On another the plane had fallen out of control and had attacked under the Main Force at low level when control had been regained. Once his plane had limped home with a 500 lb bomb resting on jammed bomb doors. The flight sergeant then began to complain of ear pains and was sent into hospital. While undergoing an operation his crew were lost over Germany. When the sergeant returned to duty as fit he asked to be posted to Coastal Command where planes operated at a lower altitude less injurious to his ear which he complained still hurt at heights. On being told that he would have to go into the personnel pool as a spare wireless operator/air gunner he finally refused to fly.

They sent him for 'The Chop' to R.A.F. Chessington, Surrey. There he was called before an administrative squadron leader who stated: 'I have a letter from the Air Ministry which I am required to read to you. You will be reduced to the rank of leading aircraftsman. You forfeit your flying brevet. The effective date is . . . for forfeiting your commanding officer's confidence.' The airman commented years later:

'That broke my heart. To me that scruffy, little W.Op/A.G. half-wing on the left breast of my equally scruffy battledress blouse (although immaculate on my best blues) had been won the hard way. It hurts to this day when I remember walking out of Chessington in October, 1943, the pale outline of that cherished little wing marking the spot on my left breast where it once was.'[6]

Earlier that year, 76 Squadron had been commanded by Group Captain Leonard Cheshire. As the shattered air-gunner was being humiliated Cheshire was beginning his fourth tour of operations during which he pioneered target-marking techniques. In the citation that went with the Victoria Cross awarded him later in war Cheshire's 'cold and calculated acceptance of risks' was emphasised.

But the Cheshires of this world are rare indeed. He himself was quick to take action at the first sign of any hesitation in the members of any squadron he was commanding. At one time he even suggested that rough justice should be handed out to 'cowardly' men in the shape of a physical beating; the authorities turned down his proposal.[7] When a man did crack under Cheshire he was kept apart from other flyers, perhaps even locked in his room, until his transfer, so as not to involve other crew members. The decision was often agonizing for the man who had to initiate disciplinary action, especially where the object of it had already seen operational service. In Cheshire's view to degrade a man by removing his flying brevet was unnecessary and for officers who had not seen operational service to carry through the procedure was disgraceful. Gerry Witherick, D.F.C., D.F.M., who flew 106 missions as a rear-gunner, put it much more succinctly: 'It was the most unjust thing I've ever seen. I'd shoot the bloke who invented L.M.F. if I ever met him.'[8]

Undoubtedly there were cases where fear of being classified as L.M.F. actually cost the R.A.F. valuable lives.

Someone, somewhere, had the bright idea of celebrating Hitler's birthday, (20 April) with an air raid in 1943. It was suggested that it would be good for civilian morale and excellent for propaganda purposes. The crews of 408 (Goose) Squadron of the Royal Canadian Air Force were not so certain. On any other night the weather conditions would have kept their Halifaxes firmly on the ground. But this was a special

[6] Personal account by individual concerned.
[7] Revie, *The Lost Command.*
[8] Revie, *The Lost Command.*

occasion. The most experienced of the men scheduled to fly the mission was a former fighter pilot who had been decorated for gallantry twice before transferring to bomber command. Within half an hour of take-off he was back in the mess at Leeming, Yorkshire, enjoying a cup of tea. The conditions, he declared, were so bad that he had decided the mission was impossible. There was nothing anyone could do to discipline him. Any suggestion that he was 'lacking in moral fibre' would have been farcical. Other experienced flyers also returned but seven other crews and pilots did not have established reputations. Their courage was not proven. And so they roared on through the darkness, unwilling to return. Not one of them came back. Hitler's birthday present from 408 Squadron had been the gift of seven Halifax bombers and crews.

'No-one liked turning back from their first, second or third raids' said an ex-member of the squadron years afterwards.

To men who did crack, the reaction of most operational crews was sympathetic. One Lancaster pilot flew without his mid-upper gunner on a raid because the boy had broken down in tears just before take-off. The incident was not reported.

There is no question that the prolonged air assault on Germany, the results of which are still a matter of controversy, introduced a new dimension into the realms of combat flying, R.A.F. flyers being faced, consciously or subconsciously, with the additional burden of the doubtful morality of indiscriminate area bombing. From time to time they took heavy losses damaging to morale. Yet during the whole of 1944 of four squadrons operating out of No. 14 Base of No. 1 Group (12, 101, 300 Polish and 626 Squadrons) only 197 cases were listed as 'early returns'; i.e. engine failures or L.M.F.[9]

As in World War I many men created for themselves an artificial shell of callousness, cynicism or indifference to enable them to endure the poignant sight of empty places in the mess the day after a raid, the unceasing toll from accidents caused by natural flying hazards and the knowledge that the German air defences were changing and improving all the time. With some the veneer lasted longer than others. A flight sergeant who had flown a number of operations before being downgraded medically after a severe crash served throughout the rest of the war on a crash tender. He was able to look on the most horrific sights with a shrug. One of these was the

[9] Revie, *The Lost Command.*

corpse of an airman who struck the ground vertically from a considerable height after his parachute failed to open. Years after the war the flight sergeant, back in civilian life, was greeted as he returned home by his little daughter wearing his old Irvine jacket. At the appearance of this stunted figure he broke down completely and was sick and tearful for the next twenty-four hours.[10]

There were thousands of men who managed similarly to hide their fears and emotions during the war. In the more sensitive individual the effort required was considerable. Whether the threat of being classified as 'lacking in moral fibre' was of any use at all in helping men to steel themselves for the nerve-wracking tasks they had to perform is highly questionable. Not long ago, Marshal of the Royal Air Force Sir Arthur Harris was asked by Alastair Revie, author of *The Lost Command*, what he thought of applying the designation 'L.M.F.' to flyers whose nerves gave way. His reply was 'Never heard of it'.

But it existed all the same.

In the United States Air Force operating in Europe a crisis in morale arose during the period before the long-range fighter escort could be provided for the Fortresses and Liberators flying deep-penetration daylight missions. Just as night flying presented the R.A.F. with peculiar hazards, the American tactics raised special problems, one of which was the visual impact of incidents during operations. The experiences of a bombardier (bomb aimer/nose gunner) of a Flying Fortress speak for themselves. A twenty-seven year old Massachusetts man, he served in one of the squadrons of the U.S. Eighth Air Force, flying from bases in Britain.

Mission 1   Uneventful.

Mission 2   Nose of plane riddled with shrapnel.

Mission 3   Saw Fortress disintegrate over Emden without any parachutes appearing.

Mission 4   Saw his squadron commander's plane do a loop under heavy fighter attack and collide with two other Fortresses. All crashed.

Mission 5   Watched best friend's plane spin into the sea off Bremen. Felt increasing anxiety but did not

---

[10] Personal reminiscence of veteran.

report to doctor as he was determined to carry on.

Mission 6   His gun froze over Kiel and he had to endure repeated head-on fighter attacks unable to fire back. The Fortress on one side, which contained a general, went spinning down through the clouds out of control. The Fortress on the other side was hit by enemy fire and collided with its neighbour. The ball turret was knocked off and went down 'like an apple' with the gunner inside it. Another man jumped from one of the bombers but his parachute was ablaze and he fell 'like a hunk of lead'. Not long afterwards another of the giant four-engined planes looped and crashed, tearing the wing off another Fortress. Ten out of the nineteen planes on the raid failed to return. His own crashed on landing.

A few days later the bombardier was sitting in a truck taking him on another mission when he broke down in tears. He carried on but found that he was making so many foolish errors that he asked to be relieved and was given a ground job.

Under the American regulations the description 'lack of, or deficient moral fibre' was also in use as a disciplinary measure. But an airman could, if he felt severe anxiety, request to be grounded. This step had been taken deliberately after Air Force experts had studied the 'severe disturbances' which developed in the ground forces, the infantry and armoured divisions. It was designed as a safety valve. A medical study of the U.S. Eighth Force in the period 4 July, 1942—4 July, 1943, stated that there had been no courts martial for cowardice or refusing to fly.[11] Disciplinary steps were taken, however, and men might be posted to unattractive ground duties.

During the worst of the fighting the callous veneer seen elsewhere became evident in an extreme form in some American squadrons. Veterans went out of their way to shock newcomers. They would describe in gory detail the appearance of a man's body after he had been hit by a 20 mm cannon shell. When novices set out on their first mission, old hands would ask for a piece of clothing, a cap or a scarf, to keep as a memento as he was bound to be shot down. 'Shut the door', they would

[11] Hastings, Wright and Glueck, *Psychiatric Experiences of the Eighth Air Force— First Year of Combat.*

shout as the raw airmen left the barrackroom. 'You don't think you're coming back, do you?' In emotional outbursts it was stated by observers that airmen would shoot out their room lights with a burst of tommy-gun fire. Several fliers confessed to medical officers during check-ups that they had seduced women 'in quantity' not for sexual gratification 'but for the sake of subduing and conquering their defences'.[12]

In the U.S. 15th Air Force, serving in the Mediterranean theatre, cases of 'L.M.F.' requiring disciplinary action were reported to have 'not been frequent'.[13]

In this command, airmen who stated that they no longer felt able to fly were referred to a unit's flight surgeon. It was the medical officer's responsibility, according to instructions, to confront the flyer 'with his selfishness, and his guilt, and shame must be stimulated so that it will drive him back to a combat situation.'

Where it was discerned that a genuine nervous disease was present, treatment was given, but if there was no apparent cause for a man's condition he was informed that there were no grounds for removing him from duty and he was placed on a battle schedule or given a direct order. If he failed to carry out the order, the matter could then be dealt with as a disciplinary offence rather than a medical matter, although medical reports were submitted before any court martial heard the case.

Where psychiatric conditions were diagnosed there were some remarkable successes. A tail gunner flying in a Liberator returned from his second mission paralysed and dumb. His illness was discovered to have its origins in civilian life and after treatment he returned to duty and completed twenty-three combat flights. Another pilot, aged twenty-eight, who constantly complained of headaches, made so many 'early returns' that the ground crews used to bet on it. His problem too was diagnosed and treated and he subsequently became a squadron leader with a high number of missions to his credit.

The air war in the Mediterranean theatre was less intense, however, than over Europe, particularly during the grim period before fighter protection had been properly developed. Before his fifteenth mission one pilot, a good flyer, told the medical officer that he was suffering from nausea before every raid and did not think he would ever get home to his wife. After he

12 Hastings, Wright and Glueck.
13 Levy, *Personality Disturbances in Combat Fliers.*

went down over enemy territory it was assumed that he had landed to become a prisoner of war because he had given up hope of making the flight back to Britain. Another pilot who had made 'early returns' from three previous flights without being able to give adequate cause, was seen to pull out of formation three or four times on his ninth raid and eventually flew away under control. He too was suspected of deliberately landing in enemy territory.

In the U.S. Eighth Air Force's first year of active operations eight men were reported to have baled out in a panic, three because they mistook leaking hydraulic fluid for blood. The reactions of other men to overcome their fears bordered on the superhuman. The waist gunner of a Flying Fortress was trapped in the whirling wreckage of his plane after it collided during a training flight at 20,000 feet. At about 1,000 feet he managed to burst through the skin of the aircraft and open his parachute. He saw his plane shattered on the ground and after landing a hundred yards away tried to pull out the crew, all of whom were dead. The gunner continued to fly. On one mission his plane was hit by anti-aircraft fire which blew the torn control wires round his neck, nearly strangling him. On another, as rear gunner, a Focke-Wolfe 190 appeared fifty feet from his turret. After he had seen his tracer bullets streaking into the enemy plane a vivid flash indicated that he had hit the German's oxygen bottle. The FW 190 went spinning out of control.

It was the sight of the falling enemy that finally broke the gunner's nerve. Medical investigation established that he was suffering from increased anxiety stemming from the knowledge that he had been responsible for causing another man to go through the same terrible experience he'd had to endure himself when trapped after the mid-air collision.

*   *   *

According to medical definition all human organisms are faced during their existence with constantly changing conditions in which they strive to survive in an agreeable form. To achieve this they carry out perceptual, co-ordinative and executive functions. Under abnormal pressures and stimuli, such as those created by a bursting shell or in a plane spinning down with a wing torn off, an organism may not have the time or the ability to respond successfully. A phenomenon which produces conditions to which the organism cannot find an answer may be defined as traumatic. Breaking point is reached when the organism is no longer able to adapt to the new and extreme conditions. Sometimes this is simply because the organism's resources are seriously reduced, as in a state of fatigue.[14]

In both World Wars the front line troops were subjected to traumatic experiences. As we have seen, in the first, because of diverse medical opinions and the official priority given to political and military requirements, many soldiers who broke down were punished as disciplinary offenders. As a leading British psychiatric expert wrote in 1957, with the experience of both wars to draw on, 'one may be permitted to entertain some doubt as to the mental health and stability of the "mere" eleven per cent [of men condemned to death] who were executed.'[15]

In the longer war, of 1939–45, not one British soldier was executed by sentence of court martial for a. purely military offence. Yet the experiences of the combatants, on the ground and in the air, were just as severe as during the First World War and some psychiatrists have stated that from their point of view 'in the long run' World War II placed a greater strain on the participants.[16] As no-one is going to suggest that the men who fought Hitler were braver than those who fought the Kaiser, why the discrepancy? Less than ten years had passed since the death penalty had been removed for desertion and 'cowardice'. Capital punishment was still a basic feature of British civil law. If anything the country was in much graver danger than ever before in its history. Some generals tried to bring back firing squads and there was probably never a better time to make a case for them.

The real reasons for their non-appearance, however, may well be neither medical opinion, social consciousness or enlightened attitudes, but simply political. Churchill and Attlee were fully aware of the long struggle which led to the amelioration of the Army Act. They were also aware that, unlike World War I, when a soldier who wrote to a Member of Parliament could find himself in the gravest trouble, the bolder newspapers would have aired the subject thoroughly.

With their thoughts on post-war elections no member of any

[14] Kardiner and Spiegel, *War Stress and Neurotic Illness*.
[15] Ahrenfeldt.
[16] See Laffin, *Surgeons in the Field*.

of the parties in the Coalition wanted to risk that. Unpleasant details of the injustices of earlier years might have come to light. And the Communist Party, who had made such potent propaganda out of the retention of the death penalty in the Army Act in the Twenties, would be able to do so again. None of the other parties had clean hands in this respect. The Liberals had allowed deserters to die and the Tories had clung to execution as an integral part of their creed for a time. The Labour Secretary of State for War, Stephen Walsh, had been adamant in refusing to allow any change in the regulations and in 1924 the committee set up by the Labour Government had opposed, to a man, suggested alterations.

And so the men who were shot at dawn did not die in vain. Because the politicans were afraid to raise their ghosts the dead soldiers obtained for their successors reprieves that were withheld from themselves.

POSTSCRIPT

The Hundred-year Hush-up

The barriers which still prevent investigation of courts martial files relating to trials during World War I are alien to British judicial proceedings. In the most celebrated criminal cases, where a person has been executed, an abundance of evidence is freely available. State Secrets may be placed in the Public Records Office in Chancery Lane, London, after only thirty years have elapsed. But the proceedings of courts martial where death sentences have been confirmed must remain secret for one hundred years.

When *The Times* reported this in 1972 quite a number of otherwise well-informed newspapers and television commentators expressed considerable surprise, apart from being startled to learn that so many men had been shot for disciplinary offences. But like most observers they assumed that the main reason for the 100 year rule was to protect the feelings of relatives. This was because the general impression had been gained that the next-of-kin of victims had not been informed. (Even Brigadier Crozier had been under the impression that he could conceal the truth from the relatives of a soldier whose execution he arranged in 1916.) The truth, however, is that it was not until 1917, when the Battle for Passchendaele was ending that Mr Balfour announced in Parliament a War Cabinet decision to place the names of men shot for disciplinary offences in casualty lists as 'died on active service'. Even then, from a study of later statements in the Commons, it is not clear whether the truth was always withheld—M.P.s were obliged to seek pensions for the widows of men reported as executed, as these had not been granted. Is one to assume that the widows of men whose executions were concealed from their next-of-kin were granted pensions in order to maintain the charade? If so, it was grossly unfair. For by the time the War

Cabinet took its decision to hide the truth, more than three years of war had passed during which, according to the official statistics, 226 men had been shot at dawn whose relatives had been notified by letter.

According to available information such letters stated the dates of the courts martial and executions. As has been seen, the condemned man did not know until a few hours before his execution even that he had been sentenced to death, still less that his death was imminent. The shock must have been enough to stifle most last-minute attempts by doomed soldiers to obtain help. But it is a fact that some did write last letters which led relatives to attempt to obtain copies of court martial proceedings. They were refused because the War Office took refuge behind the absurd regulation which stated that records could be divulged only to prisoners and that as the only persons to qualify in these cases were dead nothing could be done. Even when used in 1917 this excuse was flimsy. To use it today shows a remarkable lack of originality, if nothing else, especially as paragraph 94 of the Darling Committee's Report on Courts Martial stated in 1919:

'It appears that under section 124 of the Army Act the person convicted is the only person entitled to obtain a copy of the Proceedings of a Court Martial.

'Where a person is dead we think that the right might well be extended to his legal or personal representative or (if there be none) to his next of kin.'

In the event no-one has been allowed to have access to the proceedings which the War Office had locked away for the perusal of disinterested historians in the years 2014 to 2019.

There would appear to be no obvious logical argument for this secrecy. All British courts martial held in France during World War I were by law open to the public, and although there were practical reasons why this could not be implemented on all occasions, the desirability of making the conduct of the court public knowledge would appear to be undiminished.

Despite official obstruction there is enough prima facie evidence from Parliamentary reports, the Darling Committee of 1919 and the Shell Shock Enquiry of 1922, to suggest that not only did miscarriages of justice occur, but that they may have occurred on a disquieting scale. The very fact that the Darling Committee recommended the basic precaution of the presence of a shorthand writer at all trials, even on active service, implies that there was a limitation on the amount of evidence which was sent to the confirming authority. As to the physical conditions under which men were tried for their lives—A. P. Herbert did not feel that it was incredible to set the court martial scene in *The Secret Battle* in a French farm where the woman of the house occasionally interrupted the proceedings by carrying cooking utensils through the room.

A number of constructions may be placed upon the official reticence to release court martial papers during the war:

(*a*) They might have caused comment which would have had an adverse effect upon recruiting prior to conscription;

(*b*) They might have caused an outcry from the parents of teenage soldiers later in the war;

(*c*) The disclosures were not in the interests of security and would have been seized upon by enemy propagandists;

(*d*) They were bad for national morale;

(*e*) They could have led to legal action being taken against court martial officers and the confirming officers, including the Commanders-in-Chief.

As far as the last proposition is concerned, relatives of men 'rehabilitated' by Courts of Cassation in France did indeed try to institute legal actions but they were stifled by the authorities.[1] In the case of British soldiers, the Manual of Military Law (1914 edition, amended in 1916) records precedents.

Section 170 of the Army Act of the period (1914–18) clearly stated that actions against members of courts martial in respect of sentences 'shall be brought in one of His Majesty's superior courts in the United Kingdom (which courts shall have jurisdiction to try the same wherever the matter complained of occurred) or in a superior court in India . . .' Members of Parliament who tentatively raised this point in 1917 were fobbed off with a statement that 'it would be unwise to express an opinion in the absence of the facts of any particular case.'

As the same government spokesman was withholding specific facts in any relevant case, it is not to be wondered that no progress was achieved in this direction.

The tenacity with which the authorities and successive governments stuck to this policy has been stated elsewhere in this book. It has not been difficult for them. Few reminders exist of the men who died. There is nothing on the gravestones

[1] Van Paassen, *Days of our Years*.

of any of the victims of firing squads to state that they died at the hands of their own comrades. Headstones in military cemeteries in France and Belgium record the regiment, name, rank and age of the soldier along with his date of death and sometimes a few words expressing the grief of relatives. It was not thought necessary to include the words, 'killed in action' which had featured on the temporary crosses the stones replaced. The brave and those who were judged by others to be not so brave lie side by side. But the stern and controversial code of previous years is not entirely hidden.

In a large blue book at the Public Records Office dealing with Admiralty affairs, under the heading 'Courts Martial—General' are a number of undramatic entries, made in a bold round hand. Some are slightly humorous, such as the plaintive signal from the Senior Naval Officer, that because of the absence of an officer of the rank of Post Captain it was impossible to convene a court martial in Gibraltar. But one entry reads as follows:

'Temporary Lieutenant Shuter R.M. severely reprimanded; Temporary Lieutenant Watson R.M. severely reprimanded; Lieutenant de la Mothe R.N.V.R. severely reprimanded; Temporary Sub-Lieutenant Dyett, R.N.R. sentenced to death; sentence carried out on January 5th, 1917.'

Elsewhere in the same book, which listed various official messages, it is recorded that the charge against Dyett was 'when on active service deserting H.M's service.'

When, in the year 2017, some historian looks into the case, it is to be hoped that it will be indicated that this was the boy whom A.P. Herbert, with the experience of three years of war behind him, described as 'one of the bravest men I ever knew'. Indeed it would be better if long before that date the files were opened so that proper research might be made into one of the shabbiest episodes of British history. It is necessary not because of what men *did* in the name of duty and discipline. Their deeds must be judged in the context of the times in which they lived and the death penalty was part of the judicial code.

What is repugnant is the perpetuation of the wall of official secrecy which has surrounded these trials for more than fifty years, a wall bolstered by ministerial regulation rather than decision of Parliament.

On 15 May, 1972, Mr Concannon, the Socialist Member for Mansfield and an ex-Guardsman, asked that the records of trials of British soldiers shot for desertion or cowardice during World War I should be destroyed so as to prevent the names ever being released. Doubtless he was under the misapprehension that the majority of their relatives had been kept in ignorance.

Mr Geoffrey Johnson Smith, the Minister of State for Defence, replied that he was not prepared to recommend their destruction because they were historical documents and—'The present policy . . . attempts to strike a balance between the protection of the innocent from unnecessary pain and the preservation of material which is part of our history.'

Perhaps it may be possible for this policy to be extended so that the same protection will not be afforded to the guilty . . . where they exist.

There will be those who argue that an enquiry at this stage would cause relatives undue stress. But to assume that is to accept the premise that the victims were guilty of something shameful, whereas a large number of people take the view that it was the action of the authorities that was cowardly and reprehensible.

Other countries have survived the unpleasantness involved in clearing the names of the victims of ritual military sacrifice. The Soviet Union had the nerve even to 'rehabilitate' Marshal Tukachevsky and the generals liquidated by Stalin. Surely, after all these years, Parliament, which failed lamentably at the time to establish the truth about the treatment of these soldiers, can find the courage to revoke this 'damnable judgement on our own flesh and blood'.

The same yellow line which runs through us all shows in different ways at different times. To abandon the quest for truth under the smokescreen of false sentiment and before the parapets of bureaucracy is infinitely worse than desertion in the face of the enemy.

BIBLIOGRAPHY

Ahrenfeldt, Robert H., *Psychiatry in the British Army in the Second World War*, Routledge and Kegan Paul, 1958.

Anton, Sergeant James, *Retrospect of Military Life*, 1841.

Austin, Sergeant I. W., *1st/1st Welsh Casualty Clearing Station*, Unpublished Diary.

Bales, Captain P. G., *The History of the 1/4th Battalion Duke of Wellington's (West Riding) Regiment, 1914–19*, Edward Mortimer Ltd., Halifax, 1920.

Barnes, Major R. M., *A History of the Regiments and Uniforms of the British Army*, Seeley Service, 1950.

Bartlett, F. C., *Psychology and the Soldier*, Cambridge University Press, 1927.

Bean, C. E. W., (Ed.), *Official History of Australia in the War of 1914–18*, 12 vols, Australian War Memorial, Canberra.

Blake, Robert (Ed.), *The Private Papers of Douglas Haig, 1914–19*; Eyre & Spottiswoode; 1952.

Blunden, Edmund, *Undertones of War*, Cobden Sanderson, 1928.

Boatner, Mark M., *The Civil War Dictionary*, Charles Scribner's Sons, 1959.

Burdick, Charles, *Prisoners as Soldiers*, Army Quarterly, Vol. 102, No. 1.

Carew, Tim, *The Vanished Army*, William Kimber, 1964.

Catton, Bruce, *Glory Road*, Doubleday, New York, 1952.

Chapman, Guy, *A Passionate Prodigality*, MacGibbon and Kee, 1965; *Vain Glory*, (anthology).

Childs, Major-General Sir Wyndham, *Episodes and Reflections*, Cassell, 1930.

Churchill, W. S., *Marlborough, His Life and Times*, 4 vols, Harrap, 1933–38; *The World Crisis*, 5 vols, Thornton Butterworth, 1923–31; *The Second World War*, 6 vols, Cassell, 1948–54.

Clark, Alan, *The Donkeys*, Hutchinson, 1961; *Barbarossa*, Hutchinson, 1965.

Clarke, J. S., *Life of James II*, London, 1816.

Clode, C. M., *The Military Forces of the Crown*, 2 vols, John Murray, 1869.

Cobbett, William, *Parliamentary History of England*, 12 vols, 1806–12.

254

Coppard, George, *With a Machine-Gun to Cambrai*, Imperial War Museum, 1970.

Craig-Brown, Brigadier E., papers of, edited by Warman, *Army Quarterly*, Vol. 102, No. 1.

Crozier, F. P., *A Brass Hat in No-Man's Land*, Cape, 1930.

Cutlack, (Ed.), *War Letters of General John Monash*, Angus and Robertson, 1935.

Deere, Alan C., *Nine Lives*, Hodder and Stoughton, 1959.

Dickinson, A. H., *Mutiny of the 5th Light Infantry*, Imperial War Museum papers.

Eder, M. D., *War Shock*, Heinemann, 1917.

Edmunds, Brigadier Sir John, *Military Operations in France and Flanders* (various volumes).

Esson, D. M. R., *The Curse of Cromwell*, Leo Cooper, 1971.

Farrar-Hockley, Major-General A. H., *Death of an Army*, Arthur Barker, 1967.

Firth, C. H. and Rait, R. S. (Ed.), *Acts and Ordinances of the Interregnum*, 3 vols, 1911.

Fortescue, Sir John, *History of the British Army*, Macmillan, 1889–1930.

Freeman, Douglas S., *Lee's Lieutenants*, Charles Scribner's Sons, New York, 1944.

Gardiner, S. R., *Oliver Cromwell*, Longmans, 1909.

Glover, Michael, *Wellington's Peninsular Victories*, Batsford, 1963.

Gough, General Sir Hubert, *The Fifth Army*, Hodder and Stoughton, 1931.

Heneker, Major-General Sir William, private diary (unpublished).

Herbert, A. P., *The Secret Battle*, Methuen, 1919.

Hibbert, Christopher, *Corunna*, Batsford, 1961; *The Wheatley Diary*, (Ed.), Longmans, 1964.

Horne, Alastair, *The Price of Glory*, Macmillan, 1962.

Jerrold, Douglas, *The Royal Naval Division*, Hutchinson, 1923.

Johnson, James E., *Wing Leader*, Chatto and Windus, 1956.

Johnstone, The Chevalier, *A Memoir of the Forty-Five*, Folio Society Editions, 1958.

Junger, Ernst, *Storm of Steel*, Chatto and Windus, 1929.

Kardiner and Spiegel, *War Stress and Neurotic Illness*, Hoeber Inc, New York, 1941, 1947.

Laffin, John, *Surgeons in the Field*, Dent, 1969.

Latter, Major-General J. C., Imperial War Museum papers.

Levy, Norman, *Personality Disturbances in Combat Fliers*, Josiah Macy Jr Foundation, New York, 1945.

Liddell Hart, Sir Basil, *Foch: Man of Orleans*, Eyre and Spottiswoode, 1931.

Lloyd George, David, *War Memoirs*, 6 vols, Nicholson & Watson, 1933–36.

Longford, Elizabeth, *Wellington—The Years of the Sword*, Weidenfeld and Nicolson, 1969.

Ludendorff, General Erich, *My War Memoirs*, Hutchinson, 1922.

MacPhail, Sir Andrew, *Official History of the Canadian Forces in the Great War, 1914–19; The Medical Services*, Ottawa, 1925.

McLaughlin, Redmond, *The Royal Army Medical Corps*, Leo Cooper, 1971.

Miller, E., *The Neuroses in War*, Macmillan, 1940.

Montgomery, Field-Marshal Viscount, *Memoirs*, Collins, 1958.

Moran, Lord, *Churchill: The Struggle for Survival*, Constable, 1966; *The Anatomy of Courage*.

Mosley, Leonard, *Gideon Goes to War*, Arthur Barker, 1955.

Myers, C. S., *Shell Shock, 1914–18*, Cambridge University Press, 1940.

Nicholson, Colonel G. W. L., *Canadian Expeditionary Force, 1914–19*, Ottawa, 1962.

Osburn, Arthur, *Unwilling Passenger*, Faber and Faber.

Paassen, Pierre van, *Days of Our Years*, Hillman Curl, New York, 1939.

Pankhurst, E. Sylvia, *The Home Front*, Hutchinson, 1932.

Revie, Alastair, *The Lost Command*, David Bruce and Watson, 1972.

Richards, Frank, *Old Soldiers Never Die*, Faber and Faber.

Rushworth, J., *Historical Collections, 1618–49*, 7 vols, London, 1659–1707.

Ryan, Cornelius, *The Last Battle*, Collins, 1966.

Sajer, Guy, *The Forgotten Soldier*, Laffont (France), 1967.

Scott and Brumwell, *History of the 12th Division*, Nisbet, 1923.

Seth, Ronald, *Operation Barbarossa*, Blond, 1964.

Seton Hutchison, Lieutenant-Colonel Graham, *The 33rd Division in France and Flanders, 1915–19*, and *History and Memoir of the 33rd Battalion, Machine-Gun Corps*, printed by Waterlow Bros and Layton for private circulation.

Smith, G. E., *Shell Shock and its Lessons*, Longmans, 1919.

Smith and Kincaid, *The 25th Division in France and Flanders*, Harrison, 1922.

Spears, Major-General Sir E. L., *Liaison 1914*, Eyre and Spottiswoode, 1930.

Terraine, John, *Douglas Haig, the Educated Soldier*, Hutchinson, 1963.

Thurtle, Ernest, *Time's Winged Chariot*, Chaterson, 1945; *Shootings at Dawn* (a pamphlet).

Tomasson, K., and Buist, F., *Battles of the '45*, Batsford, 1962.

Ward Boulton, *Objection Overruled*, MacGibbon and Kee, 1967.

Wellington, Second Duke of, *Supplementary Despatches and Memoranda*, John Murray, 1858.

White, Colonel H. A., *Report of the Judge Advocate-General*, G.H.Q. American Expeditionary Force, 1919.

Wilkins, Harold T., *Mysteries of the Great War*, Philip Allen, 1935.
Woods-Hutchinson, *The Doctor in War*, Cassell, 1919.
Wyrall, Everard, *The Duke of Cornwall's Light Infantry 1914–1919*, Methuen, 1932.
Young, Peter, *Edgehill 1642*, Roundwood Press, 1967.

OTHER SOURCES

The U.S. Army in World War II—The Medical Department: Medical Service in the Mediterranean and Minor Theaters. Washington, 1965.
Lawes and Ordinances of Warre, Established for the Better Conduct of the Army by His Excellency the Earl of Essex. London, 1642.
Official History of the War—Medical Services: Diseases of the War, Vol. 2, H.M.S.O., 1923.
Official History of the Australian Army Medical Services in the War, 1914–19.
The Medical Department of the U.S. Army in the World War, Vol. 10, 1929.
Report of the War Office Committee of Enquiry into 'Shell Shock', H.M.S.O., 1922.
Statistics of the Military Effort of the British Empire during the Great War 1914–20, War Office, 1922.
The Report of the Committee constituted by the Army Council to enquire into the Law and Rules of Procedure regulating Military Courts Martial, published 1919—copy held by War Office Library, Whitehall.
Hansard—Official Parliamentary Reports.

INDEX

All British and German units which fought in the First and Second World Wars are listed separately on page 267.

263

BRITISH REGIMENTS

KRRC, 7th Bn, 168
Manchesters, 7th Bn, 209; 2/7th, 144; 18th Bn, 1, 5, 17, 88, 105-6, 117, 168
York and Lancs, 214
DLI, 212; 7th Bn, 164; 10th Bn, 168
Gordons, 190; 1st Bn, 104
Camerons, 1st Bn, 62, 68
R Irish R, 8th Bn, 88; 9th Bn, 83-5, 88, 91; 12th Bn, 123
Argylls, 143
Leinsters, 2nd Bn, 82
R Dublin Fus, 2nd Bn, 58, 65
95th Foot (Rifles), 35

Royal Marines, 30, 32, 147
Hood Bn (RN), 91, 168
Nelson Bn (RN), 93-4, 131

Corps:
    Royal Engineers, 100-1, 170
    RAMC, 38th Field Amb, 76; 1/1st Welch Casualty Clearing Station, 71; 200
        Field Amb, 225
    Machine Gun Corps, 206
    Pioneer Corps, 230

Indian Army:
    Baluchis, Sikhs and Pathans, 65
    5th Light Inf, 217-8
    Malay Volunteer Force, 219

Miscellaneous:
    King's German Legion, 42
    Brunswick Regiment, 40

FORMATIONS OTHER
THAN BRITISH REGIMENTS